SCAPEGOATING FOR COLUMBINE

Have an adventure
in reading !

Louise Benken

SCAPEGOATING FOR COLUMBINE

✦

Collateral Damage in the War on School Violence

Louise Benson, M.D.

iUniverse, Inc.
New York Lincoln Shanghai

SCAPEGOATING FOR COLUMBINE
Collateral Damage in the War on School Violence

iUniverse books may be ordered through booksellers or by contacting:

iUniverse
2021 Pine Lake Road, Suite 100
Lincoln, NE 68512
www.iuniverse.com
1-800-Authors (1-800-288-4677)

ISBN-13: 978-0-595-40614-2 (pbk)
ISBN-13: 978-0-595-84981-9 (ebk)
ISBN-10: 0-595-40614-9 (pbk)
ISBN-10: 0-595-84981-4 (ebk)

Printed in the United States of America

Contents

Foreword

The tragedy at Columbine High School on April 20, 1999, in Littleton, Colorado, has had far-ranging effects on the American people, its schools and law enforcement. Like other sentinel events of a generation that are frozen in memory, I recall watching the television at work in horror, and my worry because I had teenage relatives in Littleton. They were fine, and I followed the corrective actions approvingly. But as time went on, the strategy to prevent school violence with zero tolerance discipline and legal repercussions had a harsh effect on many children who had no intention of harming anyone. This has become scapegoating for Columbine. Our child became one of those statistics, and this is our story.

Many families who have experienced an ordeal or a tragedy attempt to heal their wounds by preventing it from happening to anyone else. My goal is to use our story to spur nationwide change. The names of all students, most adults, and many identifying details, have been disguised, but previous media coverage does not allow school anonymity. I have done my best to present a balanced view, because education and law enforcement professionals have difficult jobs to do. And the school deserves significant credit for the reforms enacted. But I feel strongly that many other students nationwide are at risk in schools still using zero-tolerance discipline and outdated anti-bullying programs that were initiated in response to the Columbine tragedy. My family had the financial resources to survive this ordeal, but many families with lesser resources have had more catastrophic outcomes. This book was written to stop the scapegoating in Colorado and across the country. A portion of the proceeds from this book will be given to worthy causes, including the Columbine Memorial Fund and Restorative Justice Programs in Colorado.

Introduction

Our family's experience with bullying and zero tolerance discipline, and my fight for reform spans almost a five year time frame from 2001 through 2006. The story has a large cast of characters, reading like a novel, but it is all true and contains much supportive data. It is also, I believe, compelling and instructive, and larger than us. The book is divided into three parts to help the reader follow sometimes parallel events from different perspectives, and then to switch gears into learning mode for the research chapters.

In Part One, Chapter 1 describes our family's rude awakening to zero tolerance school and legal system punishment with the sudden arrest of our 13 year old son on serious and unwarranted felony charges. Chapter 2 gives the prelude and precipitant of these events in our son's suffering religious bullying in a public charter school. And Chapter 3 describes the similar and near-tragic story of a 14 year old girl at the school one year later, showing the feminine response to severe bullying, and the courage of her family.

Part Two details the fight for justice through school reform, and the difficulties encountered when entrenched bureaucracies, and competing interests and goals collide. Chapter 4 takes the reader on my roller coaster of successes and failures in challenging the school district and charter school to step up to the plate, with an ultimately satisfying outcome. Chapter 5 gives an inside look at how the media can be extremely helpful, but sometimes you get beat up in the process, and the reporters do, too. In Chapter 6, the American Civil Liberties Union's outwardly tepid response to intolerance at the charter school is discussed, along with possible political reasons for staying behind the scenes. Finally, in Chapter 7, the struggle to understand our son's harsh prosecution in terms of my history of whistle-blowing at the charter school is resolved with recognition of the Columbine scapegoating phenomenon taking place across the country.

Part Three shifts from local events to new research in the fields of school violence, school choice, and bullying. Chapter 8 shows convincingly that zero tolerance school and legal consequences are not necessary for school safety, and are even harmful and counterproductive. Chapter 9 discusses the school choice movement, and why charter schools may not be the panacea for our public school ills and may in fact contribute to intolerance and resegregation. In Chapter 10, state of the art bullying prevention is detailed, and what families can do to participate in the new paradigm.

The Epilogue expresses very personally why I was so devastated by our family's brush with discrimination and zero tolerance discipline, and why I am determined to do something about it in my small way.

PART I

1

Our Ordeal

The Arrest of a Child

On a hot Thursday night in late August 2003, the second floor bedroom windows in our suburban Denver tract house were open to the slight breeze, and we were just drifting off to sleep, looking forward to the end of a long week. Our English Setter Shadow, our watchdog who woofs at anything, began to bark. We rolled over, annoyed, thinking for the hundredth time, we've got to train her not to bark at the neighbors. But she barked more insistently, and then it took on a vicious tone we had never heard before. Our 13 year old son Jeff quickly appeared in our bedroom doorway, saying, "I'm scared. There's someone shining a flashlight into my room!" Sitting bolt upright, we heard rustling in the bushes. Panicking, I grabbed the phone and dropped it, while my husband Mark rushed to the window and bellowed, "Who's out there!? What do you want!?" The flashlight beam blinded him as a male voice answered, "It's the police, can you come to the door?"

With a sigh of relief, thinking there must be something going on in the neighborhood, a prowler perhaps, we put on our robes, told our son to go back to bed, and shuffled wearily downstairs. We were totally unprepared for the shock of the next few hours and the seven months of hell that were to follow when we opened the front door.

Four police officers entered our home with intensely serious expressions on their faces. Both of our dogs retreated under the dining room table with tails tucked. A barrage of questions pelted us—"Where is your son? We are here to arrest him," "Do you have any guns in the house?" "Were you aware he made school threats?" "Where is his computer?" ... while I sputtered that there must be some mistake, and asked if they had a warrant. They didn't have one, but we were told they could get one in two hours and it would be easier just to cooperate, so we signed the papers. They then showed us two pages of an internet instant message printout dated three days prior, with alarming talk of suicide and

3

vague threats against the school, and said they had 30-50 more such pages. Mark calmly asked if they could search our home, our son's room, the firearms storage, and take the computer and question our son, before deciding whether arrest was necessary.

"We have to arrest him; we consulted with two district attorneys on this."

Just then, our son appeared on the stairs in his sleep shorts, his slight build silhouetted by the hall light. Mark said, "Jeff, do you know anything about this?" Jeff said, "Yes, but it's not serious," in a small voice, and led the officers to his computer.

The police did not do any search, but took our son away in handcuffs to patrol cars parked around the corner out of our sight, while we were getting dressed. As we drove several miles to the police station in the next town, we wondered what our son's crime was, and speculated that they just wanted to scare him a little, and would release him to us after a stiff talking-to, and making sure we would obtain some counseling for him. We had obviously drastically underestimated the effect that school bullying was having on him. It had been primarily religious in nature, and we had tried to address it with our son and the school, but it was now obvious that this had been a failure. We arrived at the small, nearly dark police station, and were shown to a flourescent-lit waiting area.

At 1 AM, after waiting what seemed like an eternity, our son appeared with the Police Sargent, the main arresting officer with the Lafayette Police Dept. He read us our Miranda Rights, and stated the charge: Anarchy and Sedition, Inciting Destruction of Life or Property, a felony. Our jaws dropped. He then asked to question our son. Mark said, "I think we should, to clear this up," but I said, thinking of all the TV shows and movies I had watched, "Don't you think we should have a lawyer present?" I also said to the officer, "I really don't see that these are real threats. He's just a kid." With a very patronizing, annoyed look, he responded, "M'am, I've been up since 6 AM and I don't have the time to explain it, if you don't get it." We then asked, and he began to outline what would happen next. Jeff would be taken to the Justice Center in Boulder, "but you cannot go there with him, or follow because you will not be let in. Call the Adult Jail in a few days, because that's where he'll be since the juvenile section is closed due to renovations." Terrified, Jeff exclaimed "I don't want to get beat up!" His face draining, Mark asked what measures would be taken to keep him safe. The Sargent responded without emotion, "They'll do the best they can, but I cannot guarantee his safety."

A solicitous female officer asked for our contact information, but I was in a state of shock and could not even remember my pager or cell phone number. We watched as they then put our son back in handcuffs and into the patrol car to transport him to jail, and I just lost it, in a blubbering mess of tears. Mark did a lot better hiding his feelings.

It was 2 AM. I pulled myself together and insisted that we follow the police car transporting our son to the Justice Center in Boulder, about 10 miles away, not knowing if we would get in trouble for disobeying the Sargent. We drove silently, not wanting to even voice our worst fears of what could happen to our small, prepubertal son, in an adult jail. We just could not believe what was happening, and desperately wanted to wake up from this nightmare.

It was surreal in the moonlight as we drove along Canyon Boulevard that leads into Boulder Canyon and the mountains above Boulder. Just before the mouth of the canyon, the Justice Center sits, and we pulled in behind the police car and watched the transporting officer place his hand on Jeff's head as he got him out, just like on TV. He came over to our car and surprised us with his kind offer to carry a note in for us. It was obvious this man had kids of his own by the expression on his face. We hurriedly scribbled an impassioned plea to take our son home tonight and promised to keep him on a suicide watch and obtain prompt mental health care for him. We played our doctor and psychologist cards. It worked.

We were later allowed in to see our son. He looked frightened, tired and pale. A sympathetic young female juvenile center employee, who confirmed that the juveniles would be transferred to a "roped off" part of the adult jail in the morning, sat down with us and explained that his evaluation showed no active suicide or homicide risks and that we could bond him out. How much, we asked. $1500. Fifteen hundred dollars! No checks, no credit cards. It was now 3 AM. Where would we get this kind of money at this hour to keep our son from being incarcerated with adult criminals? Our minds raced. There was a max of $200 per day on ATM withdrawals, damn.

Then it hit me, the Y2K cash, then 9-11 cash, almost forgotten. Where was it?

Mark stayed with Jeff, and I sped home to find the cash. I dug wildly through dusty boxes in the basement, finally finding a bank envelope soaking wet and musty. I brought it into the kitchen, laid out some towels and tried to pat the $20 bills dry. I counted them three times; it was only $1260! Leaving the kitchen light on and the garage door open, I flew back to the Justice Center, where we emptied our wallets. Mark went to an ATM for the last missing dollars. We handed the wet and dry dollars to the young woman who was trying to keep a professional face on, and she handed us papers with a court date and bond restrictions. We were out of there.

We drove home in exhausted silence. I kissed Jeff goodnight, and removed pocketknives from his desk and razors from the bathroom. Then I fell asleep next to his bed. It was 4 AM. Our ordeal had only begun.

The Courts and the School Exact Double Punishment

The next day the sun came up as usual. We looked at our son's sleeping face, and experienced deep love, then guilt. We picked ourselves up, dusted ourselves off, and decided that it was not the end of the world, but we've got a problem, let's deal with this situation. This was not strength, but the auto-pilot of shock. Both of us were able to reschedule our work that day, being self-employed. We started making phone calls—we needed an attorney, and a child psychologist.

One of the bond conditions set at the jail was that Jeff was not to go to Peak to Peak Charter School, the school he had attended for the past two years. I expected to receive a phone call early that morning from Peak to Peak, to explain what was going on. By 10:30 am, no call, so I called them, leaving urgent requests for a callback an hour apart. Finally, I reached Mr.Fontana, the Principal, only to receive the terse answer: "It's under investigation. We'll be contacting you when it's finished."

We tried to make that weekend as normal as possible and reassured ourselves and our son that everything would get resolved, and that he would never have to set foot in Peak to Peak again. He would get a fresh start in a new school, and the District Attorney would surely reduce the charges to something more commensurate with the "crime" of angry fantasies. We knew they would come to their senses and realize that this was just a cry for help made, as we learned shortly, to a peer counselor, and that harsh charges were not warranted.

The next week, we tag-teamed going to work and staying home with Jeff, who seemed very relieved to be out of Peak to Peak, and almost cheerfully did math worksheets. I went to Peak to Peak to meet with Principal Fontana and a counselor, at my request. I had never met "Counselor A." They both looked at me across the table with drawn, tense expressions as they admitted that they had known about the situation "early last week." Distraught and incredulous, I demanded, "Why didn't you call me when you knew he was suicidal?!" Ms. A said, "Don't worry, he'll still go to college some day ..." I got up and left the room, and the office staff stared at me, the bad mother, as I walked out in tears. Later that day, the Dean, Mr.Chandler, called to notify us that Jeff would be expelled. We asked him why we weren't called before this, and why they were expelling him. He answered, "We don't know your son." We sat there dumbfounded next to the speakerphone, while Chandler mechanically explained the expulsion process, and invited Jeff to write a student response, obviously reading from a script. Hand-delivered letters later arrived, and couriers either did not look at me or studied my face at the door. Mark was so angry he could not answer the door in a civil fashion.

We had scheduled a midweek meeting with Howard Bittman, a defense attorney in Boulder recommended by our family attorney, at Bittman's Pearl Street Mall office. As we sat silently in the waiting area, a graying longish-haired man in a bolo tie and cowboy boots carrying a raft of papers bounded up the open oak staircase. "I'll be with you shortly," he said. His office was piled with papers, and plants sat by an open window in the 19th century building. After hearing our story and looking at the court papers, he asked to talk to Jeff alone, saying, "Don't worry, I don't bite!" When we came back in, he said he would take the case, and with hands tented together said, "These are very unusual charges for a juvenile; the school and the police are working together on this. When we go to court, I'll try to get it reduced." We thought, yes, the judge will curb this overzealous DA. On the way home, Mark began to lecture Jeff, head hanging, in the back seat. I interjected that it was my fault for choosing this stupid charter school.

On the evening before the court date, we got a call from Howard warning us that the DA would ask the judge to have our son incarcerated and then hospitalized for a psychiatric evaluation: "The DA says he's more concerned with his mental health than the felony charges." Jeff had just been seen and evaluated the previous day by Dr. Gregory Steinwand, a psychologist who concurred with the juvenile center evaluation that he was not a risk to himself or others, and agreed to see him for outpatient therapy. Knots began to form in our stomachs as Howard relayed this ominous news, visualizing our son being misdiagnosed and medicated by some quack, and exposed to both seriously mentally ill and aggressive children. We prepared Jeff for this and sugarcoated it, hoping that Howard could convince the judge that hospitalization was not needed.

Outside the courthouse on a paradoxically beautiful September morning, aspens clattering in the cool wind, I paged Dr. Steinwand. I relayed my fears, and he talked me down so I could keep it together for my son. Mark and Jeff were inside waiting for me; I finished up and hurried in, putting my purse and cell phone on the xray belt at security.

We found our son's name on a docket and looked around at all the other kids waiting with their parents; Jeff was the smallest one. Then we went into the chamber, sat down on one of the hard benches, and waited and watched as orange-suited, manacled teenagers filed in. They were big and either looked sad or tough. I imagined the heavy leather belt with handcuffs slipping down and around my son's knees, and these big teenagers intimidating him, or worse. The chamber filled, people watched the clock. A strange coterie of bare-midriffed girls and sports-jacketed boys appeared from an interior room behind the bench and hurried out, giggling and laughing, oblivious to us in the gallery. The judge was late. So was our attorney.

Then Howard arrived and explained that Magistrate Cole was typically late, and went to confer with the Deputy DA "Reeves."[1] There would be no reduction in charges. "They're really going after him," Howard commented grimly. Finally, "All rise," the Bailiff called out and the Magistrate arrived. He sat down and made a joke. The court staff and the DAs politely tittered, but none of us in the gallery even broke a smile. Then all the kids' names were called who were being offered "juvenile diversion"—a routine form of probation, which is what we had initially expected for our son. There weren't many of us left after that.

When Magistrate Cole looked up over his glasses and read Jeff's full name, we stood up and took our turn at the lectern with our attorney. Jeff, clean cut in his V-neck sweater, peered over the lectern and answered the judge, "Yes, Sir, no Sir." Reeves, a young fellow with that slightly unkempt Boulder look even in a suit, began to read the most alarming statement of the internet instant messages we had been shown, "… they deserve a shotgun blast to the face! …," and the charges of Anarchy and Sedition. The low murmur of attorneys and clients in the back of the chamber stopped, and we felt the stare on our backs. I put my hand on Jeff's shoulder and began to weep silently. Cole's bored look evaporated quickly. Reeves then went on to demand that our son's bond be revoked, he should not have been bonded out, someone made a mistake, he's a danger, etc., grandstanding on the case that was going to build his career, it appeared. When he was done, Howard calmly outlined the results of the evaluations by the juvenile center and Dr. Steinwand, and that his client had been carefully monitored for the past week at home without any problems. He showed the photos he had us take of our locked firearms storage. Furthermore, a formal and detailed psychological testing was scheduled for the following week with another psychologist well-known in Boulder, Dr. Shirley Thomas.

Reeves began to bluster and repeat his demands, when Magistrate Cole interrupted him and ordered a compromise: the so-called BEST Program. Jeff would be on house arrest essentially, and required to meet regularly with a juvenile officer. We breathed a sigh of relief. The sunny blue-sky day now seemed right,

---

1.   Name has been changed, and he is no longer with the Boulder DA's office.

when we walked out of the Justice Center with our son and took him home, again.

Late that afternoon, there was a knock at our door. A muscle-shirted, husky, balding man stood there, something out of the Hell's Angels or World Wrestling Federation. We looked around for the motorcycle and hesitated to answer the door, but we did, and met Jeff's assigned juvenile officer. He showed us his badge and asked to sit down. We went to the kitchen table with Jeff and the officer spread out the papers explaining what was required.

Jeff would have to be with a parent or at school at all times, call the officer any time he left the house with detailed information about where he would be, and call when he got home, call when he went to bed and when he got up. He could not visit friends or have friends over. There would be unannounced officer visits at school and at home, and urine drug tests. Mark began to protest, and I laid a hand on his, saying "Let the man finish." The officer told us that he could revoke the program and put Jeff into juvenile detention. Mark shut up. We signed the papers. The officer searched Jeff's room with its computerless monitor and keyboard on the desk, wires still askew. He looked around and had us open a locked trunk revealing stuffed animals, another one with Legos, and sorted through his rubber swords, removing two cork popguns for us to put away, "So the neighbors won't get the wrong idea." We did what we were told, to the letter. We were lucky to be able to adjust our work schedules and take the income hit.

By this time, one week after the arrest, Jeff's neighborhood friends had picked up that he wasn't in school, and we told little fibs to his friends' parents—"Some things were said that shouldn't have been said at school and he's grounded, and changing schools." His charter school friends knew the truth, as news travels fast when a Peak to Peak Board member's son, one of his persecutors, blabs it at the lunch table. All but one of these friends never called again, which was no surprise. It was hard on Jeff to lose those friends, but the neighborhood buddies did stick with him. He was able to talk on the phone but had to be close-mouthed about his circumstances. Until we were able to get him into a school, he occupied himself with books, video games, and worksheets. He went to therapy with "Captain Greg" as he called Dr. Steinwand, and was pretty much unaware of what a serious fix he was in, which was probably a good thing. He seemed so relieved to be out of Peak to Peak, and we did not discuss our fears with him.

We went with Jeff to his 3-hour psychological testing with Dr. Thomas. A detailed history of his upbringing and our marriage was taken. It's pretty intrusive stuff, but with Mark being a psychologist too, at least we knew it was standard and necessary. My worst fear was that Jeff had developed a serious mental disorder, since he had told the school peer counselor that he was afraid he might have the same mental illness she did. She had shared her experience with him, and her suicide attempt, over the summer by instant messaging, and had listened to his suicidal thoughts in return. We were not aware of this until we saw the message transcripts and her police interview. I was sick with worry as Dr. Thomas' door remained closed for hours, it seemed. The relief came with her facial expression as she came out and began to brief us on her initial findings. He had no mental illness, and no violent or delinquent tendencies. Just acute anxiety and stress. She theorized that when he said, "I was just typing," that it showed how in instant messaging, thoughts go directly into cyberspace. It is a fast-paced private conversation but with no spoken words to hear one's own thoughts, or facial expression or intonations to act as a check. We have all sent emails that we wish we hadn't, but instant messaging is the 100 MPH version, far removed from letters of my youth that sat on the hall table until the mailman came. Also, he was naive that expressions of anger, even to a peer counselor, are dangerous in the post-Columbine era, having been 9 years old then. On the way home, Jeff said, "I'm so glad I'm not crazy." In pictures worth a thousand words, there is a stark contrast between Jeff's school picture, taken a week before his angry instant messaging, and one taken a week after he left the school under such bad circumstances. One shows an unsmiling sallow boy in his only black T-shirt, a favorite with the white words The Voices In My Head Tell Me What To Do. The other is a metal-mouthed grinning child in a colorful tie-dye shirt hamming it up for the camera. One clearly says "I'm crazy," and the other says "I'm OK!"

We started the task of finding a new school for our son right away in the first week after the arrest. We initially thought that the school district would help us change schools, especially because Jeff's bullying had been religious in nature, and that the school district would not support the expulsion requested by Peak to Peak. We officially withdrew our son from Peak to Peak and asked the district in writing for a transfer, but got no response. Later, realizing that expulsion from all district schools was probable, we asked for alternatives as required by policy, such as tutoring or home school support. Dr. King, the Assistant Superintendent, told us to go to Peak to Peak to arrange home school support! Or try "Justice High School," run by Magistrate Cole in his rear chambers! (So that's who the kids were, streaming through the courtroom. It was high school age only, and full.) The only honest help came from a neighborhood middle school, whose registrar told me bluntly: "Start looking for a private school for your son, if you can afford it." We then called almost every private school in the north metro Denver area, and got three appointments. Two we had even investigated before; both were snooty and expensive. We found out that they really get snooty when your son has been arrested and expelled. The third was just really expensive, and we just did not think our son needed all those extra services for behaviorally disturbed children.

We finally found "August Academy," a year-round school with reasonable tuition. It is an alternative school that was started as a labor of love by an educator who left the public school system after seeing it fail many children. I can say that with equanimity now. Before the interview, I was taken aback when a young woman walked right up to Jeff and I in the waiting area and said, "Are you feeling rejected?" I snapped, "That's none of your business!" and the receptionist hurried the girl back to her classroom and apologized to us. Shortly, we met with the director, a loquacious grandfatherly type who was sympathetic to Jeff's story, which was similar to other children there who had been bullied in public schools and/or had legal troubles. The school also has many children who simply got lost, socially or academically, in large public schools. Jeff was accepted to the school, and as we left we passed tough-looking youths with facial piercings smoking outside the building. A colleague told me when I confided my fears of bad influence and drugs, "It's the same at all the public schools," ironically reminding me of some of the rationale for our ill-fated charter school choice. It was a difficult adjustment for us as parents to see our bright son in a school for "misfits." But Jeff liked its computer-based independent study immediately, quickly made new friends who were not weird or tough, and minor teasing of the new kid was stopped promptly by the staff. It was still embarrassing for him when the juvenile officer showed up, especially the urine tests.

The Expulsion—Unfair, with Little Recourse

Meanwhile, we fought the school district over the expulsion. We did not want that on his record, and wanted him back in a local middle school with his neighborhood friends. However, the Boulder Valley School District showed no interest in our complaints of religious harassment at Peak to Peak, and refused to delay the expulsion hearing until after the legal proceedings were resolved, or even acknowledge that they had made an error in stating that expulsion was required by Colorado school law for the alleged offense of school disruption.

We asked for information about what to expect, and received a black 3-ring notebook containing all the materials for the expulsion hearing. I leafed through it noting a number of inaccuracies. This included the dates of the school threat assessment, done a week after Fontana was notified by Counselor A of the instant message problem but dated as if done at the Thursday meeting that led to the arrest. There was an apparent failure to follow procedure as clearly outlined on the expulsion due process checklist, with excuses for the discrepancies scribbled in the margins. For example, the requirement to notify parents of referral to law enforcement was checked "No," and in the margin was written, "Administration no knowledge of police acting on this incident," despite checking "Yes" on law enforcement notification. Under Police Reports was an interview with Jeff's friend "Zack" about his internet messaging exchanges with Jeff; he denied any involvement, and painted him almost in a trenchcoat: "wears black and talks about death." There was an interview with the peer counselor, Zack's sister "Alexi," who reported 30-50 chats about suicide but never homicide since the end of last school year. The tab for Attendance, Grades and Disciplinary Actions showed 17 excused absences over 174 school days, the A's and B's sliding into C's, D's and an F, and no disciplinary actions. No surprise to us there. But then, under the tab Witness statements, I came to an email exchange that took my breath away. It was the internet instant messages coupled with the emails between the peer counselor Alexi and Counselor A early on a Monday evening, and showing Ms.A's forwarding it to Fontana the next morning, dumping it in his lap. This fully documented what the school counselor and principal knew and when they knew it, and demonstrated that Alexi was a peer counselor who had close contact with her supervisor. Ms. A told the peer counselor that the situation should be taken seriously and would be taken care of by herself and the principal. But, unbelievably, no action was taken for a full three days from this point! No one assessed Jeff, and no one called us, as he continued to attend school that week.

I then began to understand what Dean Chandler meant when he said, "We don't know your son." We weren't part of the "Christian family" at Peak to Peak, and our son was not worthy of even a basic standard of care response to his urgent cry for help. All school personnel and health professionals know that teens are impulsive and that any statements of suicidality must be dealt with as an emergency, in this case that night. With teen boys, who have a higher rate of successful suicides than girls and do not often give any warning, it is critical to act quickly. We were outraged.

We went to the expulsion hearing with our attorney and a legal transcriptionist, hoping for reason to prevail, though we had been warned that "basically, they can do what they want, and there is little legal recourse." Jeff was kept in school that day, to avoid subjecting him to further trauma.

We were in the conference room already when Dean Chandler and Principal Fontana came in. Chandler smiled stupidly and reached out his hand to Mark, who did not reciprocate. Fontana knew better, and looked appropriately nervous. Counselor A declined to be present, as did "Counselor B," Jeff's counselor. She was never contacted by Ms. A during the crisis and pled ignorance, but did apologize in a voice mail for not getting to Jeff first thing in the school year, as promised at the end of last year. Jeff's science teacher, who seemed sympathetic to our complaints of creationist class disruption and expressed support for Jeff, had been asked to come as a character witness, and he also declined, but then unexpectedly showed up. It was then disappointing to see him sit across from the principal and subtly hedge his positive assessment by saying, "He's usually respectful of other students, but sometimes he would groan, 'Hey, let's get back to science!'" We felt betrayed. The school district's attorney was a dour middle-aged woman who only broke her poker face to snicker at the photos of my son, and to coldly pronounce his written apology "insincere." (I learned much later in my reading on expulsions, that it is a typical school lawyer strategy to question the sincerity of expressed remorse, and that it is better to grovel than fight, because being adversarial will backfire and cause the hearing officer to mete out the harshest punishment.)

As the transcriptionist tapped quietly, Howard proceeded to interrogate Chandler and Fontana on their handling of the incident. "So you had the instant messages on a Tuesday morning, and legal authorities were made aware of the situation on a Thursday afternoon? What exactly were you doing for two and a half days with this information that a student wanted to kill himself and maybe others?" Chandler said he wasn't told until the meeting on Thursday. Fontana looked down and mumbled, "I was leafing through manuals and talking to the district, trying to decide what to do." Howard pressed him on his experience—10 years as a teacher or administrator—and why he didn't take immediate action in such an urgent situation. Fontana said, "I didn't think it was serious." He was forced to admit that no one contacted Jeff to evaluate how serious it was. And no one called the parents. Only the School Resource Officer seemed to know that action was required after reading the messages at the Thursday meeting, and he did what police do. He initiated an investigation, though he admitted at the expulsion hearing that he had "no clue" what crime might have been committed.

I was given time to read my statement, pleading for my son, and to show photos of him and his hobbies: collecting Kachinas (hand-carved, feathered Indian warriors and legend figures), painting Warhammer figurines (medieval army men), playing computer strategy games, and rollerblading. I told about how he loved animals and would not hunt with us. He was so empathetic with his new Golden Retriever puppy when it whimpered for its mother on the way home in the car, that he took her out of the crate to hold her, and asked moist-eyed if we should take her back. He had never been in trouble, and was not a budding socio-path who must be kept away from other students. They were given the psycholo-gist's report to review. He had made a cry for help, and deserved that help, not harsh punishment. His self-composed statement, written immediately after being invited to do so by Dean Chandler in our earlier conference call, read:

> "At your school, I was abused by children in my own grade for two years.
> Since I am an atheist, they called me a child of satan, devil child, and other
> ridiculous names. I was put down for two years, more than I could bear. I
> looked for guidance and they didn't give me any. They turned me down. I
> had no one to turn to. Zach and I started talking about this and it eventually
> got out of hand. He said the same things I did, and he is being called the
> hero and I the villain. It got out of hand and I snapped, so did he. His sister
> thought my fantasies were threats. Zach was in on this fantasy too. There
> were no real threats, just fantasies, and I know the difference quite clearly.
> He was protected and turned into a hero, and blamed it all on me. I do not
> deserve what is happening to me. I do not have access to any guns. I would
> never, never, never ever actually use my fantasies in reality. I am 13 years old
> and stupid. I didn't think people would take my thoughts and hunt me
> down for it. I am sorry for all the trouble I have caused. Please give me a
> chance to just live. Expulsion will mean the end of my life (in the sense of
> education, not death). Would you be pleased knowing that you ruined it?
> Please just realize the truth and make a clear and realistic decision."

When the hearing was over, we had hopes that the hearing officer from the state, who makes the final decision, would recommend suspension and then admission to the neighborhood middle school, not expulsion. But legally he was only able to decide whether the school district had properly followed procedure and whether there were grounds for suspension or expulsion, either of which were options in this case, "Disruption of school operations." There were some procedural problems with the school's handling of the expulsion process, but they were not major. It was Peak to Peak that had asked for expulsion, and the district could have modified this to suspension, but chose not to, and we did not under-stand this, given the mitigating factors of religious harassment and the fact that the vague threats, rated "low or moderate" in the threat assessment, were made to a peer counselor. We had already withdrawn Jeff from Peak to Peak and certainly had no plans to return there after a suspension, but were hoping at least to salvage his school record from the damnation of an expulsion. And there was no actual school disruption, but the school expected bad publicity (according to Fontana at the hearing in explaining how the school was "disrupted") so it caused its own fuss by sending a letter home with students about the arrest, offering counseling for anyone traumatized by the news, and boasting how their Character Education made the difference in averting disaster. What BS! We found it ironic that no support, advice or counseling were ever offered to us by Peak to Peak or the district. Our family was apparently irredeemable, part of the "wave of evil" spoken of after Columbine. Our hopes were dashed when we received a letter a few days later notifying us of the one year expulsion from all Boulder Valley Schools. The district did reduce it to six months in exchange for no legal challenge, so at least Jeff could start his freshman year at his neighborhood high school on time in August.

The Legal Fight and its Resolution

At a mid-September hearing, Jeff pleaded Not Guilty to the charges of Anarchy and Sedition, Incitement of Destruction of Life or Property. Deputy DA Reeves again tried to make our lives difficult by adding restrictions to Jeff's bond: no computer or internet use, and reiterated his demand for a separate psychiatric evaluation. This alerted us to the possibility that the BEST Program juvenile officer had relayed our inquiry on supervised internet use to the DA, and may have been acting as his agent in his request for Dr. Thomas' report, which I had sidestepped. By then, the report was finished, but Howard did not want to hand it over prematurely before trial so the prosecution could pick it apart. Magistrate Cole had just handed out several sentences, in cases previous to Jeff's that day, which were harsher than the DA had asked for, with even Reeves wincing. Cole threatened to revoke Jeff's bond if the report was not given to him, but did not impose any further bond restrictions or evaluations. By this time, we were almost used to barely getting out alive from that Justice Center. A defense motion to discontinue the burdensome BEST Program, based on Drs. Thomas and Steinwand's reports, was denied.

About this time, becoming frightened by all of our close calls in court, and alarmed that our son's civil rights had been violated by the school and the police, Mark made a desperate appeal for advice to the famed Wyoming lawyer Gerry Spence, whose email address was in a book of Spence's poetry that Mark had and liked. To our surprise, Spence responded quickly and sympathetically to "get the best lawyer you can afford, and consider looking for an interested news reporter." We had already been turned down by the Colorado ACLU in a form letter. Howard was doing his best. A second opinion from another attorney was cut short when he said, "If Howard Bittman can't help you, your son is really in trouble." The Boulder Daily Camera newspaper editor did not return Mark's phone call. As described in Chapter 5, I called the Lafayette News, and Howard was quoted, "The charges are insane," but this little East Boulder County weekly probably was not read by, nor had any influence on, the DA.

By three weeks into this, Mark and I were sleep deprived, exhausted, and had lost weight. My stomach was awful, and so was my hair, with the gray showing. Interrupted dental work and a missing tooth completed this picture, but there wasn't much smiling to be done. I had not told anyone except a trusted colleague who filled in for me, and in whom I had previously confided my gripes about the school. I finally broke down and called my own doctor for some stomach and sleeping medication. I wrote letters to my family and a close friend, weeping over the keyboard in my bathrobe. I asked them to email, not call, because I would just cry into the phone. Most of our family was very supportive, but some, we could just tell what they thought of us, or maybe it was just guilty feelings. One relative tried to reassure us about our parenting by saying, "Something must be wrong with Jeff." Another said, "You should really get rid of those guns." Some relatives subtly distanced themselves from us. This was painful. Even our attorney Howard asked Mark, "Why didn't you get him out of that school?" Howard was not a hand-holder. We worried intensely about all aspects of the case, and bugged Howard too frequently, I'm sure. Another lawyer told Mark, "If you want your hand held, go see your Rabbi. Bittman is Harvard Law '72 and the most aggressive lawyer in town, without being a nut." I could relate to this; bedside manner is not the most important attribute in a surgeon, either. We ruminated in 20-20 hindsight about our son's attempts to communicate his distress to us, and I felt responsible for it all. We had nightmares and gut-wrenching fears of what would happen to him if convicted, especially after a well-meaning relative sent us online research about the horrible conditions in the detention facility for juveniles convicted of felonies. We had nightmares reflecting our anger at the DA, police and school officials; we'll just leave it at that, given what happened to our son when he expressed himself. The BEST Program was very stressful, with its threat of detention for a missed phone call, or falsely positive urine drug test, which I knew from my medical experience was not uncommon. Jeff was now out of his new school two weeks for fall break, necessitating work schedule changes again, and it was the wrong time for me to have to deal with a rash of difficult cases and pushy administrators.

We dealt with it all the best way we could, and I can't imagine what a single parent with an inflexible job and limited financial and social resources would have done. If we didn't have our work, it would have been worse, and both of us escaped our own problems by solving our patients'. I laid a flagstone pathway to expend nervous energy while stuck at home. Our juvenile officer sat at our kitchen table and asked me for advice on his red eye and shared some of his own problems. One of our neighbors put two and two together, having seen some of the press in nearby Lafayette, and made a kind offer to vouch for our son's character if needed. Jeff's grown older sister came for a visit and brought affection and remote control cars, and a good friend of mine offered to come stay during the trial. More than once I left Sunday church service in near-tears, and then I got up the energy to call my pastor. I shared with her my sense of abandonment and anger at God for letting Christians persecute us, and I bargained with God like a patient with cancer. There was no fall family camping and no homemade jelly that year. Mark did accompany his brother who came from out of state for a long planned elk hunt, but was sick with worry and altitude and was unable to hunt. It was a very dark time for us, the worst either Mark or I had ever experienced in our lives, and ordinary routines were replaced by a siege and survival mentality. But there were kindnesses extended to us, and we were fortunate to have the support, resources and time to fight for our son.

At an early October hearing, Discovery was due. All the evidence that the prosecution has must be given to the defense, which has the advantage of not being required to provide any evidence until trial. The DA had nothing. There were no "30-50 pages of emails" and no computer analysis. He announced, "We have a deal." Howard quickly corrected him "No, we don't," and proceeded to tell Magistrate Cole that the defense had received no Discovery. The DA had some excuse about the computer forensic analysis being delayed, and asked the judge for more time. But the trial date was less than three weeks away, and there needed to be a reasonable amount of preparation time for the defense. By law, a juvenile must be adjudicated (trial started) within 60 days of charges being filed. Magistrate Cole gave DA Reeves another week to come up with it.

That afternoon, Howard received a fax from the DA saying he had to dismiss the case, unless we agreed to change to a guilty plea on the felony charges, six more weeks of BEST Program, then one year of probation, and an essay on Columbine. If we didn't accept, they might refile the charges in the future. We said we would consider a misdemeanor plea bargain, but we were not going to have our son plead guilty to this bizarre felony, Anarchy and Sedition. We had studied the statute and the cases and knew he was not guilty. Howard said there were probably constitutional barriers to refiling the same charges, related to the 60 day rule and double jeopardy. The most the DA would do is take out the BEST, and reduce it to six months probation. We agonized over the decision. Howard said, "This can't be any worse than one of your patients trying to decide on cancer treatment. If you want to be done with this for sure, take it." But we just couldn't stomach the felony conviction, and said no (and go to hell, Reeves), and took our chances with a big deep breath. I learned later that this is considered by some legal observers to be an unethical prosecution tactic, that of bringing serious charges without evidence, then moving for dismissal before trial while threatening to refile and put you through it all over again if a plea is not taken. Some judges will not allow this, and Howard told the judge (not Cole, but another one who received the motion to dismiss) "We object, we are ready for trial." But the judge granted the dismissal, with a hand written note to "consider if any refiling is legal."

We left a polite message for our juvenile officer, saying goodbye. He actually turned out to be a decent guy who was devoted to his job; I'm sure Jeff was the easiest client he ever had. It took some doing to get our bond money returned, but when the check arrived, I was embarrassed to bring it to the bank to deposit, not being an ATM user. Getting the computer back was likewise labor intensive for Howard, but he said that the release meant the computer contained nothing incriminating, and "I don't think you'll be hearing from them again." It was scary to go to the Lafayette PD to pick it up. You develop a paranoia when the last two months of your life has been a Kafka-esque nightmare. We discovered that someone had played a game of Counterstrike, an anti-terrorist game that was one of Jeff's favorites, so we worried about planted evidence. I learned more than I wanted to about data scrubbing, Windows back-doors, taps on your ISP, etc. The tall red custom tower, festooned with tiny bits of hard-to-remove yellow and black evidence tape, did make quite a splash with the computer nerd crowd at Jeff's school, though. To them, Jeff was the internet free-speech anti-bully hero, with the scars to prove it. He was comfortable there with these other boys who had also found respect and success in this other world of complex strategy games in which their characters were heroes, not freaks or children of Satan.

Then we got mad and filed a Notice of Claim against Peak to Peak Charter School and the Boulder Valley School District (BVSD), for violation of our son's civil rights. The Notice of Claim is a required preliminary stage in suing a government entity in Colorado. We did it more to get their attention, which had been sorely lacking thus far, to problems at the charter school. Copies were sent to all BVSD Board Members as a formal Public Complaint, and also to the Boulder Daily Camera. The BVSD spokeperson sniffed dismissively, "We're going to wait and see if a suit is actually filed," in response to the reporter's inquiry in a small article. Nothing happened. No phone calls, no response.

A couple of months went by. We stopped holding our breath and gradually quit worrying about a refiling. We started sleeping better. My stomach settled down and I started exercising again. We got out of town for the holidays to visit relatives in Santa Fe. My referrals had dropped off, and I received some criticism from one of the nursing homes on my communication skills for the past few months. I imagine I had been brusque with the nurses, which is very unlike me. I apologized, saying that I had been having personal difficulties, and promised to do better. Jeff was settled in his school, and we were starting to trust them with our son. Things were starting to be okay again.

Not Over Yet

2004 arrived, and it felt fresh and hopeful. We had survived an ordeal that had tested and strengthened our family, and had put things in perspective for us. Jeff completed his short-term therapy for the stress of the legal proceedings, and it seemed that just getting out of the charter school was the rest of the cure. We began to plan for a transfer to the local high school next fall, by filling out the necessary paperwork at the school district. They don't make it easy to get out of a charter school once enrolled, even in our situation. And I did not trust them, so I got everything in writing.

Then one evening at 6 PM, Howard called. I cheerily greeted him, thinking that he had some communication on the Notice of Claim. "You're not going to like this conversation." I fell silent. "The DA has brought new charges of Solicitation of First Degree Murder against Jeff. He'll be arrested again soon." I could not believe my ears. "What?! That's ridiculous!" He agreed, and said he didn't know when the police would come, but would try to get more information. "Do we have to answer the door?!" "No." I hung up the phone in a cold sweat. I turned off the stove and waited for Mark to get home.

Later that evening, we sat down with Jeff to gently explain that charges were being refiled. He said plaintively, "Why are they doing this to me?! I don't want to be arrested again—that was scary!" We hugged him and reassured him that everything would get straightened out yet again. Then we closed every blind and drape in the house and cowered behind them for three days. We peered out before leaving the house each day, and started our tag-team routine again, not wanting to leave Jeff at home alone, since he was still on winter break for two more weeks. Howard called to say said he could probably arrange a more civilized arrest process if we hustled and got letters from his school about his behavior, and his therapist about the negative mental health effects of another SWAT-like arrest. We hustled. The school director wrote a glowing and true letter on very short notice, and Dr. Steinwand likewise came through for us.

I was instructed to call the Lafayette PD to arrange an intake. I did not trust them, and asked for reassurance that they would not be keeping him this time. We went to the station still very nervous about what they might pull on us this time. It did go smoothly, though, and Jeff seemed to handle the photo and fingerprints well. The officer handed me the new police report as he processed Jeff, and I flipped through it, seeing that Zach had said that Jeff had "asked him three times to help him go kill people at the school." I closed the report and said dryly, "I'm going to refrain from commenting on these charges." The officer made no reply and escorted us to the exit. We have no way of knowing whether it was true or not, but Jeff later heard by the grapevine that Zach had told friends at Peak to Peak that he would be grounded for a year if he didn't testify against Jeff.

Jeff still had one Peak to Peak friend, who wasn't allowed to see Jeff, but they did talk on the phone and "George" relayed all the scuttlebutt. Jeff was apparently now a big hero among the "outcasts" who did not appreciate the Fundamentalist Christian kids who rule the roost at Peak to Peak, and went around telling other kids that they were going to hell, disrupting science classes, and getting teachers fired. George was a tough Italian kid, who was also bullied but gave it right back, and got into trouble for it. Zach was also one of the outcasts, telling Jeff once that he, too, was an atheist, but his parents made him go to a church where he saw many of the Peak to Peak teachers and students. Lots of other students didn't like what was going on, but kept quiet to avoid becoming targets.

Jeff went back into therapy with Dr. Steinwand at his recommendation. He looked tired and pale, so I took him for a doctor visit, worrying about things like leukemia, on top of everything else, but thankfully he was just sleeping poorly. There was nothing malignant except the legal process he was being subjected to. I hunkered down in the basement and organized boxfuls, 20 years' worth, of family photos and watched our son grow up in them; how lost was the innocence of childhood, so prematurely, now. I worked out my anger and worry at the gym. It was hard to believe how aggressive the Lafayette PD was, and I couldn't help but suspect that there was some connection to the Notice of Claim that we had filed against the school, and that the school was again working closely with the police. Lafayette is a small town. The police spokesman had nastily called our town's newspaper, which printed a prominent notice on the police blotter page, boasting of the re-arrest and sensational charges.

Howard was tight-lipped about Jeff's chances this time of prevailing again. "I want to see what was in his computer before offering an opinion on that," he said stiffly. That did not sound good. He finally received the complete police report with the forensic computer analysis, and sent me a copy. In a few days would be the preliminary or pre-trial hearing, where in serious felony cases, the judge decides whether there is enough evidence to proceed to trial. This protects defendants, and the court docket, against frivolous prosecution, but 95% of cases are referred on to trial, Howard explained. But when it was, then he could file a motion that the refiling was not constitutional. We steeled ourselves to a trial. We were told that a juvenile non-violent first offense usually did not result in a detention sentence, but by this time, having experienced successive very aggressive prosecutions, we had little confidence in a reasonable outcome.

On a Sunday in February before the pre-trial hearing, I spread out all the reports on the bed and began to study them, though I almost didn't want to, feeling discouraged and helpless at this point. But being an internist, details are crucial and even irresistible. I read several sad poems and musings, and one brief angry story, all with titles and Jeff's byline. There were downloaded comics of existential teen angst. But no maps, no plans, no names and no hit lists. I was then flabbergasted to discover, as someone who was embarrassingly computer-illiterate, a glaring error in the Lafayette Police Detective's report on the forensic analysis. He had misinterpreted as Jeff's, the forensic examiner's search terms used to find evidence on the hard drive. The search terms were: "killing a person" and "killing a person with reference to a common scheme or plan." It was as plain as day to me that these were not the search terms of a child, and the chain of events leading to the second round of charges became crystal clear in my mind. The police were probably frustrated with their attempts to nail our son the first time around when they prematurely pushed serious felony charges for which they had little evidence. They scoured the computer analysis and fastened on the "search terms," called Zach back in for a re-interview, and asked leading questions. I quickly typed up a note on my findings to Howard and faxed it to his office for him to review on Monday. I was surprised to get back a fax that afternoon with the theories and cases to be used. In order to prove solicitation of murder, there must be convincing evidence of intent to act, i.e., plans and steps taken to carry out the crime. Howard did not think there was this evidence. It was reassuring to know that he was working over the weekend on our son's defense.

We made no plans for the future, spring break or beyond, not knowing what to expect, not wanting to even think about a juvenile detention sentence but these intrusive thoughts would not stay away. We made an appointment to have

Jeff's braces removed, not only because he was sick of them, but because serious injury can result from a punch in the mouth. Magistrate Cole had refused to pass the case to another court, as was standard for serious felonies. This was a bad omen, as we had come to experience Cole as unpredictable. Any challenges to the refiling had to wait until after the case was forwarded for trial.

The dreaded day finally came. The courtroom was empty that day except for our case, and the chamber echoed even with low volume voices. We sat down on the front bench, where Reeves sauntered over in front of us and related his recent bike accident to a female court employee in casual tones. I clutched my little prayer on a 3x5 card, from Psalms 25:1-5, "… they will be put to shame who are treacherous without excuse … my hope is in You all day long." Then Howard breezed in confidently, and playfully punched at Jeff, saying, "Are you ready for round 2, buddy?" Then he and Jeff went to sit at the defense table, boy and man forms in silhouette in front of us.

It was a blur, over more quickly than I imagined it could be. Howard completely shredded the Detective and made his error apparent, then turned his head and grinned at us in delight. The computer forensic report and hard drive printouts were handed to the Magistrate. Howard snarled at Reeves when he did not follow proper decorum. He was in control from the outset. Zack took the stand and confirmed that his sister, whom Jeff had confided in, was a peer counselor. He had answered "Yes" when asked by the prosecutor if he thought Jeff was serious about wanting to kill other students, but was vague when asked about any plans. When Howard patiently questioned him, Zack talked about the bullying Jeff endured, "because he was different and small." Then he recanted his previous statement and testified that if he really thought it was serious when they were messaging almost a year ago last April, he would have told someone. When Zack was done, Howard touched Jeff's shoulder and asked if he was doing ok. Dr. Steinwand testified that the internet messages were "compensatory fantasies in a child who has been literally persecuted for his beliefs." The case collapsed before our eyes. Howard's final wrap up was heart-felt, "It's just not right" to pass the case on for trial. It appeared to us that Reeves, leaning on his table and staring at his brief, was embarrassed that he had apparently not thoroughly studied the case materials. He then tried to make the argument that the speech in the computer did not come under the First Amendment. Magistrate Cole listened intently. He studied the computer contents printout and deliberated quietly for some time. I imagine now, after all the daily grind of monotonous juvenile cases, and trying to make a difference in his Justice High School, that Cole found this a lot more interesting and challenging.

Finally the Magistrate gave his decision, in a suspenseful, drawn-out statement, repeating "In the light most favorable to the People," meaning the prosecution is favored in these proceedings. "What I see here are some poems and images." And then, "I find that there is insufficient evidence to proceed. Case dismissed." And the tall black-robed figure got up and walked out.

I gave out a little shriek of relief and ran to hug Jeff, who said in an embarrassed tone, "Mom!" Reeves slumped at his table. Howard beamed, and told the young reporter rushing up from the back of the room, "Justice was done." When asked if he thought there would be a third try to prosecute our son, he said "I hope not. Enough is enough." I asked Howard if I could give him a hug and he accepted. It was all more than we had dared to hope for on that cold February day. I believe my prayer helped, even though the God I believe in does not micromanage human affairs or often interfere in our follies and tragedies.

As we walked to the car, Jeff commented on how his friend Zack never mentioned that he was also part of the fantasies. I said, he's not your friend and let's not speak of him or the fantasies again. We got to the car, just as Howard hurried past us with his briefcase tucked under his arm and jumped into his dented older model sedan and waved at us as he drove away.

Our ordeal was finally over. We treated ourselves to a spring break Mexican vacation on plastic, although we could not afford it, having taken over $25,000 out of retirement and college funds for legal fees, therapy, and tuition. It was like night to day, sitting on the beach by the sparkling water, still surreal. The paranoia stayed with us a long time. Like worrying about being stopped in customs and rearrested for trying to flee the country. Back at home, we would startle to see a police car in the rear-view mirror. Jeff would swallow hard while eating at Burger King if cops came in for lunch, or came into school. We had a fear that any minor incident caused by a friend would be blamed on him given his arrest record, and warned him, more than we normally would, about hanging out with any shoplifters, bigmouths, fighters, or potsmokers. Cars in our cul-de-sac at night elicited waves of anxiety and trips to the window. Newspaper articles on allegations of police mistreatment were read with a less jaundiced eye.

In the summer, as we prepared to enroll Jeff in public high school to start his freshman year, the school, despite knowing Jeff's situation, denied him pre-access to a counselor, and assigned him to the standard peer counseling group run by an upper classman. I took this to mean that our son was not welcome there. A relative, a school counselor herself who was dismayed at how the suicidality had been handled, had nevertheless warned us of negative effects if we initiated legal action against the school district, and she may have been right. I also worried that Jeff's past would follow him, leading to dangerous rumors that would be treated as fresh threats. When Jeff expressed that he really liked his new school and was feeling stressed about going back to public school, we listened. So we kept him at August, even though it was not intellectually challenging, but the public school was not that great either in this regard. Inquiring calls to private schools were not returned. Jeff also had an "anniversary reaction" about this time, reliving in his mind the events of a year ago. Being arrested twice for no good reason is traumatic enough for anyone, more so for a child, and it is extremely traumatic as an horrific denouement to two years of persecution. The fact that Mark and I as professionals knew we all had post-traumatic stress disorder did not make it go away. It has taken about two years for most of our symptoms to be gone, and for me to be able to put this on paper.

As I write this, it is like watching your family in a home movie, more objective but still painful, and scenes keep appearing in my mind, as if picked up off the cutting room floor and spliced back into the reel. The clothes I wore to court are hard to put on, but I refuse to get rid of them. There is more to this story, as the following chapters will tell.

2

"We don't know your son"

The Boulder Valley School District (BVSD) is known as one of the better districts in the Denver metro area, which is not surprising, given its higher socioeconomic status. However, east Boulder County schools tended to stepchild status compared with those in Boulder proper, also known as The People's Republic of Boulder. Elementary schools in our town were bursting at the seams with 700 kids, while folks in Boulder whined about the closure of tiny boutique schools of 200 or even fewer students, housed in historic buildings.

We were mostly satisfied with our son's elementary school, other than the fuzzy math, and he did well there from kindergarten on, graduating in 2001. He had lots of friends, and always had big birthday parties since he wanted to invite all of them. In the 5th grade, his teacher had 32 kids in his class. They were mostly boys, and some of the ones the more senior teachers did not want, I'm sure. The result was a beleaguered teacher who gave very little homework, and was so occupied with struggling students that he had no time to push bright students like our son to excel. The principal was stellar, and the discipline seemed generally common sense. Once Jeff broke up a scuffle between friends on the playground, and pulled one off the other who was on the ground. Jeff landed in the principals office with the other two, but reason prevailed, compared with some newspaper reports in a following chapter. All three received an after school detention, which seemed a little unfair to Jeff. He never again involved himself in others' tiffs, which is a shame. The cost of this discipline tactic of disempowering the bystander, which was later visited upon him in middle school, is that no one stands up for the bullied child. Another time, Jeff came home unhappy about classmates' snickers during the lesson on Hannukah before Winter Break, and the teacher took Mark's complaint about it seriously. During a computer lab session when the teacher was out of the room, another student approached Jeff and stuck his hand in Jeff's pocket, saying "I'm gay." Jeff pushed him away and said "Get away from me!" Discipline for the other student, who denied it but had previous

25

similar issues, was prompt and effective. This is "in loco parentis" (Latin for in place of the parent), a legal doctrine supporting school discipline, and was the traditional method in schools until recently. Nowadays, school officials seem to have abdicated this responsibility with statements such as,"We don't know who to believe," and punish bullies and their targets alike, or just call the cops to solve their problems.

The school did show signs of Boulderism, however, with "Reading to End Racism," a tolerance-teaching program that parents volunteered to do, to avoid emphasis on white male guilt. And PFLAG (Parents and Friends of Lesbians and Gays) literature began to appear, along with "pink triangle safe zone" posters about the school. We're all for adult gay civil rights and protecting students from harassment, but this was too much for an elementary school and may have been related to the above-mentioned behavior problem. I successfully lobbied to get the posters replaced with the more inclusive "rainbow circle safe zone" posters, which clearly state that all children are safe here from religious, racial, ethnic, sexual, and disability-related bullying. I also didn't like the coed sex-ed classes that taught the finer details of female hygiene management and made fun of boys' puberty issues.

All told, we were ready to try something new for middle school. I spent hours investigating and visiting public, private and charter schools. Jeff wanted to go to a neighborhood middle school that some of his friends planned to attend, but it was not our assigned school, which was new and had rumors of poor leadership. I checked out the middle school he wanted, which had 1000 students until the new school opened. I was not impressed, and the cursing, smoking, half-dressed girls in front of the school completed this impression. Private schools were, as previously mentioned, snooty and expensive, but we did apply to one and were turned down, which was actually a relief at the time. There was a highly rated charter school in Boulder that had a long waiting list. Then we heard about Peak to Peak, a new K-5 charter which had just started up that fall, and was opening a middle school next year and later a high school. We were favorably impressed by their presentation of academic rigor, character education, small classes, and a closed campus (no in-and-out nonsense during the day). There was no hint of an agenda other than a traditional college prep curriculum, which was just what we were looking for.

We had a family discussion, with Mark hesitant to try a charter school, because "that's where the troublemakers end up who can't make it in a public school." I pointed to the other high-scoring and sought after charter. Jeff was not thrilled, but game, since one of his friends, George, was going to enroll at Peak to

Peak. So we applied through the open enrollment process, and he was accepted to the small 6th grade class.

The Lafayette campus consisted of three portable buildings, with permanent buildings promised next year. We donated kitchen appliances and furniture after our recent remodel. Jeff and I volunteered our time moving the school from a rental building to the new campus, and there was a lot of camaraderie and excitement. We met one of the science teachers, and helped him unpack boxes. Jeff, being a computer nerd himself, liked the computer courses he talked about. I signed up to help serve lunch one day per week, donated the requested financial contribution, and dutifully clipped "Boxtops for Education" for fundraising. The teachers seemed enthusiastic, several had advanced degrees, and best of all, they gave homework.

But the first week of 6th grade was a disaster for 11 year old Jeff, and I picked him up to daily tales of poor classroom discipline with spitballs flying, name-calling and chaotic hallways. Jeff had been repeatedly called a dumb-ass by one kid, and his 8th grade girl lab partner in his mixed grade science class was merciless: "Oh, here's the little dork!" Mark was ready to pull him out, but I thought the situation was remediable, so I set to work, leaving messages and letters for teachers. Finally we got some results. I attended the school anti-bullying meeting for parents one evening, and the Elementary School Principal outlined the "HA-HA-SO" program in use for middle school: Kids are told to tell a teacher, ignore it and walk away, say stop it, agree with the bully and laugh it off, or make fun of yourself. I was dismayed. She frowned when I shared my experience of what worked: being insistent that staff intervene and correct the bullying. I left the meeting early. This was just ordinary bullying, the kind we had heard was common in middle school, and it seemed to get better, but then we started noticing other disturbing signs.

A whiff of what was to come emanated from bright yellow posters in all the hallways, advertising a Bible study at the home of a prominent volunteer, whom we later found out was a Peak to Peak Board member's wife. Mark didn't like it, but I thought it was harmless at the time. Then there appeared a flyer in Jeff's backpack for an overnight youth activity with Pastor "Super Dave" at a local Christian church, that had been given to all middle schoolers. Jeff was a little interested, since many of his classmates were going, but I was wary of any overnight activities with youth leaders whom I did not know personally, and thought it was inappropriate to push this at school. We held our noses, and didn't say anything to the school about it. (We later learned that there had been a huge uproar about it, a battle royale between those pro and con this practice, leading to a policy that such flyers could only be given to those who wanted them. But how do you say no to the popular kids?) We continued to hold our noses when we went to a fundraiser where there was an invocation and *God Bless America* was sung. Mark was offended. I felt less uncomfortable, being Christian, and it was just several months after September 11th, 2001, but I didn't think it was appropriate for a public school function.

The religious atmosphere became thicker when Jeff reported, annoyed, that he had to sit through three or four oral presentations of "Why Jesus is My Hero" during one class period in his English class. This teacher had also told him that his short story would be sent to a district middle school competition, but later selected a religious work by a 9th grader instead, and Jeff was disappointed. I did not question her about changing her mind or her apparent insensitivity in allowing Christian proselytism. But I'm sure that other BVSD teachers would have required that students each pick a different hero, or find some way to finesse the situation to respect the beliefs of all. I recall one situation in a BVSD elementary school in which a girl was required to change her science project because it showed that most children picked a white Barbie over a black Barbie as more beautiful. There was a First Amendment fuss made by the girl's parents, but the teacher and the district just put their foot down. The classroom is not the public square for adult-style free speech, and I wrote a letter of support to the school district Superintendent. Jeff did tell the English teacher that one of the bullies had purposefully tripped him coming in to the classroom, but she just brushed it off, saying it must have been an accident. Like the proverbial frog in a pot of slowly heating water, we continued to ignore the growing danger at Peak to Peak.

Then, in February, things came to a rapid boil in biology class. Jeff reported that several students were shouting out things at the teacher when she tried to teach animal classification systems. "No, that's not the way it happened! You weren't there, how do you know?" etc. The teacher had tried to discipline them, but they wouldn't shut up. One day, Jeff came home asking Mark for help with his assignment—he had volunteered to represent the science side in a debate on "Science vs. Creationism" that the teacher had set up.

Mark and Jeff sat down and reviewed some of the basic evolution principles in preparation. I didn't like it, and called Ms. Groves, who was the Middle School Principal then, relaying my concerns. I later found out she wisely canceled the debate, but the damage had already been done. From that day forward, Jeff was targeted for vicious religious harassment by the creationists in classes and hallways that never stopped despite all our efforts. His non-Christian viewpoint and Russian surname had made him a target.

Jeff was taunted relentlessly with "You're the child of Satan," "You're the Devil's child," "Your father is Satan," "You're going to hell if you don't believe," and other completely un-Christian religious abuse. Jeff complained to the biology teacher to no avail. When we complained to her about the disruptions at the parent-teacher conference, she said that it did not bother her and she loved the school. I complained to Ms. Grove about the harassment, and provided the offending students' names. When I followed up a week later, she said, "I haven't been able to contact all the students, too busy." The next time, she said, "The other children say he's giving it back as good as he gets." I said, "That's not really his style." No discipline, to my knowledge, and no mediation were initiated. We reiterated our instructions to Jeff to defend yourself, but do not start anything, don't say anything bad about their religion, and to just keep telling the teachers.

We decided that we would call the parents of one of the worst offenders. This was a time-tested method from Mark's youth, involving the parents if things couldn't be worked out by the kids or their siblings. The student's mom assured us that it would stop. Jeff later heard that the girl had been grounded, and he said she seemed nicer lately, but the other students were still keeping it up. We tried to emphasize with Jeff that the taunts were just ridiculous, and made them look foolish. It's clear to us now, that to be immersed in this culture every school day was too much to ask of a 12 year old. And an adult would never be asked to put up with this for one instant in the workplace.

By now it was April, and the Phys Ed classes were outdoors. These were also mixed grade, coed classes. An older boy, "Kent," began to make fun of Jeff in PE, while his friend, the girl mentioned above, would observe and giggle approvingly. It quickly escalated to rough tackling during flag football, which somehow the PE teacher never seemed to see. Kent then commenced a relentless campaign of obscene sexual comments that are not repeatable, accusing Jeff of masturbation, homosexuality, bestiality, and incest. This happened in PE, hallways, the library, and even field trips. It was extremely mortifying, but other students thought it was hilarious or pretended not to notice. I called Kent's dad, and got nowhere with my friendly heads up about his son's behavior. So I marched into school on a nearly daily basis to complain, verbally and in writing, to Ms. Grove, the PE teacher, and Counselor B. I was on the warpath, ever so politely furious with each additional incident, even interrupting Ms. B filling her plate with cookies at the Volunteer Tea to pull her aside and tell her it was still happening, and to please do something!

Sitting down with Ms. Groves early on in this siege, she told me things about the older student and her own sons that I neither needed or wanted to know, in an apparent attempt to gain my sympathy, and that I should be patient. I was taken aback, but said nothing. She said that the PE teacher will be more aware, and have Jeff come directly to the office if anything happens. She had questioned one student that Jeff knew had been a witness, but who declined to say he had heard or seen anything. At one meeting, she told me that she did not believe Jeff because there were no witnesses who would back up his story, so he must be "Paranoid." It seemed that Kent had everyone intimidated, and entertained, with his exploits. I personally observed this boy's aggressive behavior, and at one point I happened to pass him sitting sullenly outside the school office, and he gave me a stare. I had seen this look once before, in a Boy Scout who choked Jeff when he tripped over the older, bigger boy's shoes. When the Scoutmaster refused to do anything about it, and said that Jeff and another Scout must have provoked the older boy, that was the end of Jeff's Scout career, which was on its way out anyhow because of Jeff's growing aversion to religion. In a last ditch appeal to Kent's parents, Mark called them but the response was cool. Mark calmly warned them to get their kid off our son's back, or we're going to call the police.

In early May on a Friday, Jeff went to the office to report more verbal harassment. Kent was sent in unescorted, after Jeff, and they sat there together briefly while waiting for the principal. Kent looked Jeff in the eye and sneered, "I'm going to [credible threat of lethal violence], you f—ing freak!" Then the principal's door opened and Jeff went in. It was the Elementary Principal, filling in for Groves that day. When Jeff told her of the threat, she said "I'll write that down," but no further action was taken. Jeff then complained to the PE teacher, who said, "Are you sure about this? You need to give Kent a chance." Later when Mark arrived to pick Jeff up and heard about it, he, Jeff and the PE teacher were discussing it outside the school when Kent walked by and gave them all a rude gesture. Mark said, "Is that the kid?" The PE teacher said nothing, and did nothing, other than commenting that the student "was aggressive but it was hard to know who to believe." (!)

When they got home it was only 3:30, so I called the school to ask the Elementary Principal what she was going to do, but she had left for the day. I called the school district office and was advised to go with Jeff to school together on Monday and meet with staff to develop a plan to ensure his safety. Later that evening, the Elementary Principal called us to say in her best soothing-a-child voice, "The best way to deal with this situation is for the adults to model appropriate behavior."

It was just more of the same BS, and no action. We had had enough. So, over the weekend we called the Lafayette police, who gave us the School Resource

Officer's email, and we sent a detailed description of the problem. We kept Jeff home on Monday. That day, after interviewing the student, who admitted to the threat, the SRO asked us if we wanted to make a criminal complaint. We said it didn't seem necessary to arrest the kid, just warn him and get him to leave our son alone. In a Tuesday meeting with Ms. Grove, the SRO and both boys, Kent accused Jeff of lying, but Ms. Grove did not confront him about his admission, and no apparent discipline was administered. Ms. Grove's response to our inquiry about this meeting was an astonishing, "I think Kent has worked out his anger, and [more information I didn't need to know], so he won't be a problem now."

The next day, Counselor B held a special counseling session for the PE class, in which each student was asked to contribute. When Kent said loudly, "There are lying paranoid idiots in this class!" she said "That's not nice," but took no other visible disciplinary action. Mortified, Jeff said nothing, and felt completely abandoned by the continuing unchallenged verbal abuse right in front of successive school staff members. When we heard about this, we requested that Kent be removed from the PE class. They refused, so we moved Jeff out, but he ended up in a study hall with Kent! Feeling his power through tacit staff tolerance of his behavior, and apparent outright support from Ms. Grove (based on his parroting of her term "paranoid"), Kent continued to harass Jeff. He shook his clenched fist at him in the halls, and sent others to say, "Kent's gonna get you." Ms. B deferred our latest complaint about this behavior to Ms. Grove, who was not there that day.

Jeff then refused to go to school, saying, "Mom, I can't take it anymore." We called the SRO, who this time filed the complaint. We were told that Kent's mom was allowed to come pick him up from school and take him to the police station, thus avoiding the stigma of an arrest on campus or at home. It was a decency that was only afforded to us grudgingly on Jeff's second arrest. Kent was gone for a week, so we presumed he had been suspended after he received probation for misdemeanor harassment, but Ms. Grove would not share any information with us, even how Kent's restraining order was to be enforced. We soon found out. Jeff was removed from the study hall he had with this kid and sent to the principal's office for that hour, "to comply with the restraining order," we were told. Blind with rage inside, we civilly insisted they rectify this grossly unfair situation. But Jeff's, not the other kid's, schedule was changed yet again. By this time, there was about one week left in the school year, and the abuse finally stopped. How Jeff managed passing grades I don't know.

We were completely outraged by the semester of hell our son and our family was put through. I mailed formal Public Complaint letters to all six Peak to Peak Charter School Board Members, describing the incompetent handling of the religious, sexual and physical harassment of our son, and requested a response. Over the next few weeks, we waited for the phone call or letter from an apologetic and concerned board member, who would outline what they would do to respond. It never came. We waited over the summer, thinking they needed to meet, investigate, etc. No call or letter ever came.

We called the school district again in early June, asking how to transfer out, explaining that our son had been severely bullied. The official said stiffly that she would send us a form, but "administrative transfers are rarely approved," and that once enrolled in a charter, you must go through open enrollment again in January to return to your neighborhood school. Discouraged, we did not fill out the paperwork. There was no inquiry about the bullying. Our gut told us to get out. But we thought maybe we had solved the problem with Kent and his friends, by putting them and the school on notice that we wouldn't tolerate any more abuse. We decided to see how the first week of school in the fall went; if it was no good, we would just take him out and figure out then what to do next. This was the single biggest mistake we made, not going with our gut. The summer relaxed us. We considered that the academics at Peak to Peak were a step up from the public schools, and maybe things would smooth out. After all, 6th grade was notorious for being the worst year of middle school for bullying, and other parents had told us that it was the same at all middle schools.

Jeff's 7th grade year started off okay, and he made new friends who, like him, were not religious. He became an accomplished trick skater at Van's Skatepark, quickly mastered his first very own computer, attended to his hobbies, and got good grades. We talked to him about defending himself verbally (his friend George was great in teaching him come-backs), and physically if necessary, and that if he got called to the principal's office, so be it. Jeff reported that he and his friends didn't care what the Christian kids said to them. Once a kid stole some candy from him and he had to grab and twist the kid's arm to make him give it back, but otherwise verbal repartee seemed to suffice.

Later in the semester as open enrollment was approaching, there was a strange incident which we now call the "mystery picketer." One day Mark was picking Jeff up at school, and saw a man on the sidewalk holding a sign: "Don't send your child to this school." Mark slowed down and rolled down the window to inquire, but cars behind began to honk, and the man said "I'll be back tomorrow with flyers." Mark never saw him again. We suspect that he was one of the earliest parents to complain to the Boulder ACLU, but we'll never know, since the ACLU understandably doesn't divulge their sources.

The January open enrollment period came, and we had a family discussion about switching and decided to finish out middle school there, and then go back to the public high school, as did George's family. But slowly, the old problems came back. It was almost like the students were on good behavior until after Christmas and open enrollment each year. The religious harassment spread beyond the Fundamentalist Christians to other kids who felt free to call him a f—ing freak, to trip, shove or punch him in the halls, and deface his locker or steal his belongings. He complained to Counselor B a few times, but nothing changed. He didn't talk to us too much about it anymore for a while, preferring to handle it himself, it seemed. He never got called to the office, and "nor did anyone else," Dr.Steinwand said later, commenting on the apparent "Lord of the Flies" atmosphere at Peak to Peak. But George got called to the office for fighting back, and when he saw the Bible on the table while the Dean said "What would Jesus do," he replied (in his laconic way, I'm sure) "Uh, Mr. Chandler, uh, I'm not that religious." Jeff started having frequent minor illnesses that kept him home, and began calling from the nurse's office to be picked up from school early, because "my braces hurt," or "my stomach hurts."

One day his favorite teacher, a young former football trainer, read a religious tract in health class on the treatment of anorexia with prayer. Not you, too, Jeff thought with dismay, and mentioned it to me. This is the same poor teacher who caught hell when he told another student that the Bible didn't fit an assignment. The girl's family brought suit, went on the O'Reilly Factor, and got their way. I sympathized with the health teacher after that raking over. And he had been given a hard time by some parents over the sex-ed curriculum, even though it was decided upon by committee and was abstinence-based (there was reportedly board member religious pressure on that decision). But now he was cowed into reading religious stuff in class? He told me sheepishly that a student had requested he read it aloud, but he did not finish it. Ms. Grove brushed it off as a harmless mistake of an inexperienced teacher.

I had questioned Jeff's 7th grade science teacher "Mr. C" at the beginning of the year open house about how he would handle creationist outbursts in his science class. He said the students would be told firmly that "science class was the How, and religion was the Why and was not a proper discussion topic." However, April again became the month from hell for Jeff, with arguments from creationists in class about the age of rocks. Jeff reported the disruptions to us, saying, "Mr. C tries, but they won't shut up." He also mentioned, "Mr. C has studied ancient Hebrew texts showing lots of translation mistakes in the Bible." Jeff's papers and books were deliberately splashed, since his desk was by the sink. A girl told him while leaving class, "God is in control of everything, and you're going to hell." He shot back "Yeah, so I guess God gave your mom [a health problem] then!", which did get her off his back for awhile. A sticker he put on his locker was torn off. It said: "You laugh at me because I'm different. I laugh at you because you're all the same." He caught another kid defacing a different sticker, a Vans' Skatepark one, and grabbed his sweatshirt briefly as the kid turned to run. The kid wore a yarmulke, which flew off as he ran away snickering with the other bystanders. In telling me this episode, Jeff made no comment about the kid's obvious Jewish religion, but I was quietly angry that even those who should sympathize with him were turning against him, to be sadly repeated later with his teacher. And now I wonder if Mr. C contributed to it all by injecting his own opinions into the classroom.

Both Mark and I complained to Mr. C about the disruptions, and Jeff's falling grades. The teacher confided to me, "I'm pretty frustrated. I've sent students to the office and spoken with their parents to no avail, but I'll keep trying." He had not noted any harassment but said that he would keep an eye out for what went on by Jeff's desk near the sink, and also give him support privately, telling us, "I'll take him under my wing." There was no mention of any behavior problems on Jeff's part, and he said that Jeff would be placed in the advanced science class next year. We felt like at least Jeff had an ally this time around. I grumbled to a colleague about "Christians behaving badly" at the school, and envied the better choice she had made for her son in a neighborhood middle school.

In early May, we started getting letters about course grades of D's and F's due to missed assignments. We confronted Jeff, and he scrambled to get them done. I met with Counselor B, concerned about the falling grades and pattern of minor illnesses, and also told her that the harassment had gotten worse again, but maybe he had developed a thicker skin for it. She said she had seen Jeff only a few times that year, but he didn't say too much about it. There had been no behavior problems reported, and there was no record of the only contact he had with the Dean—being told to put away the Halloween-prop-like turkey claw he had brought to school to scare off tormenters and amaze friends. She confirmed what I was saying about grades and absences by looking at graphs in her computer, and promised to put him on her list to support and track in the first week of school next fall.

Summer break arrived, none too soon for Jeff, who said "I hate my school!" We found ourselves in the same position again, too late to switch, and kicked ourselves for not doing open enrollment in January. Over the summer, Jeff became more involved in computer games, and holed up in his room a lot. He still had friends over and went skating, but not as much. He didn't want to do as many day camps, which he loved in previous summers, running around in the hills above Boulder with rubber swords solving medieval intrigues. He showed me his web site and poetry, which was a little downbeat, but good writing. The comics he ordered were harsh to the eye, but I read them, and they were no worse than Mark's EC Horror Comics, banned in the '50's. Jeff became a little mouthy with Mark, and they butted heads some. It seemed like normal teenage changes and moodiness; he was 13 that summer. In retrospect, we felt guilty for not putting it all together. But health professionals are notorious for being blind to problems in close kin. We didn't know about the internet messaging or "IM", which was an evanescent new medium that is not stored in files or the hard drive without specific software. I had been working part-time for many years, and he wasn't a latch-key child, left to his own devices after school or during the summer. He always had plenty of nice friends, and their parents had similar involved parenting styles. He had two older sisters who doted on him. He just wasn't what you would think of as an at-risk youth.

As August wore on, Jeff began to squawk about starting school again, wanting to switch. I said it was too late, and besides, you're now in 8th grade, the top of the heap, so let's see how things go again, and you'll be out of there next year.

The school year started off badly, though, with what we later recognized as the last straw. On a Saturday in late August, Jeff had been invited by a friend to go to a Warhammer army-men tournament at a local hobby store, and they were dropped off by the boy's parents with lunch money to spend the day. One of Jeff's persecutors then showed up, and proceeded to denigrate Jeff's moves and play two against one. This kid, who later broadcast Jeff's arrest at school, said to Jeff's friend, "What are you doing with this freak?" and the two went off to lunch and spent all the money. When Jeff got home later, demoralized more than hungry, he said he would have called to be picked up, but the clerk would not let him use the phone. We asked if he wanted us to call the friend's parents, but Jeff said no, he would handle it himself. It was just too embarrassing at age 13 to have your parents fighting your battles for you. The boy did apologize on Monday, but it was a blow to lose a friend to the dark side. And it was reminiscent of losing the health teacher, and shades of Mr. C's future betrayal. That evening, Jeff vented with peer counselor Alexi's encouragement, and his fate was then sealed. Zach had warned Jeff not to IM with his older sister Alexi when she had her IM

Grabber turned on, but when you're making a cry for help, maybe this is just what you want.

If only we had not chosen that charter school. If only we had listened to our gut. If only we had listened to our son, and not the other parents and books saying it was just a phase. If only we had questioned authority, and just pulled our son out, and showed up on the doorstep of the local middle school daring them to turn us away. If only we had recognized the pattern as religious discrimination, so well formulated by Dean Chandler when he said, "We don't know your son."

3

Johanna's Story

Thirteen months after our October 2003 Public Complaint and Notice of Claim was made to the Boulder Valley School District detailing what had happened to our son at Peak to Peak Charter School, an 8th grade girl at the school slashed her wrists to escape the pain of the continuing culture of tacitly sanctioned religious harassment. Her story was almost an exact copy of my son's, but the feminine version with all the anger turned inward instead of outward. When I heard about it, I was incredulous and furious that nothing had been done, even behind the scenes. When her mother called me in rageful tears, I was filled with anguish as my own wounds ripped wide open again.

"Johanna" was gentle and intelligent. She loved animals, and drew the wrath of the popular girls who didn't like her criticism of their stoning a pigeon with garbage in the school courtyard one day. She had clean American girl looks in her jeans and clear complexion with no make-up. Not afraid to speak her mind, she had said once during science class, "I don't believe that God made the earth in 6 days," obviously experiencing the same "young-earth" creationist disruptions as Jeff had. From that day forward, she was targeted for abuse by the popular girls, part of the fundamentalist or evangelical Christian crowd that was growing in influence and numbers at Peak to Peak. They were different students than Jeff's bullies. Johanna and her friends were called pagans and ugly lesbians (they were neither), and hit, kicked and tripped for a year before Johanna broke. Her mother, "Pat," had complained about it the previous spring, and there was a mediation session toward the end of the school year that they thought had helped. When the school year began again in the fall, so did the abuse, however. Johanna, like my son, did the developmentally normal thing at this age, and confided in peers, not teachers or a parent, and tried to handle it herself. You're just a whiney tattle-tale if you tell, the abuse get worse, not better, and teachers don't do anything to help anyway.

One day in late November 2004, the bullies cornered her in the hallway, and told her she would "burn in hell." She went home and told her mother that she was never going to that school again, not yet able to relate what had happened to her that day. Then she pulled out a kitchen knife and began slashing her wrists. Pat grabbed the knife away from her, bandaged her and took her to the emergency room. Doctors directly attributed her desperate act to the abuse she had suffered at school.

Meanwhile, searching for answers to what had happened to her "beautiful, smart, confident daughter," Pat got the same defensiveness and stonewalling from the school and the district that I did a year ago. Various personnel blamed mental illness or choosing a charter school as the problem, not bullying. There was an official "We are saddened that this happened," while intensive damage control went on behind the scenes, but no support and no advice were given. Instead of sympathy, some blamed her as a single parent, and there were nasty emails and 2 AM phone calls from other Peak to Peak students and families. Counselor A told Johanna's friends about the suicide attempt without involving their parents, putting them at risk for copy-cat suicide, according to a close family friend whose daughter was told in this fashion. In a defensive letter to the State Board of Education,[1] Peak to Peak school officials insinuated that Johanna exhibited self-injury behavior (commonly known as "cutting"), by saying the girl "purposefully injured herself," continuing the abuse and denial.

Knowing I was a doctor, Pat called me in distress one day about problems her daughter was experiencing, and I advised her to call Johanna's doctor immediately, and get second and even third opinions. She was taken off medication and did much better. This authenticated my own fears of my son being misdiagnosed as mentally ill. Last year, Principal Fontana had told another parent, "Joe," a friend of Pat's, that my son had brought all his troubles on himself, and had serious mental problems, and the DA had wanted to hospitalize him. I told Pat that there was nothing wrong with Jeff that getting out of Peak to Peak did not cure. Our kids were not the crazy ones, but were reacting normally to persecution by calling out for help.

BVSD starting threatening Pat about truancy, and warned her to get Johanna into a school, despite the doctor's recommendation that she not return to public school yet. Pat could not afford private school, and had to work, so long-term home-schooling was out of the question. They went to their neighborhood mid-

---

1.   December 22, 2004 Letter to the Colorado State Board of Education from Peak to Peak Charter Schools, Inc. Obtained from the Colorado State Board of Education.

dle school and got the cold shoulder. And this girl had made no threat and had not been expelled, but her mother had dared to go public with calm expressions of their story. They then tried a school in a neighboring school district. "I had a melt-down," Johanna later said. Of course, as in our case, district-paid tutoring had been denied.

Pat asked for the name of my civil case attorney, Michelle Mintzer Murphy, and pursued a complaint of ethnic intimidation with the Lafayette Police, believing that her daughter was the victim of a hate crime. This was only after Peak to Peak had administered no visible discipline to the offenders, nor called Pat with the required follow-up on their investigation. The district supported the charter school's autonomy in discipline matters. Dr. Miller-Brown, a school district middle school director, had publicly said, "We are horrified about what has happened," in response to the suicide attempt and its precipitant. I called her, after reading in the paper that Peak to Peak's records of discipline were to be reviewed, wanting to know if my son's records were included, and were accurate, since Peak to Peak had told us a year ago that all his counseling records were lost or destroyed. She told me that she did not receive the individual records, but that the school's record of suspensions and expulsions was comparable to other schools. She also commented, "You should be proud of your work," in airing my concerns about Peak to Peak. When I expressed my disappointment that the girl's harassers suffered no visible punishment, Miller-Brown said that discipline was given. But since it was not visible, nor shared with the family (e.g., an apology), in my opinion it was too light, whatever it was.

The District Attorney declined to file charges in the case after the police submitted their investigation, saying there was not enough evidence. Ethnic intimidation charges in Colorado seem to be interpreted unevenly. A DA on the Western Slope stated that this charge "requires property damage or physical injury or imminent threats; repeated offensive comments don't qualify," in its decision not to file such charges in the case of a biracial girl who was told she would be hanged from a tree.[2] This is in contrast to Boulder, where a misdemeanor ethnic intimidation charge was successfully pursued against a CU soccer player who sent an email to a teammate that included anti-Hispanic epithets and a chilling threat to be dragged behind a car.[3] I was told that Johanna's bullies had denied everything, and one witness, a friend who was still at the school, changed

2. "DA won't prosecute over racial threats," Rocky Mountain News, January 13, 2006.
3. "Ex-CU athlete guilty in ethnic intimidation," article and editorial, Denver Post, June 4, 2006.

his story. One bully's father was a prominent Lafayette city employee. The police had been given my name and phone number, for a possible interview on our similar experience of religious bullying, by Pat's friend Joe, whose daughter was a close friend and a witness for Johanna. I was not contacted. When the closure of the case was announced by Peak to Peak and the Lafayette Police in a joint press conference, categorizing it not a crime, but "a disagreement between students,"[4] this unleashed a new barrage of abuse on Pat and her daughter. They were called liars, crazy, and school-wreckers. It was too much to bear, especially when the witness friend turned, and became one of the name-callers.

Pat was lucky to have an understanding employer who allowed her to work at home during this time to attend to her daughter. They had to discontinue Johanna's email and disconnect the land-line phone. Johanna was despondent over the separation from and loss of friends. Pat made the heart-wrenching decision to send her away to relatives out of state for a while to begin a new life, and told me that they would be moving out of the country after her upcoming re-marriage. "If this can happen in Boulder County, it can happen anywhere in the U.S.," she said in our last conversation.

And move they did, six months into their own ordeal. I am told by Joe that they are doing well. Joe's daughter, who was also harassed for two years despite Joe's persistent efforts to work with the school, finished the year at Peak to Peak while enduring continued abuse. She is now much happier at her new high school in another district.

I will always remember Johanna and Pat as courageous women who had the guts to expose the ugliness at Peak to Peak, in order to spare other parents and children what we went through. Joe and his daughter also contributed tirelessly and at great risk to themselves, and supported their friends Pat and Johanna, who really got the worst of the retaliation. Their bravery and sacrifice is part of what keeps me going in 2006.

---

4.   "DA: no charges at Peak to Peak," Lafayette News, February 16-22, 2005.

PART II

4

Justice Through Change

October 2003 Looking for Solutions

Our October 2003 filing of the Notice of Claim, also known as an "Intent to Sue," was done to get the Boulder Valley School District (BVSD) and its Board's attention, so it was purposefully excruciatingly detailed with names and dates over eight single-spaced pages. This is not what is usually done if one truly intends to sue, as it tells the defendant exactly what to prepare for and figure out what they can lie about in deposition, and gives them an opportunity to destroy evidence. Our criminal defense attorney Howard Bittman had warned us that we were unlikely to win any monetary settlement from the school district because our "damages" were not high (i.e., your son did not die, and was not beaten or raped in jail), the school had "governmental immunity" to most lawsuits, and that it could cost us Jeff's college fund to pursue it. So we elected to use the Notice of Claim as a Public Complaint to express our displeasure with the mishandling of our son's case and the religious culture at the school. We hoped to obtain justice through change at Peak to Peak. Howard had also once cryptically commented, "The solution to this problem is political, not legal," but at the time I didn't get it.

To our amazement, we got the same response from the BVSD District and Board that we had gotten from the Peak to Peak Board of Directors over a year ago: nothing. Two months after sending the Public Complaint and Notice of Claim to all BVSD Board Members, I called Ms. Phillips, the BVSD Board President, to inquire about it. She was kind in listening to me, but said she could not divulge anything because of the legal action. I told her we really didn't want to sue, we just wanted something done about it. This conversation was quickly followed by the school district counsel's request that we have our attorney send a letter dropping our Notice of Claim, before they would respond to our Complaint. Howard advised against this, and we forgot about it, as we were soon engulfed in the fight against the second felony charge.

When Jeff was exonerated in February 2004, Howard encouraged us to file a Notice of Claim for Malicious Prosecution (meaning without cause) against the Lafayette Police. He had actually suggested this after the first go-round but we had declined, just wanting to put it all behind us, and I was fearful of stimulating interest in a refiling of criminal charges. He said, "They have insurance for this, they almost expect these to be filed when a case is dismissed, and it protects your rights should you decide in the future to sue." We were furious at being put through hell again, so we filed the Notice, but then, it was the same problem: governmental immunity, and lawsuits are expensive and stressful. Mark's take on all this lawsuit activity was a pragmatic, "The school district and the police are too powerful, we cannot defeat them. Life is not fair. And let the other families at the school fend for themselves." We also needed a breather, to get normal again, so we pretty much let it all go for a while.

But it was not my style to let the school off the hook so easily, and I was willing to spend money to force change at Peak to Peak and save other kids from the same fate. I have since come across a term that describes this well: altruistic punishers—those who punish wrongdoing even at their own expense. In May, I asked Howard to inquire about the Notice of Claim, and we then received an offer from the district's counsel, now an outside attorney, to negotiate a non-monetary settlement that would address our concerns. Sensing that this was not Howard's cup of tea as a criminal defense attorney and that he was tiring of us, I thanked him for his excellent work on our son's behalf and found an attorney who specialized in school law. Michelle Mintzer Murphy knew all the players and was a good hand holder. I met with her in July, and showed her Jeff's picture and the Notice of Claim. My main concern was that children were still in danger at Peak to Peak with incompetent and discriminatory handling of the abuse, suicidality and possible school threats, and told her, "If something doesn't change, children might die." I had already contacted the BVSD Safe Schools Coordinator with our story, who responded, "This is my worst nightmare. I'll talk to them and encourage them to take the upcoming seminar on Suicide Prevention, but I don't want to step on too many toes, since it's a charter school."

I made a list of all the changes I wanted at Peak to Peak. We were asking for:

* Changes in board and top administrative leadership, counseling staff and peer counseling program changes
* Annual suicide prevention training for staff
* Review of anti-bullying programs
* Board and volunteer written commitment to nondiscrimination

* Changing some heavy-responsibility volunteer positions to paid positions to lessen the chances of favoritism towards their children

* Anti-bias training in the classroom via the Anti-Defamation League's World of Difference Program which was already in use in other Boulder schools

* Teacher training in sensitivity to non-Christian students (nowadays termed cultural competence)

* Adherence to current policy on extracurricular postings/flyers and teaching controversial and religious material

* More accountability to parent complaints and easier exit for unsatisfied families

Pretty reasonable, I thought, along with attorney settlement fees which were minimal at that point. The summer wore on, with no response from the school district's attorney. Our family attorney said, "They're stalling, waiting to see if you go away." So in September, I met with Michelle and her senior partner in the firm she had just joined, Alex Halpern, to review the case. I planned to light a fire under them, by speaking during the public comment period at the next school board meeting in October—is there anything I shouldn't say, and what would be the likely effect? Alex said that if I went public, they might be less likely to settle, having paid the price of bad publicity already that the settlement offer was meant to avoid. I knew that Peak to Peak's five year contract was due for renewal talks in January 2005, and the Open Enrollment season was also coming in December through January, but after that the value of going public would be greatly diminished. I took the gamble.

Before proceeding, it occurred to me to call Marvin Straus, the president of the Boulder Atheists who had called me a year ago to offer the support of his small group after reading a brief newspaper article about our the filing of the Notice. Knowing how reviled atheists were, I politely declined. But after being treated like dirt for a year, I was now ready to see if they could help. I met with him over lunch, and learned of this kindly retired man's efforts to educate the public that atheists were just people like the rest of us, and not evil. Of course, I should know, since my husband and now my son were atheists. But you don't advertise it. Marvin warned me that going public against a powerful adversary such as religious fundamentalists was fraught with hazards, and gave real-life examples of families run out of town, vandalism of homes, and poisoned pets. I went home and thought about it, talked with Mark, and decided to go ahead and take the risk. We live in a cul-de-sac, and neighbors watch out for each other.

October 2004 The Battle Begins

The first shot over the bow was made in October 2004, a year after the Notice was filed, at a nearly empty BVSD School Board meeting. I had gotten there early to make sure I could get on the speaking list, but I needn't have bothered. As I sat there waiting for the board members to file onto the dais, Evie Hudak came in with Jared Polis, both Colorado State Board of Education Members with their nametags on. Now I'm getting somewhere, I thought, it's a two for one exposure. I had spoken with and received support from Evie Hudak, on the recommendation of the Mountain States chapter of the Anti-Defamation League (ADL). They no longer gave legal assistance after being badly burned by a technicality in the notorious Evergreen, Colorado case of anti-Semitic harassment of one neighbor against another. But they did catalogue our complaint in their growing file of school discrimination cases, gave names of lawyers, and offered their school-based World of Difference Anti-Bias Program. They said Evie Hudak might be able to help. So it was exciting to meet her and Mr. Polis, and have both of them witness my statement, even if the crowd was sparse and nobody watches the local channel these meetings are broadcast on.

My name was called, and I went up to the lectern, nervous about the explosive things that I was about to say, but got through it:

> Hello, my name is Louise Benson, and I am here to give my input on the possible renewal of Peak to Peak Charter School's contract to provide K-12 education.
>
> I will get right to the heart of the matter. Our family had an extremely negative experience at Peak to Peak due to the strongly Christian culture, the favoritism towards children of Board and Committee members, and the complete lack of accountability to parents or the school district.
>
> Religious discrimination against non-Christians is rampant at Peak to Peak. While there may be no overt religious teaching, religious discrimination is present in other forms nonetheless, which constitutes a hostile learning environment for the minority of non-Christians at the school.
>
> It is religious discrimination and a hostile learning environment when:
>
> 1. Non-Christian children are forcibly proselytized by repetitive oral presentations of a religious nature, e.g., "Why Jesus is My Hero."
>
> 2. Children are disciplined in the halls by the Dean with "What Would Jesus Do?"
>
> 3. Posters for Bible Studies at a Board Member's house are in hallways, and flyers for a Christian religious activity are given to all children.

4. A Health teacher reads a religious tract on treatment of anorexia with prayer.

5. Science classes are persistently disrupted by "Creationist" outbursts and arguments from fundamentalist Christian children, who are never adequately disciplined.

6. Non-Christian children are viciously bullied for their different beliefs, and the perpetrators are not disciplined at all.

7. A third of the staff are members of the same Christian church, as are many of the children. This leads to a sense of isolation for non-Christians, and a chilled atmosphere even for those moderate Christians who may not like what's going on, but just keep quiet. There is no question that fundamentalist Christians on the board and in the classroom rule the roost.

These seven examples have been personally experienced by our family. Efforts to end the discriminatory atmosphere, and in particular the vicious religiously-based bullying of our son, fell on deaf ears, including those of the Peak to Peak School Board. When our son became suicidal after two years of verbal, sexual and physical harassment, the school counselor and principal, who were made aware of the situation by a peer counselor, put him at grave risk by doing absolutely nothing for three days. We have no doubt that had the suicidal child been "part of the Christian family" at the school, that things would have been handled far differently. This is religious discrimination at its worst.

I'm sure that the School Board will receive many glowing letters in support of the renewal of Peak to Peak's contract. Those who have left the school because they were disgusted with the school's culture are much less likely to contact you. I am asking you to consider not only the desires of the Christian majority at Peak to Peak, but to consider the rights of religious minority families to a public education that is free of favoritism, hostility and proselytism, and that has full accountability to parents and the Boulder Valley School District. Thank you.

I went back to my seat and waited for some kind of response. There was none, except a somewhat shocked look on their faces. After the few other public speakers finished, I still waited, but they went on with the agenda. When President Phillips finally turned to the Superintendent and said, "Dr. Garcia, would you please look into Dr. Benson's allegations, since they are fairly serious," I left for home, feeling apprehensive about the future, but hopeful that maybe I had been heard at last.

This had the desired effect, and in November Michelle received a Compromise Offer of Settlement. It included some of the requested changes in vague wording, but not leadership changes or anti-discrimination programs. It was the bare minimum response, and the refusal to pay attorney fees, after a previous verbal agreement, was pure insult. Michelle counseled that any counter-offer be delayed, since they took their time, we'll take ours.

Shortly after my Board statement, an employee at one of the nursing homes I practice in approached me and confided that he had seen me on TV, and the same thing had happened to his grandson at Peak to Peak, and they too were told to wait until open enrollment to get out! He offered to write a letter to the BVSD Board, and I decided to contact all former Peak to Peak families to encourage them to do the same if they had concerns about a blanket renewal of the school's contract. This was laborious, comparing 3 student directories for 2 years worth of "name dropouts," to produce 160 letters. My interest was piqued to find a much higher annual turnover rate than the 5% the school claimed in the newspaper, almost 20% in the middle and high schools. So maybe it wasn't just "isolated incidents" of discrimination, as suggested by a Peak to Peak teacher who spoke to me at a later Board meeting without knowing who I was.

December 2004 Peak to Peak as the Titanic

One day at work in early December, Michelle paged me with the awful news that a Peak to Peak student had attempted suicide under similar circumstances of religious harassment as my son. The reporter from the Lafayette News had called her about it, since I had just told him that I had received a settlement offer and gave him Michelle's name. Did we know the student, what was our reaction? I did not, but I was sickened to find out that I had been correct about the risks to students at Peak to Peak. The story appeared immediately in the Lafayette News.[1]

The rest of December was a whirlwind—talking to Johanna's mother Pat and her friend Joe, speaking out at BVSD School Board and State Board of Education meetings, and being interviewed by the local press. The State Board meeting on December 9, 2004, was especially tense, with many BVSD and School Board personnel in attendance as the school district awaited the vote on its application to have its charter school authority reinstated. This exclusive authority to approve charter schools in its district had been yanked by the State Board nine months ago because the district was judged "unfriendly" to charters for placing a moratorium on new ones after four had been approved in recent years and taken about

---

1.   "Allegations of religious bullying surface," Lafayette News, December 8-14, 2005.

7% of their students. Evie Hudak had encouraged me to come and speak, to give an example of why BVSD might be hesitant to have yet more charter schools that may present problems or resist oversight. My public statement was similar to the one in October. It surely caused some heartburn for BVSD because I now faulted them for not letting our child out of the charter school, and especially for what later happened to another student (Johanna) as a result of their failure to take effective action. After being interrupted several times and asked to finish up by Jared Polis, I hurriedly ended by saying that BVSD needed to be given a chance to reform this charter, otherwise the problem would end up in the State Board's lap. BVSD lost its bid with a 4-4 tie vote. Ms. Jones, a BVSD Board member, whispered to me as I passed by her to my seat, "You should call the ADL," and I replied, "I did, and they referred me to Evie Hudak and that's why I'm here." I recognized the BVSD in-house lawyer from the expulsion hearing, sitting there expressionless a few feet away as I consulted with Michelle, and this time her gray was showing. The Rocky Mountain News reporter got my name and number for an interview (which never materialized—more on that in the next chapter). As I mentioned before, Peak to Peak's response to my State Board salvo was to send a letter to both BVSD and the State Board which sidestepped the real issues and insinuated that Johanna was a cutter, not a suicidal child. Vicious.

The Boulder Daily Camera reporter was apparently sitting in the back of the room, and when she finally ran with the Peak to Peak harassment story,[2] her articles did stimulate quite a bit of local interest, although no mention was made of my State Board appearance. She happened to mention in an interview with me that Jared Polis, who, I found out, was a big charter supporter, had only given me one and a half of my allotted two minutes. The Boulder ACLU finally joined the fray, as well as the Boulder Atheists, and University of Colorado professors chimed in with debate on evolution and creationism in the schools. Peak to Peak held a forum[3] where many vented their frustrations at the school's culture and image as Boulder County's de facto Christian school, which even its Board Director and founder Chris Howard publicly admitted, "Maybe because character education attracts Christians."[4] Most of the estimated 60 parents attending said that their kids had witnessed or heard of religious or other bullying, and Peak to Peak's parent email group filtered and removed the negative comments, according to Joe. Camera reporters went on campus and received such comments as a

---

2.   "Family alleges harassment at school," Daily Camera, December 10, 2004.
3.   "Peak to Peak addresses harassment," Daily Camera, December 15, 2004.
4.   "School harassment debated," Daily Camera, 1A, December 19, 2004

13 year old's, "The fundies are in your face, kind of rude about it, saying 'You're going to die, you're going to burn in hell' … last year they got picked on." Others were quoted who had never seen a problem. A Buddhist mother had apparently contacted the reporter to say her "daughter's four months at Peak to Peak had been a nightmare."[5] Letters to the editors went both ways and included much community reaction. One telling letter from a junior at Peak to Peak said, "I hope I am an inspiration to the younger students … although we care about some people, they will go to hell if they are not saved."[6] Out the mouth of babes. Which prompted this response: "If this is what passes for tolerance at Peak to Peak, they truly have problems." Another student wrote, "There are some students who are not discreetly Christian and sometimes discriminate against others."[7] One of the school's founders, a self-described "capitol L liberal," hysterically critiqued the coverage as a witch hunt, and asked what was next, "complaining about students saying 'God bless you' when they sneeze?"[8] I shot back that the only witch hunts were occurring in the halls of Peak to Peak, and that the complaint was not trivial, but true religious harassment that had not been addressed seriously enough by the school.

There was much hope for change, although the school and the district did that PR dance that says, "We're taking this seriously, but we have done nothing wrong." The school proposed things like a bullying tip box, surveillance cameras, and rearranging the lockers.[9] A shrill half-page Guest Editorial in the Daily Camera by Peak to Peak Board President Shafer, "Religion Does Not Guide Our School,"[10] attempted to obfuscate the real problems by setting up straw issues that were knocked down. For example, it stated dry policies without admitting the problem with execution, denied teaching creationism but did not address creationist science class disruption, and hid behind confidentiality to avoid addressing complaints of favoritism and accountability in disciplinary action. The school's high state test scores and various awards were trumpeted. For a while, it was amusing to see the school as the Titanic, frantically pretending all was well and rearranging the deck chairs, and I was hoping it would go down when the

---

5.   Ibid.

6.   Letters, Lafayette News, December 15-21, 2004.

7.   Ibid.

8.   "Harassment story is really no story," Open Forum, Raul Campos, Daily Camera, December 22, 2004.

9.   "Peak to Peak addresses harassment," Daily Camera, December 15, 2004.

10.   "Religion does not guide our school," Guest Opinion, Daily Camera, January 9, 2005.

school board voted soon on its contract renewal. It was unfortunate that it took another student to be harmed to get BVSD's and Peak to Peak's attention, but at least no one had died yet.

Two weeks before the January 25th contract vote, Joe and I spoke at a packed School Board meeting, the only two speaking critically of the school, followed by dozens of supporters singing praises orchestrated by an intensive email campaign. Joe described the two frustrating years of trying to get the abuse of his daughter stopped without success. This is what I said, primarily in response to Shafer's editorial:

> Parents don't give a hoot if Peak to Peak's policy books are in order—they want policies enforced, and real accountability. Your vote should not be about a popularity contest, about how many like the school or how good it looks on paper or how many awards are won. This is about the civil rights and safety of children at the school.
>
> It doesn't matter what staff or volunteer religious beliefs are. It matters how children with other beliefs, and children with non-VIP parents are treated, and if their complaints are taken seriously. Four out of eight of my son's religious harassers had parents with important Committee or Board positions.
>
> This is not about the teaching of creationism or evolution in the school—this is about persistent creationist disruption of science classes and administration non-support of teacher discipline.
>
> Yes, it is about the culture of a school which contributes to some children feeling like they don't belong, and when religious bullies are not punished, they know it for sure.
>
> I complained to you a year ago about the vicious religious harassment of my son at Peak to Peak. You believed Peak to Peak's denials then; if you believe them now you are worse than gullible. Children's civil rights and even lives are at stake. Thank you.

I think I heard Joe clap, but otherwise the standing room-only crowd was silent, and the next speaker was called.

Among the parade of supporters, including teachers, students and parents, three stood out. A former Peak to Peak Board member gave the closest thing to an apology that I had heard yet, which had been no apology, or even acknowledgment of suffering. She said, "I was there in the early days, and (I clearly heard 'if children were hurt' but the mike cut out at this point) ... we want to work with the district to make Peak to Peak better." Science teacher Mr. C said, "Since Louise mentioned my class, her son was in my class and there was no harassment, and no disruptions, just a respectful discussion of differences." When he had to pass me on his way to his seat, I tried to look him in the eye, but he avoided my stare. And this was the man who had recently told the Daily Camera that students regularly snickered during his lessons on evolution.[11] His daughter got up there next, and said she was Jewish and felt totally respected at Peak to Peak.[12] Well, yes, when you're a teacher's kid, it stands to reason that you would be left alone, I thought. Then a mother told how her interfaith daughter never had any problems at the school. This was the same woman who was quoted in the newspaper complaining at the forum that "Evangelicals have a big voice at the school, so a lot of families will not send their kids here, and some have left. I'm afraid now it's been confirmed what's going on at this school."[13]

I could see which way the wind was blowing, so I left, but not before locating the Lafayette News reporter at the back of the room to give him a copy of my statement and whisper in a huff about the science teacher's apparent change from what he had told me, that his class had been disrupted. It infuriated me to have him get up there and make it personal, when I had made no mention of his identity. Then I walked out with the security guard provided by the district at my request, who actually turned out to be the night maintenance man in his plaid shirt. My tires were, unbelievably, not flat. As I drove home in the dark, I played a southern rock 'n' roll disc loud, the Allman brothers, "..sometimes you just feel like you're tied to a whipping post ...," wondering if I was crazy, knowing everyone thought I was some kook.

When I later reviewed the tape of the thinned out end of the Board meeting, I watched Mr. Ferguson, the Vice President of the Peak to Peak Board, fielding softball questions from Board member Jones about some of the allegations I had made in October. His answer about the religious flyers was at odds with a letter I had received in November 2003 from a Peak to Peak founder. She wrote that the flyers were given to all middle school students; Ferguson now claimed they were given out only to friends. As for the Dean's Bible, it was "only The Idiot's Guide to the Bible, and it was not used in discipline." The other allegations were not addressed at all. Jones said, "I know some of the founders myself," revealing mixed sympathies. The other members just tiptoed around the culture and harassment issues with platitudes about needing to make sure that bullying issues

---

11. "School harassment debated," Daily Camera, December 19, 2002.
12. "BVSD renews two charters," Daily Camera, January 12, 2005.
13. "Peak to Peak addresses harassment," Daily Camera, December 15, 2004.

would be adequately addressed. It was depressing to watch, but I held out hope that the final contract would quietly tighten up oversight on the school.

Joe and Pat had arranged an interview with Denver's Channel 9 News investigative producer, but I had hesitated in late December, fearful of sound-bite journalism. After the first of the year with the vote looming, though, I decided to go for it, it's now or never, and the three of us did the interview. Actually four, since Johanna bravely also went before the camera because "I don't want anyone else to go through what I did." But then it seemed that the piece was shelved, because we had heard nothing by January 22nd. All of a sudden, Channel 9 left a message saying it would run January 24, the evening before the contract vote on the 25th. It was the lead story on the 10 o'clock news, but a letdown, cutting out almost all references to the religious nature of the harassment. But beggars can't be choosers.

As I prepared for the board meeting on the 25th, Channel 4 called and said they would be at the meeting. I told them the school's contract renewal was probably a done deal, but they did do a similar piece anyway. The reporter interviewed me in the busy hallway before we entered the board room full of relaxed, murmuring Peak to Peak supporters. The presence of rolling cameras on the school board was dramatic, and there was not a word of discussion or comment from any board member before the vote, which was very unusual. They voted unanimously 7-0 to approve renewal of Peak to Peak with not a single symbolic "No" vote. Not even from Jones, or Phillips, who had said in December, "We need to decide if this school fits in our community." This monolithic front served to completely shut down any further major media interest in the case—why, it must just be all hype from oversensitive whiners.

I continued to write to the School Board members, in a series of letters rebutting Peak to Peak's press or school board meeting statements, pointing out that Peak to Peak's School Climate Surveys supported what I was claiming about the school, and to push for specific contract changes since these details were still in ongoing negotiations, but no responses were received. It was a losing battle. I then turned to the Charter School Institute (CSI), a new alternate chartering body that the Colorado legislature had authorized because districts like Boulder Valley were becoming resistive to charter schools biting into their funding pie. Peak to Peak could turn up their noses at BVSD's contract and go to the CSI for their contract, with the added bonus of even less oversight, and take all the per pupil dollars with them. BVSD would at least get a good portion of the money if the school stayed with them. I really didn't want to shut the school down, just fix it. And this was not going to happen if they contracted with CSI, an unelected board of pro-charter members from all over the state. They just didn't have the time, staff or expertise for the changes and oversight that were required, in my opinion. So letters went to all of them, and I spoke with the chairman, Randy DeHoff. He had known some of the Columbine families, so he seemed especially interested what I had to say about the bullying issues that we families had experienced, and the mishandling of the possible school threat.

Peak to Peak held a Press Conference on February 15th (they forgot to invite me!), and with the Lafayette Police, gave out a Peak to Peak Press Release conflating the non-filing of charges in Johanna's hate crime complaint with clearance of all culture issue claims against the school. The police spokesman said, "We found no evidence of pervasive harassment, religious or otherwise, at the school. We think it came down to disagreements between students." The Press Release also gave a lengthy denial of "false allegations," clearly aimed at me.[14] When Pat called me distraught about the renewed email and phone harassment of her daughter that the Release stimulated, I was just livid. I called V.P. Ferguson and left a polite message that if he was allowed to speak to me, would he please call. About a week later, to my surprise, he did call saying he had received attorney clearance and wanted to set up a meeting with me. I said we could meet at Peak to Peak, if no one was going to throw tomatoes at me, and he laughed and said maybe this thing could get worked out "without resorting to nasty lawyers." I reviewed the plan with Alex Halpern, Michelle Murphy's law partner: maybe if Ferguson, who was new to the Peak to Peak Board and came across in his appearances as reasonable, knew my story and how Pat and Johanna had been treated, the need for school culture change would become apparent. I had been encouraged by the fact that Dr. Miller-Brown, the school district's middle school director, had been willing to speak with me recently and had complimented my work, and I thought maybe if people just sat down and talked, things could be resolved.

I had not been on campus for a year and a half, and it was like being on an old battleground for a peace treaty. Ferguson, Pres. Shafer, Principal Fontana and I sat down in a small windowless conference room. Shafer was impeccably groomed and appeared loaded for bear. She began to type on a laptop, and I said "No notes, please," and motioned to her to close it. There was an instantaneous bad chemistry between us, and it was a good thing that Ferguson, an affable sort, did most of the talking, and he started off, "We're here to listen to you." I then proceeded to calmly and civilly upbraid them on their Press Release and how it

---

14.   "Peak to Peak Charter School Cleared of Allegations," Peak to Peak Charter School Press Release, February 15, 2005, obtained from the Lafayette News.

had stimulated further abuse of Pat and Johanna. They needed to retract it, or I would go to the media with a point by point refutation that named names. And by the way, you, Mr. Fontana, were completely inappropriate in telling another parent that my son brought all his troubles on himself and had serious mental problems. I leaned toward the principal, a short, younger man in a suit with his hands folded tightly on the table a few feet away, as he cut his reply before it came out. I challenged several points of the press release as I flipped through my rebuttal material. At first defensive, they began to demand proof, asking "Do you have one of those Bible Study posters?" I said no, I wish I did, but many had seen them. At this point, they said they had other matters to attend to and the meeting ended. As Ferguson saw me out of the building, he said someone would get back to me, and asked in a saccharine tone, "I live in _____, too, where does your son go to school now?" Not thinking on my feet quickly enough to sidestep this, I named Jeff's school. Later it felt like a veiled threat against my son. I speculated on their reason for calling the meeting; to offer some sort of fake apology like they did when they met with Joe, or just wanted to know what hard evidence cards we were holding? Michelle later received a letter from the school district attorney, requesting that I not contact Peak to Peak, stating that I had asked for the meeting, and that the Press Release would not be retracted. Pretty disingenuous, I thought, but par for the course so far with this attorney.

About a week later, in early March, just as I was about to send CSI my rebuttal of Peak to Peak's Press Release, I found out from chairman DeHoff that Peak to Peak had withdrawn its application from CSI, and signed a final contract with BVSD. This was good news, but I still had to look at the contract to see if the needed changes had been made. I held off on giving the rebuttal to the interested Camera reporter in a good faith effort to allow the school district to do the right thing quietly via the contract. During this several months of publicity strategy, we had made no response to the District's proposed settlement. I had Michelle evaluate the contract, which to my untrained eye appeared to have some good strong language in it regarding discrimination. However, when compared to the old contract, it contained only two major changes, that of allowing Peak to Peak parents unhappy with "climate issues" (i.e., culture and harassment), to go to the district for relief, and a clause stating that "teachers will not promote their own religious beliefs in the classroom." These were important changes, but not nearly enough, and I was feeling pretty defeated, since it was obvious to me that they had been flagrantly ignoring the many of the contract provisions for 5 years, and BVSD had not seen fit to call them on it or strengthen these anti-discrimination provisions.

April 2005 Hope Fades

I made a last ditch attempt in April to reason with BVSD Asst. Superintendent Dr. King about practical ways to improve oversight, and that leadership change and anti-bias training programs in the classroom were essential. In a letter, I highlighted some of the statistics I had already included in letters to the BVSD Board, including Peak to Peak's Climate Surveys showing about a 20% higher rate of religious harassment than the district average, which had been misrepresented as "only 5% higher" by Peak to Peak in its January 2005 Anti-Harassment Plan.[15] In comparison, the Lafayette public high school, Centaurus, 22% of students reported religious harassment in 2004, while Peak to Peak's was 33%, and the district average was 28%. Middle school Peak to Peak data showed 27%, and 22% for the district average. Simple calculation shows the 5 percentage point difference is actually approximately a 17% and 22% higher harassment rate, respectively, for middle and high schools. When compared to the local high school, religious harassment was an astonishing 50% higher. This district-wide annual confidential survey has 64 measures of how students feel about their school, and Peak to Peak's Spring 2004 results had declined significantly since 2003, showing that almost half the results were now worse than the district average. Also, Peak to Peak's administrative transfers (mid-year and other school transfers outside the usual processes, as we tried to get) for Fall 2004, before all the publicity, were the highest in the district even compared with much larger schools. Dr. King had previously responded to my request for this information—"It did not exist," and could not be provided, until I pointed out to him that it had been already given to a news reporter. At least they were letting kids out now, though, and I gave him kudos on the changes he had suggested in the original settlement offer, such as suicide prevention training and more rapid response to suicide and school threats. Unlike the others at BVSD I had managed to get a word in with and who gave me definite hints of support, Dr. King had no problem adhering to the party line that there was no evidence for my claims and that their investigation supported Peak to Peak's version of events. He said he had even called former Peak to Peak families, as suggested by me in a school board statement, and found no similar complaints, but would not send me a summary of it.

---

15. Peak to Peak Charter School Chronology and Action Plan for Anti-Harassment Measures Executive Summary, January 2005. Obtained from the Colorado State Board of Education. This document identifies no problems at the school, and no new actions to be taken.

I did not challenge him with what BVSD Board President Phillips had recently told me when I ran in to her at a nursing home. Wearing my professional hat, I made no mention of the school situation. She kindly inquired about my son's well-being, and after offering to help get him back into a public school, she dropped this bombshell: "I have independent corroboration of everything you have been saying about Peak to Peak. I have letters, and [other confidential information], but the names could not be shared with the Board." I about fell over. So, I was not nuts, thank you very much. She alluded to the political solution by saying, "Charter schools are not a panacea for public school problems." It was a friendly conversation, and I appreciated her words of support. Later, I recalled her announcement at a School Board meeting the previous December, expressing concern about recent events at Peak to Peak and asking parents to come forward, because "We cannot take action based on anonymous complaints." I just didn't understand why not, because it takes time, effort and intestinal fortitude to put your name out there and risk retaliation. And I knew the school board was in a tough position, but I needed to see some real reformative action!

Michelle's comment on all this was her usual dry "Very interesting, but will she say that in court." The new contract was not enough, and I had run into a brick wall with Dr. King. The school district's attorney was not returning phone calls, an old habit, according to our long-time family lawyer. I had no real hopes for any settlement, given that the publicity had taken its toll. And Michelle's firm, Children's Voices, had started a big class-action lawsuit against the state to get more money for the schools which kept her busy, and to top it off, BVSD joined the suit, raising the issue of conflict of interest. They could finish the settlement, but not file the our suit, removing important leverage. But since we really could not afford to file a suit anyway, this became moot.

The district was just not taking the need for change at Peak to Peak seriously. So I made formal, notarized complaints against Counselor A and Principal Fontana with the Colorado Dept. of Education Licensing Division, for endangering my son with their incompetent handling of the situation, because I was concerned about students still at the school. They don't make this process easy. After weeks of telephone tag before and after the complaint was filed, the investigator told me that since my son was not physically harmed, he couldn't do anything, but it was concerning so he would refer this charter school case to the Schools of Choice unit at the Colorado Department of Education. His Supervisor confirmed his decision that because my son was not physically harmed, that they weren't going to investigate! I had included some information about the 8th grade girl's incident, and I asked her, are you just going to wait for a kid to die?

The Supervisor said, "We checked with our attorney and we're within policy on this." I had read the policy, and disagreed, and took this response to mean: "Our butts are covered, go away." The Schools of Choice secretary left me a message saying, "Don't call us back, we can't help you."

By summer, I was ready to hang it up, but I thought I would get a couple of second opinions from Denver civil rights lawyers before doing so, since Michelle needed to sign off soon. To my surprise, both the attorneys consulted thought it was a strong case, but expensive, because the school district would fight tooth and nail to avoid the avalanche of me-too suits from other parents. This was made clear to one prospective attorney by the school attorney, and that there would be no settlement because I had gone public. This didn't scare him, and he offered a partial contingency fee arrangement, which cut it down by half, but that was still up to $45,000! Yikes. Howard was still right. Exhausted and discouraged, I threw the contingency fee offer into a big file box that contained the Press Release rebuttal, letters to legislators, and all the other stuff that had accomplished nothing, and planned to take the rest of the summer off from this project.

About a month later, Michelle called saying that the school attorney had contacted her and was hinting about a monetary settlement of "this nuisance case," and had called my demand items for school change "ludicrous," which really irritated me given that they had already agreed to some of them. In early August, a trimmed down counter-offer was sent: everything in the original district offer plus leadership change, anti-discrimination programs and our economic damages. I hoped that the money would give them something to refuse or reduce, since I would not budge on the other two. Again, the district was took their time responding, so a deadline was set. The answer came in one word, "No," and no counter-offer was made. They called our bluff. Michelle and I said goodbye, and she suggested I call Kimberly M. Hult, a well-regarded Boulder attorney in a large practice which was more in a position to offer contingency arrangements. I retained her, but we both agreed to put off any legal action while she was occupied in a big civil rights case.

October 2005 Some Success, at a High Price

It was October 2005. Two years had gone since we had filed the Notice of Claim. Civil rights cases for juveniles have a very long fuse, the filing deadline being two years after turning 18, so let them stew about it a while, and there will be hell to pay if there are more serious incidents in the meantime. But I really hoped not, and hoped that they had learned something despite the stonewalling PR and hardball legal tactics.

Was any culture change accomplished? As the BVSD Board President Phillips and Michelle Murphy had both commented to me separately, "Peak to Peak has been put on notice, and there is more public awareness of the issue." Since the school and the district did not seem to admit there was much of a problem, and wouldn't talk to me about what changes, if any, were planned, I've had to look for it myself. And I did want to be fair to the school, and wanted to know if any good had come of the hard work and sacrifice of the three vocal families, and of our children being the canaries in the mine of that toxic environment. Some hints of change were easily found on the Peak to Peak website. This included extensive personnel turnover, including teachers, counselors, a new dean and elementary and secondary school principals. Principal Fontana remains, but at least he was bumped upstairs to Executive Principal. The secondary school census was down about 20%, due to the loss of approximately 100 middle and high school students who transferred out after the 2004-5 year and were not replaced during open enrollment, according to BVSD.[16] The school's online newsletter Speak to Peak was now sporting tips on tolerance, student stress prevention, and a parent seminar on teen suicide. There was a Diversity Month, exhibits from a Jewish museum, and a "Respect Wall" built by students. A bullying prevention coordinator and extra counseling staff have been hired. The school hallways are reportedly lined with "Respect" posters. All hopeful steps, as long as it's not window-dressing, and I had my doubts, since in spring 2005 the only Peak to Peak Board candidate who even hinted at the need for change was not elected, in a choose 3 out of 5 race.

I have used both the terms incompetent and discriminatory to describe how Peak to Peak officials responded to the religious bullying and resulting suicidality experienced by my son. Is it possible that it is only incompetent? There are several reasons that I think strongly that this was true discrimination. First is that my complaints of ordinary bullying early on in Jeff's 6th grade year were handled reasonably effectively, but later episodes of clearly religious bullying were ignored or excused. Second is that all the involved school officials were highly experienced educators or counselors who were very unlikely to be completely unaware of correct handling of improper curricular and extracurricular material, religious-based discipline, religious harassment, suicidality and possible school threats. And third, it is just too obvious to see the "voice" of fundamentalist Christians with Board and important committee positions, without whose "free" labor the charter school would collapse. The school refuses to release to me the financial records

---

16.   "Class size relief in Boulder," *Daily Camera*, September 29, 2005.

for their fundraising non-profit arm Friends of Peak to Peak, whose Board of Directors is indistinguishable from the school's. This is despite offering these records "in their entirety" to the public on their web site prior to my request for them, and the website has been changed, removing this offer, since my request. Would these records reveal a heavy financial role of religious organizations, that, while not illegal in Colorado, would bring appropriate public scrutiny to possible changes in charter school law? And changes to Colorado Open Records statutes which exempt private organizations that support public institutions such as schools? (Just such a furor erupted over the CU Foundation's shadowy finances in regard to the CU football sex scandal.)

It is difficult to avoid the distinct impression of legal and public relations gamesmanship in both my son's and Johanna's cases. The school has maintained publicly that "We followed procedures." I recently requested a formal response from BVSD to our Public Complaint, wanting to represent their viewpoint in this book, but their lawyer's response was, unbelievably, that "You never made one—you filed a Notice instead."

The Boulder Valley School District and Board found itself between a rock and a hard place, with problems simmering at Peak to Peak since its inception and exploding only three years later, while at the same time fighting the pro-charter Colorado State Legislature and State Board of Education for local control of their schools and funding. Dr. Garcia, the Superintendent of BVSD, had told State Board of Ed member Evie Hudak when she called about my son's case in October 2004, that he was aware of problems at the school, but bullying allegations were hard to prove, and it was difficult to find a legal way to address these problems; more people needed to complain. As you can see, Johanna's case then came to light and the School Board president had inside information, but the school's contract was still renewed. The situation that was allowed to fester at the school was also complicated by typical small town personal connections, and compounded by classic dysfunctional bureaucratic crisis management.

I hoped to God that they would ride herd over Peak to Peak, because BVSD did achieve their goal of regaining their exclusive authority to approve or deny new charter schools in their district.

January 2006 Not Down Yet

As they say, it's not over 'til it's over. Events continued to unfold at the school over the winter of 2005-2006, at first gratifying, then depressing, and finally with some proof of real change that had apparently been done quietly behind the scenes.

A follow-up call to the Anti-Defamation League revealed that lo and behold, their organization had just been involved in a day-long Tolerance Teach-In at Peak to Peak! One of the settlement items that had been refused! A month later, I found a school newsletter article outlining significant revamping of their anti-bullying program. I was pleased that these things were being done, being common sense and not at all "ludicrous."

Then in late December 2005, another nursing home employee approached me, furious, about what had happened at Peak to Peak the day before Winter Break. I had no idea her kids went there, and she asked if my son was still there. I said no, we had a bad experience and left. She had read some of the press reports last year, but since her son had not seen any problems, they stayed and enrolled her youngest this year. "Something weird is going on at that school," she started out, "They call the Christmas tree a holiday tree, but then the teacher told the kids that Black Peter, Santa's helper, is going to come and take all the bad children away. My son came home scared and depressed. I made sure it wasn't another child's story. Then, my teenager says that they showed an evolution film in science class that described how in 3000 years, people are going to develop wings and fly!" She concluded, "We're getting our kids out of there!" I gave her some advice on which School Board and State board members to call, and how to get out of the school.

I could not believe my ears. Parents were still telling me stuff, and there were still problems at the school. That made three complaints to me since the new contract in March 2005. There was the report to me about the Bibles and crosses in the cabinets just after the school year ended, and I tipped the ACLU about it, but they didn't seem to care. And then there was the parent, an alternative program director in another school district whom I had called for general information, who spontaneously offered: "I can tell you where not to go—Peak to Peak. My daughter is there and she has been severely bullied." I said "I know," and told her a little about what happened to my son. I asked her if there was any religious bullying, and she said "No, but it's that group of girls." Her daughter did not want to leave her friends, but hated the school. I wanted to scream, "Get her out!" but I didn't. I had put these stories aside in my mind, thinking that the school needs time to fix its culture problem. I was encouraged by some of the changes at the school. I had had a good conversation with Evie Hudak earlier in December, who said she would tour Peak to Peak sometime and report back on its climate. I did not hear back from her. But when I heard the Black Peter story, the culture did not seem fixed enough.

It was just like last year, when things seemed to be at least proceeding in the right direction with the settlement offer, and then Pat and Joe called me with their stories. I decided to see if the school was being compliant with its requirement to include the district in its complaint pathway. A search of peaktopeak.org revealed that the September newsletter version of this flow diagram did include a final step to call Dr. King at the district, but the school handbook version of this exact diagram did not. I asked for and studied the school's 2005 Climate Survey, done in the spring as usual. High school religious discrimination was still at 34%, while the District average had dropped to 25%, and the local high school was still 22%.

My work to reform the school's culture was not finished yet. When driving in the mountains of Colorado, you will see road signs on the downhill side of the passes: "Truckers, you are not down yet. Steep grades ahead." That's how it felt. I took in some deep breaths and went to work on another school board public statement. One evening, I watched the movie "Northlands," about a female mine worker who sued the big bosses for sexual harassment and won against all odds. It really fired me up.

The February BVSD school board meeting started out nearly empty. I checked the public speaker sign-in sheet to make sure my name was on it, and it was there with my topic, Continuing Problems at Peak to Peak Charter School. Below my name was David Hazen, the only other sign-up, Secondary Principal, Peak to Peak Charter School, Soccer Team Recognition. I thought, oh sure, that's why he's here; someone at the district tipped him off so he could immediately rebut me. I saw one other person in the room, sitting across the aisle from the Camera reporter, and went to introduce myself to Mr. Hazen and said pleasantly, "You'll be interested in what I have to say, both positive and negative." When asked if he was up to speed on what had happened last year, he said, "A little, but we don't talk about it too much as we prefer to move on." I said that you can't fix problems if you don't know what they are, and returned to my seat.

Shortly, the room began to fill with dozens of jovial high school students in their letter jackets, and I felt a wave of sadness about what had been denied to my son by the unintended consequences of past charter school decisions made by those I was about to address. My attention then snapped to a knot of distinguished-looking men in suits making their way through the athletes to sit down across the aisle from me. I looked at the program and saw that sports award recognitions would be given to championship-winning teams, and that the board would vote on Magistrate Cole's Justice High School becoming a charter school. Yes, it was the judge sitting over there, and my stomach tightened briefly before I forced all that out of my mind and studied my statement. The meeting finally got started with the Pledge of Allegiance—yes they do still say the Pledge in Boulder schools, but at Boulder High it's done in a small room before classes start and only a few show up each day.

Then the sports award recognitions were given, and I thought it was odd that only two Peak to Peak soccer players had shown up with (now) Coach Chandler to share the spotlight, when all the other sports teams from other schools had most or all their members present. Later events would give possible context to this. After a few agenda formalities it was my two minutes, and I first praised the contract and school changes. Then came the negatives: the fact that parents were still complaining to me about climate and for the first time there were racist over-tones, the Climate Surveys that remained poor, and the evidence of contract non-compliance. I finished with "It has been almost 5 years since my son was targeted for religious harassment after volunteering for science in a creationism vs. science debate in his 6th grade biology class," and my recommendation for the top lead-ership change that is required for true culture change. As I sat back down, I looked up to see Magistrate Cole turning around to briefly make eye contact with a faded recognition of who I was. Hazen then went up to defend his school and said that the 2006 Climate Surveys would be the "best ever." As I left the meeting and walked by the Camera reporter's aisle seat, she did not ask for my statement, but took a copy when I offered it.

Less than a week later, Dr. Miller-Brown called me from the district to assure me that the Peak to Peak Handbook flow diagram guidelines on harassment complaints would be fixed within the week, and said, "You probably won't believe this, but the school said the missing district piece was an inadvertent error." I was pleased with this responsiveness, and offered to give advice to the school and district based on our negative experience, saying, "I'm trying to be positive about this," and she said that this was appreciated. It was a disappoint-ment to check the school web site six weeks later to find that nothing had changed, and my phone calls were not returned. Another trip to the school board was made, noting the possible connection between the missing pathway piece and my receipt of parent complaints. I was again swallowed up in a crowd, this time rancorously pushing BVSD not to allow military recruiting on its campuses. But the online guidelines finally got fixed.

At work, the mom who told me of the Black Peter story relayed that they had met with five school officials including the teacher, who defended her use of this "Southern legend that originated in prejudice." With a sigh, she said that the class was being taken on a field trip to an area church, and was this the one that helped start the school? I didn't ask whether she had done the open enrollment process to get her kids out … she had mentioned concerns about the neighborhood schools. I thought of our family's similar decision process, and our mistake in ignoring gut feelings, but did not say anything.

The DOJ and the End of the Road

During my research for this book several months prior, I had run across information on what parents can do about discrimination against their children in schools (in chapter 8), by contacting the Office of Civil Rights (OCR) in the U.S. Department of Education. Because of the continued complaints despite the appearance of change at Peak to Peak, I decided to contact them. Looking in the blue government pages in the Denver phone book, it was uncharacteristically easy to find, and even more amazing, I got an immediate callback! They were very concerned but they only handled racial, sexual and disability-based complaints, and referred all religious cases to the Department of Justice (DOJ) in Washington, DC. I negotiated bureaucratic phone trees and finally got a live person who gave me an address to send a complaint letter. It was sent off half-heartedly with a copy of the Notice of Claim in early January 2006. To my pleasant surprise, an investigator called a few weeks later and interviewed me at length. He needed to speak with the other parents, so I made a phone call to Joe, who agreed, saying "I've heard nothing has really changed much at Peak to Peak," and also that he would speak with Pat. Letters were given to the two work acquaintances who had approached me a year apart. They were taken aback—"You want me to call the Justice Department?!" their faces said. I made no further approaches to these co-workers.

No one called the investigator. I recalled Joe commenting how busy he was, and I thought that Pat probably wants to forget about the whole painful experience. Was I becoming a nuisance in people's lives? Jeff had said after my latest school board statement, "Mom, I'm so over this, you should be too." Somehow, though, it felt like people were telling me things for a reason.

About this time, I noticed a photo series on the front page of small local public-input print/online newspaper, YourHub.com. It showed several of the Photoshop pictures for a Peak to Peak digital photography class assignment called "Place Yourself in Paradise." Several of these photos appeared religious. For example, a kid flying high over a satellite photo of the earth in what might be imagined in the Rapture, an end-of-the-world belief that all Christians will ascend to heaven, and everyone else gets blown up at Armageddon; as in the popular bumper sticker "In case of Rapture this car will be unmanned." There was also an Asian boy in apparent meditation, titled "Nirvana." Oh boy, I thought, the school is still actively promoting religious expression in the classroom. And in Bennett, a small town east of Denver, an elementary school teacher was suspended for showing snippets of a 1973 children's video series, "Who's Afraid of Opera," that had a puppet version of Faust. Parents had complained that the teacher "was teaching about the devil." And then there are CU professor Ward Churchill and Denver high school teacher Jay Benning with their leftist rants. This is the mixed up red state-blue state craziness we have in Colorado, with its own little microcosm of the same in Boulder County. I was feeling very discouraged, and Mark and I began talking about moving after Jeff was in college. Mark said, finish the damn book and let's be done with this.

Then the Lafayette News reporter, who did not attend any of the latest school board meetings I spoke at, called after I had faxed him a copy of my school board statements. The reporter wanted to talk to the mom who complained of racist teaching, because another parent, "Luis," had called him "on the record" about the atmosphere of racism at Peak to Peak that he felt also pervaded the sports program. I recalled there were some Latino names being called off as Chandler and two Anglo boys received the school board's recognition at the board meeting months ago, and a possible reason why the other boys might not want to be there occurred to me. Against my attorney's advice, I told the reporter about the DOJ preliminary investigation and asked him to pass it on to Luis. He didn't feel comfortable doing this. And I didn't feel comfortable asking my co-worker to call the reporter.

I found Luis in the phone book, and sent him a letter asking him to call the DOJ investigator. He did, and phoned me to say he was happy to have the contact, because he had been working in parallel to me in Lafayette, speaking to the city council and writing legislators about racial intolerance at Peak to Peak. He had taken his two older boys out, and was very happy with their neighborhood high school, but was struggling with a decision for the younger children because that local school wasn't good, but Peak to Peak was "not that much better." He liked some of the teachers a lot, and had a more positive opinion of Principal Fontana than I did, but also some of the same negative ones towards others. I sensed the same angst the rest of us had in balancing educational goals with protecting your child, and not really wanting to be run off by the bullies and bigots at the school. He said that Peak to Peak built a big fancy school in the trailer neighborhood, but "they don't want us there—it seems like a school for rich people." He believed the school would eventually fail under the weight of complaints and financial strain of the bond payments, and the school district would then take over the school. I agreed this would be for the best, and we promised to keep in touch. Hanging up, I recalled the line of expensive SUV's that snaked through those streets twice a day.

When none of my other contacts called the Justice Dept. investigator, he began to talk about having limited resources, which I interpreted as the beginning of a soft letdown that nothing much was going to happen. He offered to call them, so I provided the information for Pat and Joe, whom I knew would probably not mind being called, but not for my work colleagues because it seemed too intrusive. He researched the newspaper articles I referred him to, with the suggestion that he contact named parties. He did succeed in contacting Pat and Joe as well as a former teacher's aide, but the named parent who complained at the forum about evangelical influence at the school did not want to talk. A wider net needed to be cast.

So, I wrote Ms. Phillips, now off the BVSD School Board due to term limits, entreating her to talk confidentially to an interested party who was not my attorney. I had told the investigator about her statement to me of having independent corroboration of my claims. No response, pretty much as expected.

I sent a letter to the editor, printed in the Lafayette News,[17] generically encouraging parents to call the OCR if they felt their child had been discriminated against in a public school, both as a public service and thinking there might be more complaints about Peak to Peak.

I called Marvin Straus of the Boulder Atheists, who last year had placed a newspaper ad soliciting an informal survey on religious harassment at the school. He had gotten about 16 calls, half of which were supportive of the school, and half knew of problems. One caller referred him to a former school official who reportedly had kept records of such events, but she refused to talk to Mr. Strauss when contacted at her new school. Another parent gave him the name of a second church reportedly involved in starting the school. He asked me why I was still beating my head against a wall. He had contacted the school to do a brief program on atheism after I told him the ADL was having some success there, but he had gotten no response. He thought that if there were still significant problems at the school, it would have been in the papers. I told him about Pat's family being run out of town, the latest racial complaints, and my school board statements that had not made it into the paper. And people kept telling me stuff, maybe knowing I was willing to speak out, and the Justice Dept. seemed interested in the situation. He scoffed at my naivete, and threw cold water on my

---

17.   Speaking Out, April 5-11, 2006.

hope. "They have an Office of Faith-Based Initiatives at the Justice Dept., just like within the Departments of Education, Labor, and Health and Human Services. Nothing will come of this. When they get a complaint, they're required by law to respond. They're making you do all the work, aren't they?" I sheepishly responded, "Kind of." He said he'd be happy to talk to the investigator, though, when he got back in town after his vacation.

These new contacts were given to the investigator, as well as an offer for names and phone numbers of former school parents and sympathetic individuals at the school district, school board, ACLU, ADL, etc. who might be willing to speak confidentially. In one of our last conversations, I tactfully asked whether the Faith-Based office had any influence on these investigations, as I had heard. He said "Nothing could be further from the truth." I'm afraid I may have insulted him.

Two weeks later a letter arrived in the mail: the investigation of my complaint had been closed due to lack of evidence to proceed. After calling immediately to get the investigator's rationale, it was explained that the Justice Department adheres to the standard of "deliberate indifference," which requires evidence of discriminatory intent on the part of school officials. He said that intent is one of the hardest things to prove, and gave the example of murder charges being dropped to manslaughter if there was no evidence of intent to kill. This hard line, consistent with a 14th Amendment approach, seemed in contrast to one of our earliest conversations in which we discussed my reading that Title VI, the federal law against ethnic discrimination in education, has been interpreted to require a lesser standard of evidence that includes statistical and circumstantial evidence, and he had requested that I fax him the Climate Survey results. He now explained that the DOJ uses the higher standard because "the legislative intent is that school officials should not be responsible for the actions of children over which they have no control." He confirmed that none of the new contacts I had sent him had been followed up on. When asked why the OCR did not process our complaint and instead refers all religious discrimination complaints to Justice, he said it's a "division of labor." He expressed sympathy by saying, "I realize this is a disappointment, and your child and other children experienced wrongful acts, but we have to go by the law." I politely offered my opinion that if he would pursue the other leads he might find the intent he was looking for, but I realized his time was limited and he must have other important cases. We amicably ended it and I thanked him for his time. He had been very accessible, friendly and patient over the three months of the preliminary investigation. Luis told me that his case remained open, and other parents planned on speaking with the investigator, so I hoped that a full investigation would still be pursued.

Within a day, the Lafayette News called to say the DOJ story[18] was being published next week, were there any new developments? It had been a month since we had talked last. He said he had not until that week spoken with charter school officials to get their response to parents complaining to the DOJ. After a deer-in-the-headlights moment, I left a couple of awkward messages about my case being closed. The story went to press anyhow, and while it finally gave a muted voice to Luis' complaints about Peak to Peak, I was still tilting at windmills.

Summer 2006 The Gold Standard of Success

A week later, I attended a Boulder County Youth Summit as part of my volunteer work on an advisory board and had the amusement of seeing school district officials scurry to avoid giving me the cordless open mike, and quail when I finally got it. But I said nothing personal or off topic, and in focus groups later, I was able to look into some of the faces and eyes of these people. Hopefully they realized my sincerity, and I tried to see theirs.

I sighed when I checked the results of Peak to Peak's spring 2006 board elections: some of the original board members, the ones who never responded to my first complaint letter in 2002, were back. Another co-worker confided during a friendly sidewalk chat that his kids had experienced racial bullying at Peak to Peak, and were now at another school, commenting that he had trained his children to walk away from this kind of ignorant foolishness.

But then refreshing news arrived in the dead of summer. Expecting confirmation of the latest parent complaints to me, I requested copies of the Peak to Peak Spring 2006 Climate Surveys. I re-read and underlined across columns to make sure my eyes weren't fooling me: there was dramatic improvement! Peak to Peak was closer to or better than school district averages on many important measures. High school religious discrimination rates were down 7 points, from 34 to 27%, closer to the district average, now at 24%. And middle school rates, 20%, were now equal to the district. Racial discrimination data, never as dramatic in disparity in the past surveys as religious data, was improved up to 5 points at both the middle school and high school levels and equal to or better than district averages. Assuming the survey was administered without bias and the results are valid, this

---

18.   "Justice Department attorney interviews Peak to Peak parents," Lafayette News, May 10-16, 2006.

is the gold standard proof of the changes I have been working for these long, nearly three, years. I followed up with Luis at the beginning of the new school year. He had decided to keep his younger kids at Peak to Peak and had kept in contact with the DOJ investigator. So far they were being well-treated, and he commented that the school had made many positive changes. I agreed, and remembered that the school had given open enrollment tours in Spanish and applied to become an ESL (English as a second language) school. Although we had experienced religious intolerance, some met intolerance based on actual or perceived sexual orientation, and others had endured racial intolerance at this charter school. It was gratifying to see the statistics improving! The school still has a ways to go, but so do many other schools here and across the nation. The credit for this one small success here in Boulder Valley goes not only to those of us who spoke out, but to the media who helped us speak out, and those who worked behind the scenes at the ACLU, the ADL, the BVSD School Board and the Colorado State Board. And these results could not have been obtained without the school district and charter school itself finally getting on board with the needed changes.

The important message here is that a rapid turnaround in school culture is possible! As Chapters 8 and 10 will explain, a school culture of inclusiveness is paramount in reducing bullying and the use of zero tolerance discipline while improving safety and achievement. Chapter 9 shows that charter schools in particular need to meet the challenge of inclusiveness. It's all connected. And that is where it stands at press time. I have done all I can do. It is someone else's turn, in another school, another town, and another state.

"There may be times when we are powerless to prevent injustice, but there must never be a time when we fail to protest."

—Elie Wiesel, philanthropist, author, and Nazi hunter

5

Small Town Press Shut Down?

Over the September weekend in 2003 when we were reeling from the first arrest, I picked up a voice mail from Quentin Young, a reporter from the Lafayette News, wanting to speak to the parents of Jeff _____, using his correctly pronounced, unusual Russian last name. On top of everything else, just what we needed, publicity. And how the hell did he get our name? Fuming, I had no intention of returning the call. But as we began to see that we were clearly being aggressively mistreated by the school and the DA, I reconsidered. Never being one to keep my mouth shut when my buttons get pushed, I decided to call the editor. I would only do a Guest Commentary, no editing, and no interviews. It was printed promptly, and forcefully indicted the school for its domination by fundamentalist Christians, the bullying of non-Christians by their children, and for putting my son at grave risk by ignoring his cry for help for three days.[1]

I thought for sure there would be letters of support or confirmation of my observations of culture, but was I wrong. Instead, there was an outpouring of school support and critical comments towards us, such as, "A doctor and psychologist should have known their son was suicidal," and "The lawyer calls the charges insane, however the mother is angry at the school for not acting sooner because the threats included suicide. So which is it?"[2] The paper did not print my response that it is well known that family members, even those who are health professionals, are often blind to suicide risk; that teen suicide is common and easily accomplished but true school threats are rare and difficult to carry out; and that prompt school and police action does not require bizarre felony charges. I also thought that maybe some of the volunteers I had worked with, who knew my son was a good kid who had been bullied, would call with sympathy. Nope. We were pariahs.

---

1.   Guest Commentary, Lafayette News, September 10, 2003.
2.   Speaking Out and Town Talk (letters), Lafayette News, November 6-11, 2003.

After we filed the Notice of Claim, a letter arrived in the mail from a Peak to Peak founder who cried crocodile tears for us: "Oh, how awful that this happened to your family!" She went on to say "Peak to Peak was not a good fit for your son," before threatening that "many will come forward to say negative things about your son to defend our school," if we went forward with the lawsuit. "It could be worse than anything he's been through yet," the letter said. It is illegal to make a threat to dissuade someone from pursuing civil rights remedies, but I'm sure she didn't know that. I even wrote her back asking for dialogue with the school in order to improve it, but got no response. We never experienced the viciousness that Pat and Johanna did. I have no explanation for it other than the fact that we were no longer in the school directory. Or who knows, maybe newspaper reports of guns in our home[3] suggested that we were gun nuts, and dangerous to fool with in the age of caller ID, or perhaps my outing of the above letter writer in the Lafayette News chastened others.[4] Pat's friend Joe felt it prudent to have the local police in his town do extra surveillance on his street.

Quentin Young followed both of Jeff's arrests and the court proceedings closely and reported reasonably accurately and fairly, and I began to trust him with interviews. He would not reveal who had given him the name of a juvenile, but I suspect it was the school because of the correct pronunciation. The Boulder Daily Camera did not do any more in the fall of 2003 than report the possible civil rights suit,[5] but it was ok, since I did work in Boulder. But when Johanna's case in December 2004 made the school's problems with religious harassment more than an isolated incident, I was non-plussed to have my tip to their reporter initially shrugged off. When she finally could not ignore the story any longer, she did dive in with several articles and a lengthy, page one above-the-fold Sunday piece.[6] It started off by calling the whole thing "hype," but did seem overall balanced and quoted many on both sides. The local brushfire picked up briskly after this. But the reporter alienated Pat by misquoting her in the first article and subtly slanting her language towards the school,[7] and Pat never spoke with the Camera again. As a frequent letter to the editor writer, I knew too well the hazards of print media, and they can really make you look stupid when they want to by editing. Reading these articles now, with the perspective of time, it is still easy to see how some even seemingly balanced articles were "front-loaded" with the infor-

---

3.   "Boy made threats to let off steam," Lafayette News, September 10-16, 2003.

4.   "Allegations of religious bullying surface," Lafayette News, December 8-14, 2004.

5.   "Parent alleges religious harassment,", Daily Camera, November 1, 2003.

6.   "School harassment debated," Daily Camera, December 19, 2004.

7.   "Family alleges harassment at school," Daily Camera, December 10, 2004.

mation favoring the school, and burying the negative towards the end. I am familiar with this tactic, being a newspaper junkie. None of the explosive allegations I made in school board and state board statements were printed, nor was there any attempt to get the school's counterpoint on these allegations.

What really disheartened me about the news coverage was the Rocky Mountain News, one of the two Denver dailies, not picking it up after their reporter showed such initial interest in my State Board of Education statement and said she would call me. When I called in follow-up, she said she would check with her editor, but never called back. Even though the Rocky is pro-charter school, it still surprised me. Neither could I get the Denver Post to bite, with letters and phone calls, even after our TV interviews. The only coverage the Post afforded this story was via Barrie Hartman, the Post's Boulder free-lancer and a retired Boulder newspaper editor, who had written a piece about tolerance using the Peak to Peak situation as a springboard. He expressed his "skepticism about the validity of the accusations," because he "know(s) parents who founded the school."[8] Hartman did not bother to contact any of us to get the other side, which would not have been hard to do. The Post did print my letter pointing out this omission, but no further interest was forthcoming. I asked the Channel 9 producer why their lead story was not picked up by the big papers, and she said they never want to be second fiddle on a story, unless it can't be ignored.

I believe that BVSD and Peak to Peak PR professionals used the powerful people they know to blackout the story, just like the school board probably planned their monolithic contract renewal vote, to shut this down. Evangelical control and religious harassment in a charter school after the November 2004 election, during which there was much media attention paid to evangelicals' growing clout, should have been a wildfire issue, and was followed soon after by the media storm over the exact same problem at the Air Force Academy. But I had no real proof of a blackout. I thought sourly of the huge coverage of the Peak to Peak Bible book report brouhaha in early 2003, when even the Denver Post jumped on the bandwagon to defend the girl in poorly researched editorials and stories. I still have the unsent draft of an email castigating Bill O'Reilly for his contribution to Peak to Peak's hubris by sympathizing with the girl on his show, which certainly boosted the untouchability of the religious culture at the school. Even when a Peak to Peak parent wrote to one of the Rocky Mountain News' editors about the abusive tactics of a counselor, the editorial excused the school and blamed rogue staff.[9] A counselor had done a variation on the infamous and mis-

---

8.   "New year, new level of tolerance, perhaps?" Denver Post, January 2, 2005.

guided "blue eyes-brown eyes" classroom experiment in which children are sent home believing they have failed an assignment because of eye color, to teach children about discrimination. In this case, tags of two different colors were passed out. Peak to Peak's coverage, which was more than any other charter school in Colorado, seemed to be Teflon-coated.

When I contacted Denver media critic Jason Salzman to investigate the non-coverage issue, he commented that media coverage choices were not always rational. His book *Making the News*, explains just how mercurial it is. Both print and TV news reporters are constrained by their editors and producers in what actually sees the light of day. Complicated stories are difficult to cover. Mistakes and sloppiness happen. There are times when complaints to the editor are warranted in cases of gross inaccuracy, but you are largely at their mercy. Pat learned that they can burn you, and talking to the editor does not help. I guess no one could really believe something like this could happen in liberal Boulder; columnist Hartman had expressed just this sentiment. Still, if only local coverage would do the trick to change the school's culture that was ok. And big coverage comes at big cost, and my family's and certainly Johanna's family's wounds were still relatively fresh, so it was probably for the best. My lesson was that you take what you get, so don't burn your bridges with friendly reporters. And the local coverage did raise awareness of the problems at the school, for which I was grateful.

But I do know, because school insiders told me, that Quentin Young was treated badly by Peak to Peak officials, who were vociferous in their charges of bias against the school, and told his editor in early 2005 that he sat next to me at a school board meeting, which was completely untrue. He was criticized for doing investigative work into the background of a Peak to Peak principal at a Waldorf school, and into why there was a church van parked outside the school cafeteria for days on end after sound equipment had been borrowed from the church (free advertising?).[10] I challenge anyone to read all of his articles on the scandal and say that he showed any overall favoritism towards us or the school. The paper, to my surprise, quoted the science teacher's school board statement about no class disruption and my response to Young about it. I expected fireworks, but none occurred.[11] He has also reported aggressively on stories negative to the Lafayette police and mayor.[12] Lafayette is a small town with typical alli-

---

9.   "Teaching sensitivity can be a disgraceful exercise," Rocky Mountain News, June 19, 2004, 13C.

10.   Email from Sheryl Shafer to all Peak to Peak families on Dec.10, 2004, and personal communication, "Joe."

11.   "Peak to Peak contract weighed," Lafayette News, January 12-18, 2005.

ances and politics, so pressure to shut down bad publicity doesn't surprise me, but it was just wrong for Peak to Peak to give this young reporter so much hell.

When I tried to give my typed rebuttal of Peak to Peak's Press Release to him after being disappointed in the new Peak to Peak contract, Young said that his editor would not print any more stories on the subject, unless it was "big, like the ACLU taking the case."

While the school's press release was not extensively quoted by either the Lafayette News or the Daily Camera, their last articles on the story were front page and headlined with the main points of the release. The Lafayette News bold print headline was: "DA: no charges at Peak to Peak; Investigation into reports of harassment, bullying at school finds no crimes committed."[13] The Camera's was "Bullying not widespread, police report."[14] Both articles appeared to further the school's conflation of no charges in Johanna's criminal complaint of intimidation with clearance of all civil complaints about culture and harassment. It didn't seem to matter that the school's climate data, which I had pointed out to reporters, supported my claims. The Camera also allowed parent claims to be called "wilder allegations ... not true" by Peak to Peak Board VP Ferguson in direct proximity to two paragraphs recounting the suicidality of two children in response to religious bullying. An intriguing line, that I was not interviewed by the police about bullying at the school despite being the most vocal critic, was not further developed. This left Peak to Peak with the last word, and I simply wanted a chance to reply.

"I am under a lot of pressure.... I've got to go to a meeting," Young said in ending the conversation. He had become slow to return my calls, so I took the hint. Joe heard from other sources that it may have all came down from the top. Disheartened, and wondering what good it would do at this point since the renewed charter school contract was a done deal, I did not give my rebuttal to the Daily Camera, and stuffed it back in the growing "gone nowhere" file box.

This pressure from Peak to Peak on the local press was paralleled by a dramatic cessation of community and school parent negative comments in the Lafayette News, and a big front page aerial photo of the students in formation spelling "UNITY" accompanying a boosterish article,[15] just prior to the contract vote in January. As noted before on the comments of Peak to Peak supporters at

---

12.   Lafayette News, January 14-20, 2004, A-1.
13.   February 16-22, 2005.
14.   February 16, 2005, A1.
15.   "Peak to Peak students, parents, teachers share support for community school," Lafayette News, January 19-25, 2005, A1.

the school board meeting, those who had strayed were brought in to line. I know they felt their school was under attack, but it was just sickening to see the photo, and then later hear from Pat and Johanna that they were being literally run out of town.

In the fall of 2005, I contacted Quentin Young to see if he was still at the Lafayette News. He was, and I said, "I'm surprised you're still there, I thought you would have moved on to a bigger paper." I asked if he would be willing to be interviewed about the criticism he had received from Peak to Peak. He said he couldn't talk about it at work, since an interview was a personal matter. When I contacted him at home, he said, "The school made a concerted effort to discredit me, but ethically I can't talk about it while I'm still in a position to report on Peak to Peak." He would have to be "very far away" before he would consider talking about it. No reporter wants to become part of the story, but Peak to Peak made it so. I resigned myself to the fact that this is a part of the story that won't be fully told. I thanked him for his coverage of the story from both sides, and he said, yes, it had an impact. I said yes, it did, and said goodbye.

In early 2006, when things began to heat up again with the racial complaints, the Camera showed no interest. It failed to mention Peak to Peak's role in the resegregation of Lafayette schools in an extensive and otherwise excellent article on the topic.[16] When I called their reporter to compliment her on it, but also point this out, she sidestepped my question about any pressure to keep coverage positive. A later article did acknowledge briefly that the school was attracting many area students, and an on-line review of this reporter's articles shows that the Camera did address charter schools' contribution to the "socioeconomic stratification" of Boulder schools.[17] The Lafayette News, to its credit, did finally wade back into these dangerous waters by printing my letter encouraging parents to call the OCR as described in the previous chapter, which dovetailed with their coverage of immigration issues in this town with a high percentage of Latinos, and with the DOJ article on a back page. When I went in to the paper's office to obtain a copy recently, I happened to look up on the wall of Colorado Press Awards. I was not surprised to see Quentin Young's First Place 2004 Best News Story.

I am grateful for every scrap of coverage we got, and I wrote both papers to thank them after the 2006 Peak to Peak Climate Survey showed improvement.

---

16. "BVSD tackes segregation," Daily Camera, February 6, 2006, A1.
17. "Schools try to promote diversity," Daily Camera, June 18, 2005, A1. Additional articles addressing "stratification" on 8/14/05, 4/12/06, 5/7/06, and 5/12/06. More discussion on resegregation in chapter 9.

But it is hard for me not to conclude that the media were under pressure to stem the negative coverage of the school. I can't blame the messengers because they were in the middle, just trying to do their job. They took heat, too, for the unflattering stories about powerful institutions. This is just the way things are when the solution is political.

6

Where Is The ACLU When You Need Them?

The American Civil Liberties Union has a long and illustrious history (or notorious, depending on your point of view) of advocating for First Amendment causes. These causes tend to be liberal, but sometimes conservative. Lately, the ACLU has been best known for picking on the Boy Scouts, defending pedophiles, and tearing down the Ten Commandments, but they have also advocated for Rush Limbaugh's right to privacy of his medical records, which is a Fourth Amendment issue. I do understand the reasoning behind staunch defense of free speech and the separation of church and state, because one of these days the winds of political fortune will be blowing against you. I cringe to see them defending the speech rights of pedophiles to push for changes in the law, and I think anyone talking to a terrorist should be wiretapped, but intellectually I get it. And running the Boy Scouts out of public school sponsorships is based on objections to tax-supported institutional help to a group with membership requirements for belief in a higher power. But they were wrong, and the Supreme Court said so, to attack the Boy Scout's freedom of association rights in leadership and membership requirements as a private club. I think the Scouts are a great organization even though my son outgrew it. If you don't like the religious or anti-gay stuff, join Campfire Boys or any number of other groups instead. Recently in Boulder, the ACLU came out against starting a city hot-line for the reporting of possible hate crimes and hate speech, because it was on the slippery slope towards criminalization of thought, and this upset the liberals. I was surprised and dismayed to hear of the National ACLU filing suit to protect conservative religious protestors who defile soldiers' funerals, because there are free speech rights on government property. But I guess you can't accuse them of just taking on left-wing cases.

77

Mark first contacted the Colorado ACLU after our son's first arrest, requesting legal assistance in the religious harassment aspect of the case. A letter of decline came quickly, stating that they only took cases that affected large numbers of people. A follow-up letter was sent to them, giving more detail and also raising the issue of the Ashcroft Justice Department encouraging local Districts Attorney to use anti-terrorism laws against ordinary crimes, which seemed apropos in our son's bizarre charges.[1] This had already occurred elsewhere in the case of a drug dealer, and there was discussion of use of anti-terrorism laws against a Colorado man who allegedly vandalized a 9-11 flag display.[2] We received no further response from the Colorado chapter. I had some connections in Washington, and even the National ACLU told us, "We don't get involved in bullying cases; you have our sympathy, but try to get on with your life."

After the second arrest, I doggedly tried the Boulder ACLU and spoke several times with their lawyer Mike Ruderman, and we were even interviewed at length by another volunteer attorney, who also sympathized with us, but thought that bullying cases were difficult due to the "he said-she said" factor. Ruderman said that the Boulder chapter had received similar complaints before, and would investigate. He told me that one of their members was also on the BVSD Board and she had had similar issues at a private school with her son; two of the personnel from this school had moved to Peak to Peak. I knew who they were, having seen their photos and names in a private school yearbook when we applied there. And he had been told that about a third of the board and teachers at Peak to Peak belonged to the same church! All pretty juicy stuff, but circumstantial, and not illegal or immoral. When Joe tried to get a member list at this church, he was turned away. In a later conversation, Mr. Ruderman would not reveal his source for this information, so I got brave and went to the church and was easily able to pick up a roster (which only includes those willing to have photos taken for it) from a visitors display in the lobby. Several Peak to Peak board members (2 of 6), staff, founders, and volunteer names matched school staff lists I had from the second and third years of operation. "A third" of the teachers may have been old history from the first year (for which I had no list), possibly because the then K-5 school almost did not open, and last-minute teachers were needed when it did?

---

1.   "Patriot Act also used to fight regular crime," Rocky Mountain News, September 15, 2003.

2.   "Flag case probably won't fly," Rocky Mountain News, September 1, 2003. "Summit County officials may pursue flag desecration or terrorism charges against the person who burned a U.S. flag flying atop a mountain in memory of the Sept.11th victims…"

"Peak to Peak has gone right up to the line separating church and state, but we cannot prove that they have crossed it," was Ruderman's comment to Evie Hudak, the State Board of Education member. She told me that there was another charter school that was doing the same thing, and they were very skillful at this, and even private investigators sent in could not catch them stepping over it. And it was not illegal in Colorado for a church to start or contribute to a charter school if no one stepped over this line. But I think the charter school law should probably be amended.

So Ruderman ended up telling me, "The district said they couldn't find anything in their investigation of your claims. We'll keep the file open, and keep our eyes and ears open. We need more people to complain. The state chapter also says that they have no position on charter schools." None of the four people I had asked to contact him, had done so. I couldn't blame them because their kids were still at the school, or they were former employees who probably feared retaliation or legal repercussions. But when Ruderman said he had talked to former Peak to Peak Principal Groves and said she seemed like a "straight shooter," I had to disagree. When she left Peak to Peak early 2003 due to a broken leg, Fontana, the Assistant Principal, took over, but in retrospect he was even less attentive to religious bullying and other problems at the school, as indicated by declining school climate surveys.

So, another dead end. I did not hear from the Boulder ACLU until a year later when they joined the fray after Johanna's incident caused such furor. Their chairman Judd Golden said publicly, "We believe they're (Peak to Peak) failing to adhere to religious neutrality, and students' religious beliefs are being demeaned," and that "repeated complaints lead to the conclusion that there must be tacit support for Christian religious bullying at the school." I was approached by one of the Boulder ACLU Board Members, after one of the school board meetings, and she gave me support and her phone number. Joe spoke with the Director of the Colorado ACLU, who encouraged us to send letters requesting legal assistance, so we hustled and Joe hand-delivered them. But no response was ever received, despite numerous phone calls by Joe and myself.

Six months later, Ruderman told me that the BVSD Board was under "tremendous pressure," and I finished the sentence for him, "to appear charter-friendly." He said that the whole problem of charter schools was best addressed at the state level, trying to get me to see the big picture, the political solution. I was starting to see the big picture, I just didn't like my son and other children being sacrificed in the meantime. He didn't even react when I told him that about the report that there were still Bibles and crosses in cabinets at Peak to Peak. (I researched policy on this, assuming it was for the convenience of a church using the school, and found that storage of religious materials was not allowed by BVSD policy, but Peak to Peak had substituted a much weaker policy in their charter documents. How convenient, again, right up to the line. Or over it? (Shortly after our conversation, a church moved out of the school.) Ruderman said people shouldn't send their kids to the school if they didn't like the atmosphere. Just like the district, he seemed to say it's your own fault for choosing a charter school, and I snapped, "But you don't find out about the religious stuff until you're enrolled, and then it's hard to get out." I asked him to check on the status of our request for legal assistance with the state chapter, but never heard back. Pleading letters and follow-up calls to the Boulder ACLU to forget about Ward Churchill, who already had a good lawyer defending him, and help us out, got no response.

When I started on this book, I called Ruderman for the official Boulder ACLU position on the Peak to Peak matter, wanting to give them that courtesy. He referred me to Judd Golden, who spent a good 30 minutes explaining the Boulder ACLU's failure to get more involved, and what they interpreted as BVSD's position. The ACLU only gets involved when "the facts are not in dispute," and the only question is legal interpretation of First Amendment issues, because the organization has limited resources. Peak to Peak was disputing our claims and it didn't matter if they were blatantly lying; this is what courts of law were for, to sort out who was telling the truth. As far as what they understood BVSD's position to be, it was that the families were "being oversensitive," that these were "isolated incidents" and that "they don't know who to believe." He said the district planned to be more vigilant and provide more oversight. He denied that a BVSD Board member being one of their members had any influence on the matter. I finished up by saying that I had hoped that the ACLU had been a little more of a bulldog on it, and why did they just limit themselves to the low-hanging fruit (e.g., keeping local jail inmates from volunteer landscaping work at a church and getting one inmate kosher meals) but thanked him for his time. His group was all-volunteer, and had no responsibility to do anything, he replied, but "You did a good job bringing attention to the issue, and good luck on the book."

I follow the types of cases the Colorado ACLU gets involved in, and it's not all when "the facts are not in dispute." For example, they recently filed suit for two Bush protesters who got thrown out of a town meeting, and hired a private investigator to get evidence because indeed plenty of the facts were in dispute. In late summer 2005, I got lucky and caught its Director Cathryn Hazouri on the phone to get her view on our case for the book. She apologized for no written response to our requests for assistance and promised to look into it and have a response sent, but it never happened, and further phone calls have not been returned. Reporter Quentin Young told me that he had spoken with her over the summer, and happened to ask about the Peak to Peak matter. She said, "No smoking gun."

So that's what it came down to in three words, but I think their interest in the case may have dissipated for big picture, political reasons. I was disappointed in them until the 2006 Peak to Peak Climate Survey showing improvement came out, and now I believe their behind-the-scenes advocacy contributed to this result.

7

Law Enforcement And The Courts—Just Doing Their Job

It is with hesitation that I criticize those in law enforcement who put their lives on the line everyday for public safety, and those in the judicial system who make the difficult decisions to administer justice on the public's behalf. We have, and Joe has, friends who are policemen and women. We have seen the constant second-guessing of their split-second decision making in the press, that only took a brief time-out after the heroism of September 11th.

But there are those in every profession, including my own, medicine, who do not exhibit the highest professionalism, get sloppy and make mistakes, are susceptible to outside pressures, or rarely, who are plainly malignant towards those under their power. It has taken awhile for me to settle on where the Lafayette Police Department and the Boulder District Attorney fit in to this continuum with regard to their repeated attempts to prosecute my son.

The feeling that we may have been singled out for harsh treatment arose from the fact that I had made three reports of possible illegal activity on school grounds over the two years of my son's attendance at Peak to Peak. These reports made by myself and a teacher, which indirectly or directly involved the Lafayette Police Department, resulted in arrests for narcotics on campus, and in one report that was unsubstantiated, changes in school internet use policy. I want to make clear that no officer was arrested. But these good faith reports, which in good conscience could not be avoided, probably caused significant stress for the police and the school. None of this information was shared with anyone except Mark. While the details may add interest to this tale of my journey to understand what happened to my son, they do not contribute to my final analysis that he was the victim of Columbine scapegoating rather than retaliation, and therefore will not be recounted here.

We were pleased with the responsiveness and professionalism shown by the School Resource Officer at Peak to Peak after our failed attempts to get the school to put a stop to the vicious bullying of our son, and I thanked him for it at a school open house. And we do credit another SRO for recognizing the seriousness of the later situation of suicidality and possible school threats when school officials seemed paralyzed to act. But we were very traumatized by what we saw as an overzealous arrest and prosecution the first time around, and did not understand why a misdemeanor plea was not offered. And the re-arrest on even more serious felony charges the second time, based on less than careful police and prosecution work, seemed over the top. Always big police supporters and ready to give them the benefit of the doubt in critical press reports, we were ready then to file the Notice of Claim against the police for Malicious Prosecution.

We had learned from Howard that DAs are virtually immune from legal repercussions of their mistakes and excesses, and deputy DAs must be fired or their bosses voted out of office, but the police can be sued on a number of grounds such as excessive force or false arrest. Also, a badly mishandled investigation or arrest without sufficient cause can be malicious prosecution. Recent press articles detailed the case of a Colorado man who filed suit after an investigation that resulted in no charges. The man claimed that the police secretly interrogated his teenage son about him, leading to the boy's suicide. In addition, the failure to remove his address from a "no-go" list caused an ambulance company to refuse service, and the man almost died.[1] Our case was certainly not that egregious, but we thought it was worth looking into.

I consulted several months after Jeff's exoneration with civil rights attorney David Lane, who came highly recommended, and since has become nationally known for his defense of CU Professor Ward Churchill. He met me in his not-fancy downtown Denver office in shorts and a Hawaiian shirt. He listened patiently to my story, and kindly explained that unless I could prove that the error in the computer report interpretation was intentional, I had no case because the police were given wide latitude to make mistakes. And even if the jury sided with us, it was unlikely to return any damages to a plaintiff who had not been raped, beaten or killed while in custody. He had represented many such clients, and our case was probably small potatoes to him.

So our basic lesson continued to be: In confronting government wrongdoing or errors, anything less than grievous harm was a big ho-hum. Life is not fair, and

---

1.   "Cops block ambulance," Rocky Mountain News, November 28, 2003.

we were lucky that our son was ok. You could say that justice prevailed both times, so didn't the system work as it should have?

The problem is that this has not just happened to a family of professionals who had the umbrage and money to fight for their son. This is happening to children and families all over Colorado and the nation, often with far more negative outcomes than ours. It is Columbine scapegoating: the scorched earth approach to school violence prevention, as demanded by society.

PART III

8

Scapegoating For Columbine

Searching for a Quick Fix in Retribution

Our nation was so horrified by a string of school shootings in the 1990's culminating at Columbine High School here in Colorado, that it was like 9-11 in its "This changes everything" effect, from police response planning to classroom and school design to attitudes toward bullying. It also cemented recent changes in 100 year old concepts of juvenile justice that had been developed by Denver Judge Ben Lindsey,[1] from the rehabilitative model to a more adult-style punitive model. Schools practiced an even harder form of zero tolerance discipline, which had been initiated earlier in the decade, and began to hand students over to law enforcement, resulting in the "no nail-clippers, no bomb jokes" equivalent of school discipline.

According to Elliot Aronson, author of *Nobody Left to Hate: Teaching Compassion after Columbine* (2001), quick fixes were sought. Then-Governor George Bush said, "There's a wave of evil passing over the land." Many saw the problem as a lack of moral or religious training, and Congress voted right after Columbine to tack on an amendment to a crime bill to allow the posting of the Ten Commandments in schools (which failed), and there was blame placed on the Supreme Court decision three decades ago to ban organized school prayer. Movies, and video games in particular were blamed, and legal attempts to clamp down on them were debated but ran into First Amendment problems. It also strained common sense because of the huge numbers of children who were exposed to these media forms yet did no harm to their peers.[2] Lax gun laws compared to other countries were thought to be the culprit, but this effort ran into Second Amendment problems, and school shootings in Scotland and Germany seemed to disprove this theory. Some observers blamed anti-depressant medications for turning troubled kids violent, since shooters in several well-known school killings

---

1. *Anton Wood: The Boy Murderer,* by Dick Kreck (Fulcrum Publishing, 2006).

were taking them. There is evidence that these drugs blunt emotions, including empathy, and it is possible that such effects may tip some people over the edge. But millions of kids take these drugs and don't become murderers. Or was it the school misfits and the "pathological loners" who needed to be identified and watched, and removed from schools. This found widespread support, did not violate adult civil rights, and states and communities seized on the criminal model to cleanse their schools of the evil ones.

Heavy Collateral Damage

For several years after Columbine, I noticed a steady litany of depressingly similar news reports: teen was bullied, got mad, fantasized revenge, drew pictures/wrote a story/made a list of enemies, someone told, teen got arrested and sent to juvenile detention. Even younger children were suspended, expelled and arrested for minor infractions or innocent mistakes. It became so commonplace that these reports have dropped off the major media radar except for the youngest children of 5 and 6 being put in handcuffs for having a tantrum or finding a butter knife in the backpack. Will somebody please stop this madness?! Even putting aside the most ridiculous examples that have made the national news, in Colorado there have been multiple cases such as our son's, that indicated a need for investigation, but the failure to find anything serious did not stop the meat grinder of overzealous prosecution for the child and his family, including the child spending time in detention, before being spit out in a heap.

Clipping newspaper reports from the Rocky Mountain News and Denver Post for the past two years since our own traumatic experience, the following is a selection of what I have found. In some cases, the final outcome was not later reported. No doubt readers in other cities could come up with a different, but all too familiar, list of expelled and arrested students.

Louisiana—Two high school students who had no discipline or criminal records were charged with terrorizing, a felony, after poems about being bullied and drawings of shooting a teacher, but no weapons, were found after an anony-

---

2.   The evidence that videogames are associated with violent behavior is weak, according to a 2004 review in the Journal of the American Medical Association (Vol. 291, No. 15), which concluded that excessive gameplay was a symptom, not a cause, of social and emotional problems. The most comprehensive study to date, from the Universities of Illinois and Michigan, showed that gameplayers did not become more belligerent (Wall Street Journal, June 2, 2006). The positives of videogames are outlined in Prensky's *Don't Bother Me, Mom, I'm Learning* (Paragon House, 2006).

mous tip. The charges were dropped after a grand jury found insufficient evidence.

Georgia—14 year old girl expelled for private journal entry describing a dream about the Columbine shooting, after a teacher confiscated it in class. The family had lived near Columbine at the time of the tragedy.

Colorado—A 13 year old boy was arrested for felony possession of an explosive device, after putting fireworks powder in a plastic pop bottle in a field behind his house, but did not explode it.

Florida—A seventh grader is suspended in preparation for possible expulsion after a "hit list of people he wanted dead" was found. No charges were filed because no specific threat was made.

Colorado—High school girl arrested on weapons charges, and suspended for six months in her senior year, after a pocketknife was found in her purse during a routine traffic stop off campus, and the girl admitted to having the purse at school earlier in the day.

Ohio—Sixth grader suspended for bringing Sports Illustrated swimsuit issue to school.

Iowa—15 year old arrested for felony terrorism, after wearing a T-shirt with images of the Columbine killers to school, and spreading rumors about a shooting. It was later reduced to a misdemeanor.

Kentucky—A 60 pound second-grader was charged with felony assault after kicking his teacher, who was not injured. Charges were later dismissed.

Colorado—A 15 year old boy was arrested on solicitation to commit first degree murder several months after allegedly asking two friends to help him bomb the cafeteria, who said they didn't think it was serious. He was described as despondent, and there was no plan, explosives or bomb-materials found. He lived with his grandfather on a farm, who kept locked up hunting rifles. "He had access to fertilizer and nails," said police. He was held without bond in a juvenile detention center until his hearing a week later. His grandfather accused the school of intimidating the boy into making a written confession. "He had no intention of carrying this out … I can't believe the Columbine scare has got people this goofy." The teen was bound over for trial; he later agreed to a plea bargain of misdemeanor disruption of an educational facility.

New Jersey—A 12 year old was suspended for 6 weeks, after making a joke about the peanut butter cookies in his lunchbox being dangerous to a teacher with a peanut allergy.

Georgia—Two middle school students were charged with making terroristic threats and conspiracy to commit murder after telling classmates they planned to kill the teacher. No evidence of plans or weapons were found. The boys were put on house arrest, and later found guilty of terroristic threats.

Colorado—An 11 year old boy was held on $50,000 bond for setting three houses under construction on fire. The parents couldn't make the bond, and he remained in detention until sent to psychiatric facility, and faced up to two years in youth corrections. The boy's father cried uncontrollably as he was taken into custody. A relative said the family was caring and had sought treatment for their son's problems before he sneaked out one night and set the fires.

Texas—A 17 year old boy was sent to prison for 4 years in a plea agreement for charges that carried a maximum life sentence, after writing in a spiral notebook whom he wanted to attack at school.

Texas—Two boys were held in a juvenile detention facility after being arrested for making terroristic threats, after talking about a Columbine-like attack and said they could get weapons.

Virginia—15 year old boy arrested and charged with possession of a explosive device, a felony carrying a maximum of 10 years, after making and exploding a series of baking soda-plastic pop bottle bombs in his backyard.

Colorado—11 year old boy arrested for ethnic intimidation and assault, after a shoving match on the playground in response to another boy harassing him in Spanish and he told the principal, "Maybe he'll start speaking English now." Charges reduced 7 months later to disorderly conduct.

New York—High school student arrested and expelled after school security guard found a Civil War musket and uniform in his car. He had participated in a re-enactment over the weekend.

New Mexico—After hitting another boy with a basketball at school, a tearful 8 year old boy was arrested, handcuffed, and booked into an adult jail where inmates banged on his cell window and told him they were going to get him. He was later released to his parents, who filed a civil rights lawsuit on his behalf. The suit alleged that it was not the first time school officials had called police to temporarily detain students as part of school discipline .

Florida—8 year old boy arrested for battery after slapping a boy who then picked up a rock; a sister separated the two.

Pennsylvania—A 10 year old girl was arrested, handcuffed, and taken away crying, for bringing a 8 inch pair of scissors to school, but did not threaten anyone. She was suspended, and may be expelled to a special disciplinary school.

California—11 year old girl suspended for doing cartwheels during lunchtime. No one was kicked.

Florida—Two boys, 9 and 10, were arrested and charged with making a written threat to kill or harm another person, and suspended, for drawing stick figures of a classmate being stabbed and hung.

Colorado—A 12 year old with a speech impediment who had been severely bullied but never fought back, as his mother worked with the school to stop it to no avail, finally said to the bullies, "Remember Columbine?" and was suspended for 5 days; a police investigation revealed no writings or weapons.

Colorado—11 year old charged with theft for taking a lollipop from a jar in his classroom.

Colorado—A 13 year old boy with a fever who was upset that he couldn't go home was arrested for disruption of an educational facility after throwing papers and breaking a mug. The school had cleared the rest of the students out of the building.

Colorado—Three middle school students were arrested for interference with an educational facility and expelled after allegedly making threats against a teacher that were reported by another student. No hit lists, writings, plans or weapons were found. They received probation.

Colorado—17 year old charged with carrying a concealed weapon and suspended when a 4 inch folding knife was found in his pocket by the principal who suspected alcohol on his breath.

Georgia—Two 13 year old girls who served glue-laced cake to classmates as a prank were initially charged with attempted murder, later reduced to disrupting a school and given probation.

Colorado—A 14 year old girl was arrested on felony charges of carrying a weapon on school grounds after a letter opener was found in her locker during a search because she made an unspecified threat to another student and wore a necklace with photos of the Columbine shooters.

Colorado—Bullied 7th grader arrested and expelled for hit list.

Colorado—16 year old arrested for passing on a rumor about bathroom graffiti mentioning Columbine that was originally reported by the custodian, but could later not be found. It was senior skip day and low attendance contributed to the rumors.

Kansas—17 year old boy arrested for battery and expelled for throwing up on a teacher.

Colorado—High school student arrested and lodged in juvenile detention, for playfully shooting his friend in the leg with a toy weapon that caused no injury.

Pennsylvania—A 14 year old boy was arrested and charged with making terroristic threats and harassment, and was expelled, after writing a rap song at home that had violent, but vague, lyrics. The school learned of the writings in March, and contacted police. He was expelled in May, but a judge reversed the expulsion, saying the school was not actually disrupted by its investigation, and did not immediately call his parents or search his locker. However, the legal charges were still pending as of August 2005.

Colorado—14 year old boy who brought a pellet gun to school and showed it to a friend was arrested for felony menacing, even though he did not point it at anyone or make a threat.

Colorado—Three highschool girls were suspended for leaving nasty messages on a web page created off campus, after a falling out with two other students.

Colorado—High school boy suspended for 16 days after posting jokes, without any names, about his school on a popular internet site. The ACLU is taking his case.

California—11 year old girl charged with assault with a deadly weapon, a felony, after throwing a rock at a boy during a water balloon fight, causing a wound that required stitches. Police responded with three cars and a helicopter. She was placed in detention for 5 days, and spent a month under house arrest after police said she resisted arrest and scratched the officer's arm. A plea deal involving mediation was reached.

Colorado–A 14 year old boy was arrested for unlawful sexual contact after a school resource officer filed a routine report about several boys and girls playing a consensual game of "boob tag" on a middle school playground. The school had found that no actual contact had taken place. The boy's mother, who said the game was inappropriate and warranted punishment but not prosecution, feared the up to two years in youth detention for conviction and did not want her son labeled a sex offender.

New York–An 8 year old boy was taken into custody and charged with negligent homicide after sneaking on to an unattended school bus and releasing the parking brake, resulting in its rolling forward and killing a classmate. The judge refused to release him and instead ordered a mental evaluation.

Colorado–A 16 year old boy was kept in detention for 62 days awaiting trial on juvenile possession of a handgun after posting Myspace.com pictures of himself posing in his home with several of his father's firearms. The boy had been given extensive safety training by his father, a retired Air Force pilot, and had been given permission to handle but not load or fire the weapons without supervision. No threats were made and no other youths were present. He received probation and his father planned to appeal the conviction.

Massachusetts–A 6 year old boy was suspended for 3 days for "sexual harass-ment" after putting two fingers inside a classmate's waistband after she touched his shirt. Experts commented that only in rare cases can children so young sexu-ally harass one another.

And of course the most ridiculous of all which we all saw on the national news, handcuffed in tears, the Florida 5 year old arrested after having a temper tantrum in her kindergarten classroom.

In Colorado in the 2004-2005 school year, there were 71,000 suspensions, 2400 expulsions, and 11,000 referrals to law enforcement.[3] Nationwide, roughly 1% of all public school students are expelled in any given year, according to the U.S. Department Education; it is unknown how many involve school referrals to the police. In the first half of 2006, there have been numerous cases of arrests and expulsions for ill-considered or naive internet postings on popular teen social sites such as Myspace.com. The collateral damage in the war on school violence con-tinues.

In Colorado at least, arrest is used to stop a crime or respond to a complaint, and then to initiate processing and set court dates. It is not to be used to inflict punishment, according to a specific law prescribing its limits,[4] but this seems to be largely ignored here and elsewhere in the case of children. An arrest of a child for the most of the behaviors described above is punishment, because charges are often reduced or dismissed, and the frequent denial, delay, or the setting of a high bond compounds this punishment. Bond is used to ensure court appearance or in the case of denial, to protect public safety. Most of these children do not appear to be flight or safety risks.

Before and since Columbine, school shootings unfortunately continue sporad-ically. A more recent case in Red Lake, Minnesota, involved a boy who had been bullied and, it is said, rumors that circulated about the boy's plans were not fol-lowed up. The Columbine shooters telegraphed their anger for at least a year. In October 2006, while the nation was riveted on television coverage of two aber-rant cases of psychotic adults killing students, a bullied 15 year old also shot a hole in his school ceiling after becoming angry that teachers would not stop the bullying. We know that not only must bullying not be ignored, but any reports of threats must be immediately assessed for seriousness. The vast majority will be cries for help, and not serious. Children who make cries for help should not be

---

3.   Denver Public Schools Superintendent Jerry Wartgow, a member of Common Good Colorado, a group seeking better schools and reduced legal entanglements. www.cgood.org/Colorado

4.   Colorado Revised Statutes 16-5-207

further bullied by being arrested and harshly prosecuted. To the extent that a school is truly disrupted by any incident (e.g., a closure or lockdown) that proves to be a false alarm, school consequences can be applied in a fair fashion. Negative publicity alone should not be categorized as a school disruption. The main appropriate action by the school is to call the parents, and assure counseling to address root causes of the cry for help. Suspension during a threat assessment may be appropriate.

But schools have largely chosen to abdicate their traditional in-loco-parentis responsibility and have turned a discipline issue—behavior problems, failure to curb bullies, support victims and counsel both—into a criminal matter. When the police are called, they will investigate and arrest; this is their job, and after Columbine, the public expects them to get tough on school violence. The schools increasingly see their public mandate as suspension or expulsion, not counseling, of troubled non-violent students.

In getting tough after Columbine, and in the public backlash against actual or perceived soft sentences of the '80's and '90's for juveniles committing violent acts, law enforcement has overreacted against non-violent juveniles, more so than against adults. Adults are rarely arrested for threatening speech not accompanied by attempts to carry it out. Bob Grant, a former local District Attorney and Executive Director of the Colorado District Attorney Council, was recently quoted in the case of a published story of a plot to kill a real person who had harmed the author: "People are arrested for what they do, not for what they write."[5] A local judge said during a trial, "One of my thoughts ran to holding a blowtorch to (the defendant's) foot,"[6] and no one arrested him. Until recently speech was not a crime unless a direct, credible threat is made to another individual, or an indirect threat of violence is made with evidence of intent and plans to act. For example, in the chapter on Jeff's harassment, an older boy made a direct threat of lethal violence that was credible, i.e., it was an act using ordinary PE equipment that could be easily accomplished at that moment or any school day. A non-credible threat would be, "Aliens are going to zap you dead." Writing stories, journal entries, on-line rants and drawing pictures are not crimes unless they describe credible, detailed plans to harm real people, and steps are taken to implement the plan. Finding pipe bombs and school maps with plans and a hit list in a kid's bedroom would fit, but simply having a shotgun or rifle in the home of a student who expresses vague threats would not fit this requirement.

---

5.   "Writer accused of stalking Broomfield man," Daily Camera, June 2, 2005.
6.   Rocky Mountain News, February 10, 2004, A6.

The mistake many in the public seem to make is that there is not a dichotomous choice to do nothing or to arrest a child who appears to make a threat. This was illustrated in Chapter 5 by the letter writer who said, "The lawyer calls the charges insane, however the mother is angry at the school for not acting sooner ... which is it?" In our son's case, the school, either through incompetence or discrimination, took no substantive action for three days while in possession of alarming instant messages. A competent process would have included an immediate call to the parents that night, arrangement for urgent professional assessment and counseling, temporary school suspension, and a police investigation into whether the threat was credible. If it appeared that the parents were not cooperative or did not have the resources, social services should be contacted. Arrest of children should be reserved for clear cases of a committed crime, or public safety/ flight risks.

In the case of the 15 year old Colorado boy who expressed a fantasy of making a bomb to explode at school, school officials apparently were more on the right track in not initiating an arrest. They arranged for counseling and an expulsion study program which the boy was doing well in for two months, when the school security guard's request for a restraining order, based on the original tip to the school by other students, alerted the police to the incident. The boy, who had no previous record of trouble, was then arrested, put in detention without bond for at least a week, and put through the same hell our son was, until prosecutors came to the same conclusion 6 months later that they had no evidence for the felony charges they had initially pressed.[7]

In a 2001 Colorado case, which was reviewed in a 2005 newspaper article,[8] three 14 and 15 year old boys were arrested for "planning a Columbine-style attack" on their junior high school. The boys, who also had no previous troubles, had verbalized vague plans to girls who were friends, drawn some stick figures with guns and drawings of hanging bodies, and an untitled list of names was found. Firearms were seized after the arrests from one of the boys' parent's ranch, and one of the girls reported that one of the boys had once pointed a shotgun at her. It appears that when one girl's brother beat up one of the boys, some angry words were exchanged, and the girl called police to relate the boys' "plans." They were charged with conspiracy to commit first degree murder; later each pled guilty to conspiracy to commit first degree assault. Two of the boys were sentenced to 1-2 years of detention plus 2 years probation and the third boy to 2

---

7.   Rocky Mountain News, June 9, July 14, and November 11, 2004.
8.   "A tragedy averted," Rocky Mountain News, April 16, 2005, 21A.

years probation. Contacted in 2005 for interviews, the now 18 and 19 year-olds said: "We were just stupid junior high school kids. We made a stupid mistake." "I just needed attention ... I wasn't getting what I felt I needed at the time." "We didn't know how to deal with our feelings in a socially acceptable way." Of the two boys who served detention, one is working in a sandwich shop and hopes to become a mechanic; one is still in alternative school and wants to help counsel other students to avoid his fate. The boy who received probation is in college. It is hard to avoid the sense that juvenile detention has derailed the lives of two of these kids. Did they deserve it, and did society require protection from them? Would all three have been more fairly treated with probation and counseling?

In both of these last two vignettes of teen boys placed in detention for varying time periods, we do not know what they experienced there; it was not discussed in the articles. But it is well known that in male prisons there is a pecking order of strongest to weakest, and it is enforced brutally, with the smallest and weakest becoming "girlfriends," while guards turn a blind eye.[9] Violence in prisons is a serious problem, according to a 2006 report of the Commission on Safety and Abuse in America's Prisons, and prisoners recounted gang violence, rapes and beatings.[10] Frighteningly, juvenile facilities have 10 times the reported rate of sexual assault that adult prisons do, according to a study done by the Justice Department's Bureau of Justice Statistics, released in 2005.[11] A 1994 report says that 50% of these facilities are not up to minimum standards.[12] Here in Colorado in 2006, many youth facilities are crumbling, detainees sleep on thin plastic mattresses on concrete benches or the floor, the interviews are not private, and the furnaces and sewer system are below code standards,[13] suggesting that things haven't changed much. While the three boys discussed above do not appear to have been hardened or embittered by their experience, this is not an uncommon response to detention in a poorly run facility, and case reports of wrongfully incarcerated youth suggest long term negative effects on children and families.[14]

---

9.   "Prison rape may be underreported," Rocky Mountain News, July 30, 2006. Details findings of the National Prison Rape Elimination Commission. In some confidential studies, one in ten inmates report having been raped.

10.   "Crisis in our prisons," NewsMax magazine, August 2006.

11.   Ten incidents reported per 2000 youths at state-run juvenile facilities. Reported in the Rocky Mountain News, August 1, 2005.

12.   *Conditions of Confinement: Juvenile Detention and Corrections Facilities, Parent.et al.* Office of Juvenile Justice and Delinquency Prevention report, Washington, DC, 1994.

13.   "On the edge of obsolete," Rocky Mountain News, March 13, 2006.

A 14 year old boy who was allegedly beaten and suffocated to death by guards in a Florida boot camp is a chilling reminder of the risks of youth detention.[15] This boy's original crime had been to take a joy ride in his grandma's car; when he violated probation by trespassing at a school he was sent to the camp.

The girls who told on the three boys were also profiled in the 2005 newspaper article. Because the boys were treated harshly, the girls were ostracized and run out of their school, for ruining the boys' lives. There are consequences of over-zealous prosecution for the accused, the witnesses, and society. The next time will someone, usually a girl, think twice, or the better of it? Knowing if she tells, all of their lives will be ruined, and if she doesn't tell, there may be a tragedy? If she knew that the situation would be handled sensibly, wouldn't that encourage more telling? In the Santee, California school shooting just after Columbine, it was reported that other students did not tell because they knew that the boy, who had been severely bullied, would get expelled even if it wasn't serious. In fact the Secret Service, in a 2000 study of school shootings, reports that there had been some forewarning in 75% of these incidents![16]

If all the stories of the many cases I have listed could be told in as much detail as ours, I'm sure ours would not be even close to the worst. What is mostly innocent childhood behavior, acting out of problems, immature judgement, and honest mistakes has been criminalized.

Brain Research Supports Juvenile Rehabilitation Model

New information in brain research supports the rehabilitative model of juvenile justice and common-sense school discipline. It has been shown that the brain is not fully developed until about age 22 in girls and 24 in boys. Auto rental companies are way ahead of us, since 24 is their minimum age to rent. The brain undergoes dramatic changes of neuron pruning, similar to pruning a tree to make the branches stronger and more productive, beginning at about age 11 in girls and 12 1/2 in boys, at the onset of puberty.[17] In addition, different areas of the brain mature before others in a back to front fashion, which results in an "acceleration over brakes" effect on teen behavior, according to a recent Boulder talk by

14.   "Testimony and interrogation of Minors," Owen-Kostelnik et al, *American Psychologist*, May-June 2006.

15.   "Second autopsy shows youth was suffocated," Rocky MountainNews, May 5, 2006.

16.   www.edu.gov/bullying

17.   "How teen brain develops," Rocky Mountain News, September 30, 2005, 5A. Details research at UCLA and NIH.

Dr. Ken Winters, Director of the Center for Adolescent Substance Abuse Research at the University of Minnesota. The base of the brain, or cerebellum, experiences growth first, and is responsible for physical coordination and sensory processing, so it is no wonder that the best gymnasts are teens and that video games and music become alluring. Next in development is a structure called the nucleus accumbens, which is responsible for motivation. There may be a reason why your teen seems lazy and has no self-motivation! Many parents have seen a lackadaisical attitude toward schoolwork, especially in middle school boys, that improves in high school given the right supportive factors. The amygdala controls emotion and this brain area develops next; this accounts for the teen tendency to run hot and cold, say things before thinking, and to misinterpret facial expressions, e.g., fear as anger or hostility. Last is judgement, seated in the prefrontal cortex or front of the brain, which is pretty mature about age 18 for structured decision making, e.g., where to go to college. But judgement with emotional input such as delaying gratification (drugs, alcohol and sex), or resisting impulses (e.g., beating up the guy who winked at a girlfriend), is not mature at this age.

This research relates directly to the teen behavior that is getting mostly boys in trouble with schools and the law. It is common knowledge that boys tend to be more competitive and say more crazy, aggressive things than girls; it's called trash talk, boasting, tough talk, etc. While most older kids know about Columbine, many younger kids don't, and they don't read the newspapers to see what happens to boys who trash talk, so there is a steady supply of unwitting victims and their families caught in this web. What a pain in the neck for schools and police! Well, Colorado has just joined other states in making speech a crime. At least they don't call it terroristic threats. Colorado House Bill 1014, passed in 2005, made it a class 1 misdemeanor (the most serious) punishable by up to a year in jail, to make a credible threat against a school or school official.[18] Credible threat is defined using the "reasonable person" standard, which means that if the threat should be reasonably be investigated, it fills the bill for arrest charges. No need for intent, plans or steps. I think prosecutors were just sick and tired of not succeeding with their bizarre felonies in these fantasy threat cases.

At least the charges are misdemeanors, and that's a step in the right direction. But it does not solve the teen boy trash talk problem, by turning students into the equivalent of airline passengers, and subject to arrest for joking, letting off steam, or making a cry for help. If they post signs at the schoolhouse door like they do at

---

18.   Colorado Revised Statutes 18-9-109 (5)

airports, "It is a Class 1 misdemeanor to make a threat," will this shut down all trash-talk and cries for help, as well as that urge to confide the awful plan that says "please stop me!"? This indeed could be the perverse effect, and there will be no warnings, about real attacks, about suicides, about dire need for relief from bullying, depression, and mental illness. Just keep it to yourself, kid, and don't bother us, society seems to be saying.

The equivalent of Columbine scapegoating by the legal system is known in the schools as Zero Tolerance Discipline, defined by the American Bar Association as a specific response to student misbehavior where a school automatically and severely punishes students for a variety of infractions, often resulting in expulsion or suspension and criminal charges. The ABA officially opposed zero tolerance school discipline in a 2000 resolution, and issued its *Zero Tolerance Report* in 2001.[19] The school and legal systems are meting out double punishment for both the seriously misbehaving and those with minor infractions, as well as the merely unlucky or naive student who said the wrong thing or didn't know what was in his backpack.

The History of Zero Tolerance Discipline

Zero tolerance as a guiding philosophy in school discipline and violence prevention got its start with the 1994 Gun-Free Schools Act. This was passed by Congress in response to the epidemic of urban gun violence around and on school grounds. Zero tolerance seems to have arisen from the 1982 "Broken Windows" theory of crime prevention of George Kelling.[20] This famous theory states that a breakdown in societal order as evidenced by broken windows, graffiti and petty crimes will beget more serious crime, and if small crimes are punished consistently and firmly, there will be a decrease in major crimes. Proponents of this theory point to successes in New York City and elsewhere, while detractors point to other factors bringing down crime, such as concentrating police efforts on "hot spots" of serious crime. Mandatory sentencing, "three-strikes" laws, and trying juveniles as adults also became part of the program to get tough on crime in the '90s. The Ashcroft Justice Department (2001-04) pushed maximum, uniform sentencing, and the use of the Patriot Act in ordinary crimes such as drug-deal-

---

19.   A comprehensive review of major legal issues relating to school violence, zero tolerance, student rights and due process, *School Violence: From Discipline to Due Process,* was published by the ABA in 2005.

20.   Skiba and Noam, Eds., Zero Tolerance: Can Suspension and Expulsion Keep Schools Safe? *New Directions for Youth Development,* Winter 2001, p.20.

ing.[21] There has also been a trend towards paramilitary tactics in domestic policing, including the use of SWAT teams for minor drug and gambling investigations.[22]

Juveniles tried as adults often receive longer sentences than adults for the same serious crime, and do not receive the intensive attempts at rehabilitation in adult prisons that would be afforded in juvenile lock-ups, according the Pendulum Juvenile Justice Foundation.[23] This organization is working to change laws that charge juveniles as adults, based on brain development as discussed, and the recent Supreme Court decision that the death penalty cannot be applied to juveniles. In Colorado prisons, this means that there are 46 "lifers" who went in for murder committed as a juvenile, out of 346 total.[24] The Foundation does not want to let them all go, but wants juveniles given rehabilitation, and if successful, a chance at parole. While brain immaturity cannot be used to excuse violent criminal behavior such as murder, it is thought to mitigate culpability. The insane person is hospitalized, and the juvenile deserves a rehabilitation trial, is the thinking. In addition, research and specific case studies have shown that children, especially those with below average IQ, are much more vulnerable than adults to false confessions with resultant wrongful convictions, according to an extensive review of the topic in the journal American Psychologist.[25] Children will say what the investigator wants to hear, in the hopes they'll be then allowed to go home! Happy Meals and candy were used to obtain a false confession in a famous Chicago case. This article also comments on media exaggeration of youth crime rates and pressure on law enforcement to find and prosecute youth "predators." In a survey of police interrogators' attitudes toward youth, one comment was, "The juveniles I interrogate aren't kids; they're monsters."

When I went to a hearing at the Colorado State Capitol on proposed legislation to give youth lifers a chance at parole after 40 years, I sat for hours with families in their Sunday best and grandpas with their canes who had waited for the

---

21.   "Ashcroft: go for max," September 23, 2003, and "Patriot Act also used to fight regular crime," September 15, 2003, Rocky Mountain News.

22.   "Wrong Door," by Balko and Berger, Wall Street Journal, September 2-3, 2006. Balko is the author of Overkill: The Rise of Paramilitary Raids in America, Cato Institute.

23.   www.PendulumJustice.org

24.   "Teen crime, adult time," Denver Post, February 19, 2006. Extensive review of topic.

25.   "Testimony and Interrogation of Minors," by Owens-Kostelnik et al, May-June 2006.

chance to address the legislators about their loved ones in the graves of the earth or of the 23 hour lockdown. The DAs went first, on the clock, while we, who had taken time off work and school to have our two minutes, just sat there and listened to them go on at length, describing these youth as monsters. The bill later passed, but was not retroactive. My guess is that some of the youth lifers are monsters, and some aren't, and some of them are innocent.

The decision to try a juvenile as an adult is often a politically motivated one, as in the recent Colorado case of a 14 year old who shot and killed a playmate, possibly accidentally according to a third youth present while the three boys handled the gun. The DA was under intense criticism by colleagues for incompetence and nepotism before she made this decision. The child was charged as an adult with first degree murder.[26] After the DA was recalled, the new DA negotiated a plea bargain of 5 years in the juvenile system followed by 4 years in adult prison, an improvement over life without parole, but still quite harsh for what may have been an accident. In another recent case, a 14 year old who with unclear motivation wounded a young neighbor girl with a pellet gun was charged as an adult. The parent of the girl, who recovered completely, feared the boy would not be rehabilitated if sent to prison, agreed to a plea deal for juvenile corrections for 5 years, followed by 12 years in prison which would be suspended if he successfully completed the juvenile sentence.[27] In this setting of more severe punishment for serious juvenile crime, it is no wonder that legal consequences for minor offenses and even behavior that used to warrant non-legal punishment (e.g., after school detention, essays, community service, a lecture, and parent consequences such as grounding), has been ratcheted up as well.

Proponents of these tough-on-crime programs point to the fact that violent crime has dropped to a 30 year low per the FBI's annual crime report of October 2005. Further data show that in 2004, murder, robbery and aggravated assault were at 39, 37 and 20 year lows, respectively. Preliminary 2005 FBI data show the biggest one year increase in violent crime since 1991, but it may be just a statistically insignificant blip. Credit has been given to all of these: mandatory sentencing; new strategies including community policing in which cops get to know the people on their beat, Hot Spot and Broken Windows strategies; demographic shifts in population aging (young men commit most crimes); the decline of the crack epidemic; and lastly, the spread of right to carry gun laws.[28] Record num-

---

26.   "Critics question DA's motives," Rocky Mountain News, October 17, 2005.
27.   "15 year old pleads guilty in shooting with pellet gun," Rocky Mountain News, November 22, 2005.

bers of people are imprisoned, about 2.1 million nationwide in 2004, up from 1.2 in 1994. This costs the nation 35 billion dollars annually.

While this broad broom keeps truly dangerous criminals out of society longer, it also sweeps up the less dangerous and non-violent offenders who could be dealt with in other ways, particularly drug cases, and longer sentences are producing an aging and less dangerous prison population. The Sentencing Project, a research group that advocates alternatives to prison, believes that no two crimes or defendants are alike, and flexibility is key. To be fair, mandatory sentencing always gets a boost from judges who give too-easy sentences in well-publicized cases. DNA testing continues to exonerate some who were wrongly convicted. Tight state finances are forcing new looks at ideas to reduce recidivism, alternatives to incarceration for non-violent offenders, and introducing some flexibility into mandatory sentencing. Unfortunately, newspaper reports also indicate a growing criminalization of adult judgement lapses and errors. Recently a Colorado mom was arrested and charged with contributing to the delinquency of minors for allowing her 16 year old daughter to have erotically shaped lollypops at her all-girl birthday party,[29] and a doctor was arrested for an unintentional medical mistake that resulted in a death.[30] Traffic deaths resulting from judgement errors are more often bringing charges of manslaughter, and drunken driving deaths that were previously prosecuted as manslaughter are now increasingly being prosecuted as second-degree murder.[31] Recently an accidental home fire that killed two responding firefighters was prosecuted as manslaughter.[32] Parents have been prosecuted for hosting supervised drinking parties as safer alternatives to avoid graduation and prom night tragedies. There should be consequences for bad judgement, but in all these examples, it seems excessive.

The same get-tough philosophy was applied to school violence, and as mentioned, actually predates Columbine by five years. What began as an well-intentioned and appropriate effort to remove guns from school environs became a rush to evermore types of weapons included in this policy, then drugs, in a 1997

28.   Bernard Harcourt, a University of Chicago Professor, is the most well-known critic of the Broken Windows theory. His books include *Illusion of Public Order: The False Promise of Broken Windows Policing (2001).*

29.   "Mother jailed for teen party," Rocky Mountain News, November 17, 2005.

30.   "Doctor arrested in breathing tube fatality," Denver Post/9News Team Coverage, December 4, 2005.

31.   "Murder trial starts in N.Y. crash," Denver Post, September 17, 2006.

32.   "Pot-grower guilty in fire that killed two firefighters," Rocky Mountain News, November 22, 2005. Grow-lights set the house on fire.

amendment to the Gun-Free Schools Act. Then fights, then threats, then poetry and art, and honest mistakes and events away from school grounds were all were swept up in the rubric of zero-tolerance to keeps schools safe. Schools have also installed technology such as metal detectors and security cameras, hired security personnel, used drug-sniffing dogs and put phones in classrooms and locks on doors. There has been a drop in school violence of 50% from 1992 to 2002, according to the Bureau of Justice Statistics and the National Center for Education Statistics.[33] In numbers of crimes, this is a reduction of 140 per thousand students to 64 per thousand. About one-third is non-fatal violent crime (assaults, rapes, robbery), and two-thirds is theft. There has also been a corresponding 50% decline in self-reports of weapons carrying at school from 12% to 6% from 1993 to 2003. The Center for the Prevention of School Violence in Raleigh, North Carolina, believes that the drop is due to schools focusing on the issue more, including technology-based approaches, school violence prevention programs and implementing anti-bullying programs. I believe another possibility is under-reporting, as schools are now publicly graded on this criteria (more on this later).

As with adult crime, some combination of factors seems to be working. So does this mean zero tolerance has worked, or contributed? The apparent improvement in rates of nonfatal school crime is extremely welcome. Unfortunately, school fatalities and multiple school shootings have remained steady, but rare, which is similar to workplace shootings. Deaths cannot be under-reported. According to the Secret Service study of school-related deaths since 1974, there have been an average about 34 per year. The National School Safety Center's Report on school-associated violent death is quite informative, and has tracked every single event since 1992 through 2005 in detail. Most of the 387 deaths are due to interpersonal disputes (102) or "unknown" (119); there were 71 suicides, 41 were gang-related (separate from interpersonal disputes), and 14 were accidental. Twelve were categorized as bullying-related, but I believe this is an underestimate, and reports of highly publicized events including as Columbine, Santee, and Red Lake have been predominantly bully-related. Suicides, according to bullying experts Barbara Coloroso and James Gabarino are often bully-related as well. The report's bar graph shows spikes in '92-'93 and '93-'94 of about 40 deaths, since then an average of 20-30 deaths; '04-'05 and '05-'06 show 1 death each reflecting incompleted reporting. Multiple shootings are very rare. Children are 70 times more likely to be murdered or die violently away from school, with

---

33.   http://nces.ed.gov

about 24,000 homicides and 17,000 suicides of children occurring off school grounds in the period of 1992-2000.

It is the violent deaths and multiple shootings, even if rare, that parents and the public fear the most for obvious reasons, including the seemingly sheer random nature of these events. Fights and theft we sort of understand, but not shootings and death. And zero tolerance was meant to address this, but it has not worked. Why not? Does the broad broom of sweeping out "troublemakers" only go so far?

This was the heart of my search for answers to the why of what happened to us, and as I discovered, many other families. This is the question of whether all the collateral damage is a necessary evil in the war on school violence, like the civil rights violations and innocent deaths of those mistakenly targeted or caught in the crossfire in the war on terror. In my research, I found three books or reports directly related to this issue. One, *Zero Tolerance: Can Suspension and Expulsion Keep Our Schools Safe?*, discussed below in detail, took a scholarly approach, and another, *Zero Tolerance*, edited by Ayers, Dohrn and Ayers, took a populist essay approach primarily focused on the unequal application of zero tolerance to minorities. A report of the Advancement Project, *Education on Lockdown: The Schoolhouse to the Jailhouse Track*, profiles three large school districts that have used harsh law and order approaches to school discipline: Denver, Chicago, and Palm Beach, Florida. All of these sources give ample evidence that unnecessary harm is being done, and that there are other, effective ways of keeping schools safe. Several books I read on the topic of bullying discuss these same issues, and bring up the controversial topic of school staff contributions to poor culture and abuse of misfits, which will be more addressed in the chapter on bullying.

If Zero Tolerance Does Not Work—What Does?

A 2001 review of zero tolerance includes a lengthy list nearly identical to the one given earlier, of children suspended, expelled and arrested for similar nonviolent acts prior to or contemporaneous with Columbine. In this scholarly research series of six monographs in the journal New Directions in Youth Development (Winter 2001), edited by Skiba and Noam, *Zero Tolerance: Can Suspension and Expulsion Keep Our Schools Safe?*, the topic is explored in detail, and the answer is that there is no evidence for effectiveness of this practice in reducing school violence or improving student discipline. The major findings of this issue[34] are:

1. Zero tolerance is a political, not an educational, solution.

2. Practices and policies used for school discipline and school safety prevention must be evaluated as educational interventions. Zero tolerance has failed to demonstrate effectiveness.

3.There are alternatives to the use of zero tolerance that have been demonstrated as effective at both the national and local programmatic levels. Since 1997, no fewer than five panels have been convened or supported by the federal government that have extensively reviewed the literature on youth violence prevention in order to make recommendations concerning effective practice. Not one of these panels has designated zero tolerance as effective or even promising. Rather, these panels, like the distinguished authors in this issue, have found that addressing the problem of school violence requires going well beyond rhetoric to understanding the complexity of the personal and systemic factors that increase the probability of violence and designing interventions based on that understanding.

4. Effective strategies for violence prevention and school disciplinary improvement are comprehensive and instructionally based, and they are effective precisely because they seek to keep students included in their school and community.... the programs and interventions with the best record of reducing youth violence are essentially instructional, teaching students methods for solving their personal and interpersonal problems ... The data consistently show that the best, perhaps the only, way to solve the complex problems of violence and disruption in schools is not to put certain children out of sight or out of mind, but to make the commitment of time and resources to help all children succeed.

In conclusion to their major findings, the authors also recommend smaller schools, which have been known from research in the 1950's and 60's to reduce school violence. Despite this, the trend to larger schools began in the 1970's and 80's, often for financial reasons, and was felt to contribute to the school violence problems of the late 80's and 90's. It is obvious that when all teachers and administrators really know each child, and there is individual advising and mentoring, a child is less likely to fall through the cracks, and feel so desperate that violence

---

34.   Reprinted with permission of John Wiley and Sons, Inc. Copyright 2002, Wiley Periodicals, Inc.

against self or others is contemplated or acted upon. Other sources also support what educators know to be common sense, that students learn and behave better in clean, well-designed,—equipped and maintained schools.[35] As we learned, however, even attention to these factors cannot override a school culture which supports student abuse.

Since each article has something important to say, I will quote from the Editor's Executive Summaries of these six monographs, and place my comments in parentheses. Some conclusions are omitted from later chapters because they are similar to preceding ones. It's a little dry, but bear with me, because the availability of details may help parents convince their schools to change.

1. Zero Tolerance, Zero evidence: An Analysis of School Disciplinary Practice, by Skiba and Knesting.[36]

* Although punishing both major and minor incidents is central to zero tolerance philosophy, community and national reaction has grown as increasingly trivial incidents receive progressively harsher penalties.

* Although expulsion may be reserved for more serious incidents, school suspension is used for a wide range of misbehavior, including disruption, attendance-related issues and non-compliance.

* Suspension and expulsion are used inconsistently across schools, often primarily as function of classroom over-referral or poor school climate.

* Minority overrepresentation in suspension and expulsion has been documented for over twenty-five years. There is no evidence that this is explainable by either student poverty status or increased disruption on the part of minority students. (I believe students who are "different" or do not further the school's identity or mission, are targets as much as ethnic and racial minorities.)

* A high rate of repeat offending indicates that school exclusion is not a particularly effective punishment. In the long term, suspension and expulsion are associated with an increased risk of school dropout and juvenile delinquency.

Emerging data indicate that preventive strategies to school exclusion hold a great deal of promise for addressing school violence and disruption. Schools and

---

35.   "Schools built for learning," Rocky Mountain News, November 6, 2005. Details how school design has measurable effect on behavior and learning.

36.   Russell J. Skiba, of the Indiana Education Policy Institute, is probably one of the foremost authorities and critics of Zero Tolerance. This monograph is based his Policy Research Report #SRS2, 2000.

school districts wishing to replace zero tolerance policies with research-based policies and practices might begin by:

* Reserving zero-tolerance disciplinary removals for only the most serious of disruptive behaviors and defining those behaviors explicitly.
* Expanding the array of options available to schools for dealing with disruptive or violent behavior.
* Implementing preventive measures than can improve school climate and reconnect alienated students. (There are many programs that do this by giving all groups of students, not just the elites, ownership in the school, and providing safe methods of conflict resolution.)
* Evaluate all school discipline or school violence prevention strategies to ensure that those strategies are truly addressing student behavior and school safety. (Rather than being political solutions that ensnare the unwitting or transfer the school's problem to the community.)

2. School Expulsion as a Process and Event: Before and After Effects on Children at Risk of School Discipline, by Morrison et al.

* Although a variety of behavioral pathways may lead to expulsion, one commonality appears to be poor school performance. The majority of expelled students do not appear to pose a threat of serious danger to the school environment.
* Students with disabilities appear to be over-represented in school expulsion. (This was apparently despite the greater protections offered these students through the Americans with Disability Act or ADA, but may have changed since this was published.)
* The availability of alternative programs is inconsistent at best, and their effectiveness is for the most part unstudied. (Only a few states mandate educational alternatives for expelled students who do not qualify as special education students under the ADA. Many are left to their own devices if parents cannot afford private school, if one can be found to take the student, or are unable to homeschool their child.)
* Support and implement comprehensive prevention programs to enhance the protective nature of schools. (Anti-bullying programs, character education supported by congruent adult behavior, conflict resolution programs, after school activities, tutoring, etc.)
* Offer educational options when expulsion is necessary. (Practical, high quality alternative options should be available to all students, not just the disabled.)

3. Zero Tolerance: Unfair, with Little Recourse, by Browne, Losen, and Wald.

This chapter examines racial disparities in the application of zero tolerance and harsh disciplinary codes and the impact on minority children. It describes the legal avenues available to parents and children's advocates interested in challenging these policies and summarizes recent court decisions issued on zero tolerance and other school discipline cases.

* African American and other minority students may perceive these disparities as a sign of rejection by the system, contributing to increased misbehavior or school dropout.

* Protection against discrimination on the basis of color or national origin is through the equal protection clause of the Fourteenth Amendment to the U.S. Constitution and under Title VI of the Civil Rights Act of 1964, which prohibits discrimination in education based on race or national origin. (According to this monograph, Fourteenth amendment claims have been successful when the school did not follow their own procedures or made a ridiculous decision, such as expelling a boy who found a knife in his backpack and turned it over to the teacher without incident. For discrimination claims, there must be proof that it was intentional, a high standard. Title VI claims do not require evidence of intentional discrimination, and can use school statistics or culture, but in practice more parents seek administrative remedies to "fix the school" through the Department of Education Office of Civil Rights (OCR), rather than going the expensive judicial route. Oddly, we found out that there is no specific religious component to Title VI, but there may be judicial precedent for Jewish ethnicity being equivalent to national origin. Sexual harassment claims, including those based on sexual orientation, are through Title IX.)

* Challenges to zero-tolerance policies can be made under the First Amendment, but protections afforded students are not as expansive as those that are extended outside educational settings. (For example, a boy was suspended for uttering an expletive while alone at the school bus stop after missing the bus, but was overheard by a teacher. The judge upheld the school's right to regulate speech, but lamented the lack of common sense in discipline shown by the school. The elementary or secondary school classroom of minor children is not the public square for adult-style free speech, while the college classroom of young adults is more properly so. This is discussed further in Chapter 9. But the above example is zero tolerance and punitive, not corrective.)

The success of some parent and advocacy groups in bringing about changes in disciplinary policy suggests that although strategic legal action remains an important avenue for parents and advocates to pursue, they might well be advised to do so in concert with other public education, lobbying, and organizing efforts. (Such as this book!)

4. Alternative Strategies for School Violence Prevention, by Gagnon and Leone.

This chapter reviews the efficacy of programming in three areas: universal or school-wide approaches, targeted or intensive interventions for individual students or groups of students, and the use of security measures such as metal detectors and surveillance cameras. Effective programs include:

* The Resolving Conflict Creatively Program, a social cognitive intervention in which students are taught conflict resolution through modeling, role playing, interviewing, and small group work.
* Project ACHIEVE, a universal intervention for elementary and middle schools that trains school personnel in effective methods of teaching social competence, effective instruction (to all types of learners to reduce frustration of students in acquiring academic competence) and organizational planning.
* Positive Behavioral Interventions and Supports, a team-based model that seeks to restructure school-based discipline, including a common approach to discipline, positive expectations and continuum of procedures for rule violation.
* Early detection through school-wide procedures such as the Systematic Screening of Behavioral Disorders, and early identification of students experiencing difficulties. (I am against profiling students, but identification of troubled students could be done in order to support them, not label them as "time bombs" or "pathological loners," and it is critical to look for school contributions to the problems of students!)
* Intensive behavioral interventions, such as the Functional Behavioral Assessment or alternative schools, that provide support for students who do not benefit from universal interventions or that target small groups of at-risk students. (These assessments are currently only required to be done on Special Ed students facing discipline.)
* Data documenting the effectiveness of school security technology or security personnel are both less extensive and less promising than universal or student

centered approaches. (Students feel demeaned and mistrusted in prison-like schools, and tend to test or game the system. However, more caring adult supervision in halls, locker rooms, and even bathrooms is what students want for safety, according to bullying experts.)

5. The Best Approach to Safety is to Fix Schools and Support Children and Staff, by Osher, Sandler and Nelson.

Zero tolerance presumes that removing some students is necessary for school safety. In contrast, two national reports, Safe, Drug-Free and Effective Schools for All Students: What Works, by the U.S. Dept of Education, and The Role of Education in Systems of Care by the Center for Mental Health Services, find that commitment to maintaining all students in school and ensuring the success of those students can make the school safer for all students. Many schools were studied for successful methods. Notably, not one of these schools relied on discipline approaches that exclude, alienate, and discard students to create a compelling learning environment.

* Safe schools provide all students with the supports and skills they need to develop appropriate behaviors and healthy emotional adjustment.
* Schools that are most successful establish a caring culture that provides a sense of belonging for students and helps them identify with the school community.
* Successful schools address challenges of disconnectedness by building a school community grounded in the culture, knowledge and interests of diverse students.
* Interventions, including temporary exclusion from the classroom, are based on problem-solving and continued membership in the school community.
* Alternative settings emphasize a positive environment, instruction in positive behaviors, and a quick return to the classroom.

6. Beyond the Rhetoric of Zero Tolerance: Long-term Solutions for At-risk Youth, by Noam, Warner and Van Dyken.

This monograph proposes an alternative to zero-tolerance policies without compromising school safety. The RALLY Program, Responsive Advocacy for Life and Learning in Youth, dealing with high-risk youth, is an in-school prevention and intervention program combining mental health and educational practice to support students inside and outside the classroom.

When schools become places in which to learn instead of institutions of estrangement and marginalization, the overall safety of schools and quality of education will increase.

The other book I reviewed, *Zero Tolerance* by Ayers, et al, (2001) is worth reading for the eloquent and moving essays that narrate real life stories of minority children caught in the zero tolerance web, and whose families had far fewer resources to call on for help than we did. The expulsion explosion, from 10 per year to 1500 per year in the Chicago school system over a 6 year period, for example, has dumped these kids on the streets in many instances, effectively ending their education when many then turn 16 and can't imagine returning to school. One teacher's essay made it clear that principals want high enrollment during the October count season, because school funding and their own paychecks are based on numbers, then strive to get the poor performers out before the state testing in March. (A 2006 University of Florida report by economist David Figlio confirms this impression.[37] And education experts such as Harvard professor Gary Orfield calls these students "pushouts."[38]) In Texas, the juvenile justice system is in charge of the education of expelled students; how does that make them feel, I wonder. Some of the cases are heart-breaking, including those with untreated mental illnesses who were expelled, arrested and entered a spiral of decline in the juvenile system. More than one million kids come in contact with the juvenile justice system each year, over 90% of them for non-violent offenses. One essayist faults the sensationalist media for making it seem that juvenile crime and school violence is more common than it really is, fueling public fear, and pushing legislative and school officials to become ever more punitive. After looking at the statistics of the National School Safety Center, I would agree with this. Another laments that it has taken the ensnarement of the children of white suburban conservatives to horrify those who initially supported zero tolerance for other people's "bad" children. He is right, and that hit home with me.

Dorhn argues for two basic principles: No child should be punished by being deprived of an education, and all school disciplinary procedures must be fair,

---

37.   "Student pool manipulated for higher standardized test results...," Washington Times, National Weekly Edition, June 19-25, 2006. Report originally published in the Journal of Public Economics, May 2006.

38.   "Colo. schools ditch pushy attitudes towards dropouts," Denver Post, August 20, 2006.

equitable, and individualized. Seven recommendations are given, my comments again in parentheses:

1. Small schools are safer schools.… Relationships and trust, rather than hardware and militarization, lead to safety and learning opportunities. (Adults must feel obligated to intervene when they know a student is in distress, according to another essayist.)

2. Open all schools after school, with rich programming.… Most youth crime occurs in the 3pm-6pm time immediately after school. (Denver now is floating this idea. Much bullying also happens after school, and there are fewer eyes on the street and parents at home to provide supervision and protection.)

3. Employ community justice sanctions within schools for school offending, such as peer juries, teen court, restorative justice, and mediation. Involve youth themselves in sanctioning misbehavior. (These methods have pitfalls, as discussed later)

4. Transparency requires schools to track and report all schools suspensions annually by school, including race, age, gender, and reason for exclusion. (This requires reasonable and standardized definitions of prohibited behaviors to prevent schools from gaming the system.)

5. Offer excellent alternative education only as a last resort for every child expelled from school, with opportunities to return to the home school at the earliest possible moment.

6. Remove guns from the environment of children. This is an adult responsibility. (As a Second Amendment supporter and hunter, I believe all firearms should be locked away from children, and supporting laws should be passed. Children should be trained to leave the area and tell an adult if they see a gun. Teens allowed to use even a BB gun should be trained in firearms safety.)

7. It is a human rights obligation to provide children with an education … and to utilize a standard of "best interests of the child" in child sanctioning.

It all seems like common sense to me. Why aren't we doing more of this stuff?

The third publication I reviewed, the Advancement Project's 2005 report,[39] *Education on Lockdown: The Schoolhouse to the Jailhouse Track*, gives a

---

39. www.advancementproject.org; click on publications. The first report, in 2000, was "Opportunities Suspended: The Devastating Consequences of Zero Tolerance and School Discipline Policies," by the Advancement Project and the Harvard Civil Rights Project.

full review of zero tolerance discipline, including the evolution of zero tolerance in schools, an examination of the changing role of police in schools, how minority children are disproportionately impacted, and gives details on the collateral damage in three large urban school districts where zero tolerance is in full force. In this 2005 report, expert opinion on the ill effects of zero tolerance has not changed from 2001, yet it continues apace.

The Denver Public Schools cracked down between 2000 and 2004 (due to Columbine, I believe), with a 71% increase in student referrals to law enforcement, most of them for nonviolent behavior and use of obscenities. These referrals typically resulted in a visit to juvenile court and probation or a diversion program, which is essentially probation. Palm Beach County School District has its own police force, as does Houston and Los Angeles. The report's summary says, "Research has shown that prevention and intervention programs are the most effective methods for addressing school violence and creating a productive learning environment. It is also more cost effective than hurling students into the juvenile justice system." Initial solutions are almost identical to those previously cited: limiting suspensions, expulsions and arrests to student conduct that poses a serious threat to safety, adopting clear school discipline guidelines that provide notice of potential disciplinary actions for specific offenses, and establishing oversight committees to handle complaints about school discipline practices and review discipline and arrest statistics to ensure that discipline is meted out in a fair and nondiscriminatory manner. The last recommendation is not mentioned in the other two books cited, and is a welcome addition to what parents should be pushing for, but is likely to get a fight from school districts hiding behind confidentiality.

Social psychologist Elliott Aronson's book, *Nobody Left to Hate, Teaching Compassion After Columbine*, mentioned at the beginning of this chapter, while not directly addressing zero tolerance, does explain how schools can be made safer by changes in the social environment of schools. This is done by attending to root causes with both central and peripheral interventions. He believes that while some of the peripheral interventions such as restricting youth access to firearms have merit, and others such as profiling have little merit, they do not address the fact that middle and high schools are very stressful places for millions of kids, and much of that stress is unnecessary. The number of students who respond to that stress by killing their classmates is miniscule, but the number of students who respond by becoming depressed, some to the point of contemplating (one in five), attempting (one in ten) or completing suicide is much larger. Rejection by peers or failure at sports at this stage of development can be extremely painful.

Addressing this stress and alienation is a critical central intervention. Aronsen proposes structural changes such as the "jigsaw classroom," a variation of cooperative learning for a small portion of the classroom day that allows students to get to know each other, while avoiding the pitfalls of group learning such as passive students who become resented by the harder workers. This model has a good track record, according to the author, and if done correctly, everyone brings a piece of the project to the table, and while learning the strengths and weaknesses of others and themselves, students develop empathy for classmates who may be different. In that way, there is "nobody left to hate."

On the other hand, authors such as Christina Hoff Summers and Michael Gurian point to adverse school conditions for boys, and the growing male gender gap in academic achievement, that are contributing to the school failure which often precipitates behavior problems. Boys receive as much as 70% of failing grades, create 80% of discipline problems, account for 80% of dropouts, and have 70% of learning disabilities and 80% of behavioral disorders including attention deficit and hyperactivity disorder. 42% of boys are suspended from school at least once before the age of 17, as compared to 24% of girls. Young men make up less than 44% of America's college population.[40] These are disturbing statistics. While a full discussion of this issue is beyond the scope of this book, it is beginning to be addressed. Boys may need a more traditional competitive classroom with behavior standards, leeway to move about more, and restoration of recess and daily P.E. to let off steam. Experimentation with single-sex classrooms was recently given the green light by the U.S. Dept. of Education,[41] but adversaries fear a "separate and unequal" problem with this approach.

All of these authors seem to be saying the same thing: educational inclusion, not exclusion, is the answer for troubled students, most of whom are boys.

Discipline Alternatives

It is time to turn to a discussion of some of the discipline alternatives such as Restorative Justice. The following is primarily taken from the 2002 Colorado Mediation Project's Restorative Justice Training Manual.

Currently, schools run the gamut of a continuum from very punitive to fully restorative, with most leaning mainstream/punitive. 80% of schools use some

---

40. "Academic underachievers: Schools said to neglect boys," Washington Times National Weekly Edition, January 30-February 5, 2006.

41. "U.S. Eases Rules on Educating Sexes Separately," Wall Street Journal, October 25, 2006.

form of zero tolerance.[42] Punitive schools utilize demerit systems and public shaming, focus on obedience and order, and there is an adversarial relationship between disciplinarians and students. Today's mainstream discipline sets out clear expectations for behavior and predetermined punishments for any violation of the rules, with little room for individual consideration.

Restorative Justice is a new paradigm of discipline being used in schools and communities for less serious school behavioral problems and crimes. (It is my opinion that this model makes sense for students and juvenile offenders, but not for serious adult crime; this issue having been raised recently in the media by the Vermont judge who used restorative justice reasoning to give a rapist only 60 days in jail.) The usual approach has been retributive, and asks what rule was broken, who broke it, and how do we punish the one who broke the rule? Restorative Justice asks what is the harm that was done, how can we repair that harm, and who is responsible for the repair?

The principles of Restorative Justice are:

1. Crime and wrongdoing is understood primarily as an offense against human relationships and the trust and safety within a community.

2. The offender is held directly accountable, not only for breaking the rule, but for the harm done to the victim and the community.

3. To repair the damage as much as possible.

4. Balanced participation of victims, offenders and the school community.

5. To help the offender develop empathy and make better choices.

6. To develop creative solutions outside of traditional criminal justice constraints.

7. To build sustainable partnerships between schools, police, courts, and the wider community.

Recently, many schools across the country have begun to explore the use of restorative justice processes as part of a more comprehensive approach to school discipline. The goals of these school-based efforts are to:

* Reduce reliance on punitive discipline (suspension, expulsion, police charges, etc.)

* Enable offenders to make amends directly to their victims and the school community.

* Develop discipline protocols where victims, offenders parents, and staff are all active participants.

---

42. "Beyond Zero Tolerance," by Susan Black, *American School Board Journal*, September 2004, Vol. 191, No. 09. www.asbj.com/2004/09/0904research.html

* Reintegrate offending students successfully back into the school community.

Not every school offense will be appropriate for Restorative Justice discipline. The types of cases usually referred to a school's Restorative Justice panel includes theft, graffiti and vandalism, bullying, minor physical assault, verbal assault, truancy, disturbing the peace, and defiance of authority. I believe that non-serious school threats fit well in this model. Panels include a trained facilitator, the involved students, parents, and affected school and community members. Participation is necessarily voluntary for it to be successful; the offender(s) must have admitted the offense, and any victim(s) must not fear re-victimization during the process. Participants design an agreement that addresses the harm, and can include apologies, counseling, community service, replacement of property, etc. Agreements are specific and measurable, with one participant selected to help monitor the offender's progress. When the terms are fulfilled, the case is closed. If they are not fulfilled, the case is referred back to school officials for traditional punishments including suspension.

Other models of Restorative Justice in schools are:
* Restorative Class Meetings—When wrongdoing occurs in class, the teacher convenes an open forum to assess impact on fellow students and decide if repair is needed.
* Offender Competency Sessions—Offending students participate in classes or mentoring sessions to learn pro-social skills, e.g., anger/conflict management, decision making, etc.
* Victim Impact Panels—Panel of surrogate victims testify to harm done by other students in similar situations, e.g., clique of students being bullied.
* Peacemaking Circles—Used in situation with no clear victim and offender, e.g., conflict between groups or cliques.
* Talking Circles—Used to discuss a broad range of issues facing a school community, not necessarily tied to a particular wrongdoing.

There can be drawbacks to Restorative Justice models, according to newer anti-bullying thought, as further discussed in Chapter 10. Sometimes the offender is not sincere, or uses the session to re-victimize the victim, e.g., "he deserved it." While the offender is allowed to tell his side, it is up to a skilled facilitator to prevent abuse of the victim. Re-victimization is exactly what happened to Jeff on several occasions at Peak to Peak (although the school did not then purport to use restorative justice methods), when the bully was allowed to call him a "liar" and a "paranoid lying idiot" without effective challenge. Another problem is dual punishment. Sometimes, the offender goes through the process and an agreement is reached, only to have the police decide to arrest anyway. This has happened locally in a fledgling program. Also, if the whole school community is not invested in the restorative justice process, victims can be retaliated against in subtle ways such as shunning and secretive damage to property. If the culture of the school is not inclusive, restorative justice can be used by in-groups to punish out-groups. Mediation is not always effective when the school culture supports popular bullies; this is what happened in Johanna's case. And peer counseling is only as good as its peer counselors and supervision by competent adult counselors, as we saw in Jeff's case. Tip lines and boxes also have pitfalls in that false reporting can be used to harass. Columbine killers Klebold and Harris were harassed in just this manner, by intentional false reporting of their use of marijuana which instigated a humiliating locker and personal search.

Teen Courts are a hybrid model of traditional juvenile justice and Restorative Justice, in which students are prosecuted, defended and sentenced by peers in a supervised courtroom setting for such low level offenses as fighting at school. Punishments are often community service and essays. Several of these programs have started up in the Denver metro area recently, and hopefully serve to avoid suspensions and detentions. A 13 year-old was given a typical sentence of community service after fighting with a girl who had spread sexual rumors about her—unfortunately the other girl did not show up.[43] Another juvenile model being developed locally is the "Graduated Sanctions Council" to improve collaboration across agencies to more effectively intervene with appropriate consequences for at-risk youth.[44]

A word here about two current rages in mainstream school discipline, police ticketing on campus for minor offenses, and school official strict confidentiality of discipline. Ticketable offenses are fighting, use of obscenities, failure to carry student ID, and alcohol use on or off campus. In Denver, groups such as One Nation United and Padres Unidos are working on reducing the number of offenses that are ticketable, reducing suspensions and expulsions, and increasing referrals to Restorative Justice programs. Regarding confidentiality of discipline, the restorative model does not require broadcasting its work, but does require that the offender be open and apologizing and make visible amends to the school

---

43. "Teen Court debuts in Commerce City," *Rocky Mountain News*, January 6, 2006.
44. Developed by Judge Melonakis, 17th Judicial District, Adams County, Colorado. YourHub.com, June 8, 2006.

community. In my opinion, visible but reasonable consequences are good-behavior reinforcing, as well as serving as a fairness indicator to other students. It is community-building for students to know that consequences for wrong-doing are sure, individualized, and fair. Too much confidentiality fosters rumors and can hide favoritism in discipline, or give the impression of no discipline. While I would not favor going back to the days of my youth when kids were paddled in front of the whole class, and one poor kid who lived on a pig farm behind the school was mercilessly picked on by the teacher for this humiliating treatment, some visibility of consequences is a good thing.

If done properly by trained facilitators, who are usually volunteers from the community, and all participants adhere to the rules, Restorative Justice models can replace much of the zero tolerance discipline in a school, greatly reduce collateral damage, and be an educational and character-building experience for students.

Experts Continue to Search for Effective Programs

School violence prevention is an area of intense ongoing research. What do the top experts say in 2006?

Del Elliot, a professor at the University of Colorado and the director of the Center for the Study and Prevention of Violence (CSPV), says that while many schools have made significant improvements in school safety procedures, and most have crisis response plans, many schools are reluctant to implement new programs such as anti-bullying measures and other programs to make kids feel safe, because of the focus on academic improvement and test scores. "This is a very short-sighted approach, because if your children do not feel safe at school, they are not going to learn. Schools that don't pay attention to student safety tend to also have higher dropout rates and lower test scores."[45] At a seminar of Western Attorneys General, Elliot pushed for identification of teens who might be at risk of Columbine-like attacks via "interagency social support teams" assessment of confidential information to identify which teens are at risk and to choose the right way to intervene, whether it be counseling or a search warrant.[46] I do not, as mentioned before, favor this type of intrusive labeling or profiling based on what teachers, counselors, local police, and social workers might think about a student prior to that student causing trouble or showing clear signs of distress.

---

45.   "Robbing Peter…Expert says CSAP focus can hurt efforts as making Colorado schools safer," *Rocky Mountain News*, April 13, 2005.

46.   "Cooperation urged to ID troubled teens," *Denver Post*, July 14, 2005.

Identification may lead to more zero tolerance school and legal repercussions if a student tells honestly how he feels. Counseling and getting at root causes is the way to go, but students also need greater protections from capricious and over-zealous school and police personnel. We must find a middle way between this new police state approach and the do-nothing approach of the past to the Columbine killers' violent web sites.

As Elliot says, there is interplay between the new emphasis on academics and school safety. In Colorado, as in other states, mandatory standardized testing is done to assess how well schools are teaching basic subjects such as reading, math and science. Schools are under intense pressure to improve scores and school ratings; failing schools will be taken over. While accountability is a good thing, there are many things that contribute to a school's performance including socioeconomic status and mobility of students, percentage of English speakers, and school and neighborhood safety. Schools are rated on a 5 point scale from Excellent to Unsatisfactory, and the results are published. Parents who are able, pull their kids out of low-scoring schools even if their child seems to be doing well, due to social pressure and the natural desire to have the best for their child. The result is those left behind are more likely to score lower. It is a downward spiral. While some low socioeconomic schools, primarily elementary schools, have become shining examples of achievement and deserve close study to find their secrets, middle and high schools generally have not seen much improvement with ratings pressure. It does not help students' self-esteem or pride in their school community to have their school labeled Low or Unsatisfactory, and alienated students are at the highest risk of dropout, behavior problems, and violence.

The CSPV has developed the Safe Communities—Safe Schools Model to assist each school in Colorado to design an individualized safe school plan, with the goal maintaining a positive and welcoming school climate that is free of drugs, violence, intimidation and fear, "where teachers can teach and students can learn." The basic components, available on their web site www.colorado.edu/cspv/include:

* Establish a clear Code of Behavior that includes the rights and responsibilities of both adults and students within the school community.

* Include all youth in positive, rewarding activities and relationships at school.

* Control campus access and establish uniform visitor screening procedures.

* Promote ongoing relationships with law enforcement, businesses and community organizations.

* Provide a hotline for anonymous tip reporting.

* Establish guidelines and procedures for identifying students at risk of violence.

* Identify effective violence prevention programs, both in school and community. (The web site gives extensive resources, including bullying prevention.)

* Establish a school support team, to help improve the climate at the school and to support students at risk.

* Develop a crisis response plan that covers natural disasters and emergencies (required by law in Colorado).

A similar organization, the Center for the Prevention of School Violence, in Raleigh, North Carolina,[47] stresses student involvement in schools, and gives links to programs to encourage this such as SoundOut.org, and an article on reaching out to include youth in school and after-school activities, because posters and flyers may not be enough. Multiple approaches may be needed including drop-in programs, allocating slots for at-risk youth, recruiting youth in pairs of friends, and offering opportunities for leadership and paid employment. I was reminded of my husband Mark, a so-so student who didn't do much homework but aced the tests, and would rather be in the woods. He was collared by the high school wrestling coach who said, "Our team needs you," leading to a successful four-year experience, and fostering other school involvement such as theater. His graduating class was 110 students. Small schools need all their students and they try harder to include everyone, even those who'd rather be down in the woods or out on the streets.

This North Carolina organization also has extensively studied alternatives to suspension and expulsion after noting an approximately 25% and 50% increase, respectively, in North Carolina in the 2001-2002 school year (Columbine related?), with a high risk of entering the juvenile justice system. There is also the effect of rewarding poor behavior, by not having to attend school. Some of the options, called Alternative Learning Placements, or ALPs, that were developed include centers where academics and homework help are combined with counseling and community service, and Juvenile Structured Day Programs for youth who are sanctioned by the courts, which provide a similar but more intensive program, and have a 60% return rate to public school. Ensuring that these ALPs are not dumping grounds to warehouse "bad kids" is of critical importance to the child as well as society. Characteristics of successful ALPs include: dedicated teachers who are also mentors who believe their students can succeed despite the

47.   www.nscu.edu/cpsv.org

sometimes enormous odds that can include difficult-to-modify environmental and family risk factors, a maximum 1:15 teacher to student ratio, a longer well-planned program that is also flexible and open to student feedback, and support from outside agencies, such as social services and mental health, in the community. Actually many of the keys to success of these ALPs are the same a recommended for the educational mainstream: a safe and stable learning environment, smaller classes, 1:1 instruction as needed, caring teachers and administrators, and adequate resources.

As previously mentioned, few states mandate alternative placements for suspended and expelled youth, but voluntary programs such as in North Carolina seem to be a growing trend. In Colorado it is not mandatory, and seems to be a patchwork depending on the school district. Boulder Valley's regulations require alternative educational options, but they seem quite limited and subjectively doled out. As mentioned before, we were offered a high school placement for an 8th-grader, or homeschool support from the expelling school, neither of which we could imagine doing under the circumstances. By the way, Justice High School was recently approved as Boulder Valley's newest charter school, having exhausted its grant start-up funds. Hopefully this will let Magistrate Cole excuse himself from close involvement, since kids who have been punished by him deserve teachers with fresh eyes on their pupils.

While all this study and expansion of options is highly desirable, the best solution is to keep kids in their schools if at all possible, and minimize the suspensions and expulsions requiring alternative schools, because these harsh sanctions often derail or even ruin young lives.

A number of states and school districts are trending in this direction. Texas passed House Bill 603 in July 2005, which mandates that school districts consider factors such as self-defense, lack of intent, and disciplinary history, before initiating suspension, expulsion or alternative education placements.[48] The Knox County, Tennessee, school board changed its zero tolerance policies after a student committed suicide following his expulsion for the friend's knife found in his car. Florida's Clearwater High School replaced zero tolerance with a system of graduated discipline and counseling, and cut suspensions, expulsions, and its drop-out rate.[49] The California Department of Education has a website outlining

---

48.   www.katyzerotolerance.com

49.   The Knox County and Clearwater changes are discussed in "Beyond Zero Tolerance," by Susan Black, in *American School Board Journal*, September 2004, Vol.191, No.9.

zero tolerance and alternative placement related law so that school districts can avoid harsh, incorrect application.[50]

Here in Colorado, Attorney General John Suthers, who pushed through the new school threat law previously mentioned, favors such programs as threat assessment teams and crisis plans in schools, as well as information-sharing agreements between schools and law enforcement, the juvenile justice system, social services, and mental health agencies. New statutes passed in 2005 mandate certain information sharing between schools and law enforcement, outlined in the October 2006 Revised Colorado School Violence Prevention and Student Discipline Manual prepared by the AG's office. This document take the expected zero tolerance approach, but also gives the caveat "School districts would be wise to limit the use of suspension and expulsion to conduct demonstrating a relationship to the school or the health or safety of students." The Safe2Tell Hotline set up by the AG after Columbine to collect anonymous tips, does not get frequent calls, about 40% of which are from parents calling about bullying, and is staffed by the Colorado State Patrol.[51] These types of programs, while well-intentioned and important to manage emerging threats or crises, do not address the underlying school problems that give rise to poor school safety. At a gathering of educators and police at the recent Safe Communities-Safe Schools Conference, Suthers talked about continuing problem of serious school violence and touted the above measures. To his credit, he made note of Colorado's higher than average rate of bullying. He said that two-thirds of Colorado youths report having been bullied at least once in the past month, and 29 percent admitted bullying, compared with 23 percent nationally.[52] The revised Manual contains an extensive section on bullying, including the critical importance of adult involvement in bullying prevention.

Van Schoale, Executive Director of the Colorado Children's Campaign, an advocacy group involved in the Colorado Small Schools Initiative, recently commented on the minimal improvements found in a Denver inner city high school after breaking the school up into three smaller schools. "All three schools suffer from low student achievement, a lack of counseling, ineffective teaching, poor student discipline.... It is very much the same culture as the large high school. Culture is the driving force behind good high schools."[53] The Bill and Melinda

---

50.   www.cde.ca.gov/ls/ss/se/zerotolerance.asp

51.   "Vocal Columbine parent backs phone line...," *Rocky Mountain News*, April 20, 2006.

52.   "Prepare for crisis, AG tells schools," *Rocky Mountain News*, April 12, 2005.

53.   "Manual experiment gets mixed reviews," *Rocky Mountain News*, April 15, 2005.

Gates Foundation has invested $11.8 million in Colorado to make schools smaller. Its Colorado director Thomas Vander Ark, acknowledged at the same gathering how difficult it is to change entrenched culture and pedagogy in schools. But we must at least try. A recent Gates Foundation study using focus groups of dropouts, found that students were emotionally disengaged from school and described teachers that were burned out and boring, not enough tutors and no one to talk to about problems, poor discipline, and parents who were uninvolved.

What do the parents of the Columbine victims think would help reduce serious school violence? Five of them met with former Attorney General (now Senator) Ken Salazar to relay their ideas, which included changing juvenile diversion programs (such as the killers graduated from just weeks before the attack), presumably to better evaluate risks to the community, creating school safety report cards to make it easy for parents to evaluate campuses, and raising the amount of money that parents would have to pay for wayward children's actions (the killers' parents' insurance paid out small amounts to victims' families).[54]

With all respect, I just don't think these suggestions would help much. The school safety report cards were implemented under the No Child Left Behind Act, but are completely untrustworthy, because the categories are not consistently used, and most school don't want to look bad, and underreport, and while a few over-report. If a school is labeled a "persistently dangerous school," a parent can move to their child to another school within the same district. But the Colorado State Dept of Education made the definition so lax that a school would have to report over 135 violent serious crimes (1st and 2nd degree assault, rape, robbery, murder and arson) in a school of 600-900 children before it could be so labeled.[55] This is an idea that could still work if better standardized, and a law was recently passed to this effect.[56] Mr. Salazar, before he went to Washington, was involved in a statewide campaign to reduce bullying, and said "A predicate to good achievement in our schools is having the kinds of learning environments where students feel safe …" This is where a difference can be made, I also believe, and it will be further discussed in the chapter on bullying.

The American Psychological Association convened a panel in 2006 to summarize research on zero tolerance discipline and concluded that these policies are

---

54. "Safety at schools discussed," Rocky Mountain News, September 24, 2003.
55. "Dangerous schools definition murky," by Colo. U.S. Representative Marilyn Musgrave, Rocky Mountain News, November 3, 2003.
56. "Law pinpoints school fights, assaults," Rocky Mountain News, April 7, 2006. Senate Bill 55.

backfiring, and make students feel less safe and more anxious, reduce academic performance, and are steering more teens into the juvenile justice system. The panel called for more flexibility and common sense, reserving harsh punishments for the most serious infractions. As this chapter recounts, these are not startling new recommendations. When are we going to start implementing what experts have been saying for at least five years?

Summary

In this chapter on Columbine scapegoating, which is zero tolerance discipline on steroids, I have discussed its ramifications for youth and families in both the school and legal systems. It has been over ten years in use nationwide, and has not abated in the five years since studies have proved its ineffectiveness and harm, precisely because of Columbine. Zero tolerance is a totalitarian system that uses excessive force on a few to keep others fearful and in line, and is inimical to our American democracy and common sense. Children have become easy targets in the spillover effect from the war on terror, and the victims of harsh tactics such as profiling and pre-emptive arrests and detentions. One original goal of zero tolerance, to make punishment consistent and non-discriminatory, has been turned on its head and has become quite inconsistent across and within schools and discriminatory, particularly towards minorities and those who "don't fit."

Like nascent mandatory sentencing reform, zero tolerance discipline is overdue for common sense course corrections. There are humane alternatives that actually improve school safety, largely positive and supportive school culture, and programs that involve all students and refuse to give up on those who are troubled or different. Are we ready to challenge our societal attitudes and entrenched bureaucratic school districts and district attorneys to finally change the scorched earth approach? I certainly had no idea how harmful it was, and read newspaper reports of harshly punished children, thinking "They must have done something to deserve it," too. But as the reports became ever more ridiculous, and then my son was suddenly a victim, I was forced to face the truth. Public pressure must be brought to bear to prevent the derailment of more young lives. Get involved in your schools, and encourage culture change if needed, and speak up when children are subjected to zero tolerance in the schools or the courts by calling community leaders, writing letters to the editor, and organizing advocacy groups. Let them know there are alternatives that do not ruin lives.

"Pay attention, get involved, and never ever look away."

—attributed to a Holocaust survivor

9

The Charter School Movement
And The Columbine Connection

"Modern education does not seem adequate to teach compassion ... "

—The Dalai Lama, 2006[1]

The Rise of the Charter School Solution

Charter schools are part of the schools of choice movement that has been developing over the past two decades in response to the failure of public schools to educate our children to international standards, and I believe, to the failure to assure safety. Urban schools in particular are producing many students who cannot read, write, spell, or do basic math well enough to perform in entry level jobs, or even compose a resume, make change or balance a checkbook. And those who make it to college often need remedial courses. Standardized testing under the No Child Left Behind Act has revealed achievement disparities in detail, embarrassing the education establishment, which is now howling in protest. In years past, school dropouts and semi-literate youth could go out and get decent union factory jobs. But in our global economy, the education stakes are now dramatically higher, and a solid high school education only gets you in on the bottom floor of the wage scale. Trade careers can be well-paying, but even vocational education programs require solid math, science and computer skills these days.

A detailed discussion of the fault for America's public education failure is beyond the scope of this book, but is, in my opinion, roughly apportioned among the following factors. First, social and family upheaval due to the transition from the industrial to the information age, environmental regulatory overkill, and globalization. According to Francis Fukuyama, in his 1999 book, *The Great Disruption*, a similar period of social disorder occurred in the early 1800's

---

1.   Rocky Mountain News, September 16, 2006, A1.

when the industrial age overtook the agrarian age. The Victorian Age was society's overcorrecting response, which itself was then moderated in the early 20th century. Educators today point to broken, overstressed, mobile families who have trouble keeping the bills paid, much less supporting their child's academics. Blaming "lazy parents" is an excuse. Second, the teacher's unions are partly to blame, with their emphasis on politics and members' security, paychecks and benefits, rather than student achievement. We probably need to trim bloated administrative education bureaucracies, and expand the current 180 day school year as have nations such as Korea whose students outperform ours. Third, teacher's colleges must become more rigorous, and stop pushing educational fads such as whole language and fuzzy math. Middle and high school teachers should have degrees in their subjects. Fourth, portions of non-minority and minority communities need to recognize education as the road out of poverty. And fifth, schools must be made safe and inclusive, as discussed in the previous chapter.

States, cities and school districts have responded to educational failure with voucher programs, magnet schools, splitting up large schools, and charter schools. A 2006 Harris Interactive poll of parents shows this: 62% reported their children attended traditional public schools, 20% private religious, 8% private non-sectarian, 8% homeschool, and 7% charter schools. All of this experimentation is introducing some energy and innovation into the public education establishment. Denmark and Sweden have voucher systems, New Zealand is all public charter schools, and Britain is experimenting with school choice. Are Americans late to the party? The Center for Educational Reform,[2] a pro-school choice organization, seems to think so, and is the source of much of the following basic data about voucher and charter schools, except where noted.

Voucher programs, which give tax dollars to parents towards private school tuition, have run into opposition and legal setbacks, and remain very limited in the number of students served, about 36,000 in 40 states. Voucher programs were dealt a blow recently with the July 2006 release of a U.S. Department of Education report that analyzed results from the 2003 National Assessment of Educational Progress. It found that public school students perform as well as private school students when test scores are adjusted for factors known to affect achievement, such as socioeconomic status, ethnicity, and English language abil-

---

2.   www.edreform.com

ity.[3] There is preliminary evidence that voucher schools may not contribute to resegregation problems,[4] a charter school issue to be discussed later.

It is charter schools, privately run by community volunteers, non-profits, or corporations such as Edison, with tax dollars, that have seen explosive growth in the past decade. Is this something whose time has come, or are we allowing the Balkanization of our treasured system of free public education, our great equalizer?

For simplicity, I will refer to traditional public schools as public schools and public charter schools as charter schools. Charter schools operate independently of local school boards under contracts to provide nonsectarian educational services to all students who apply on a space available basis. They must comply with state and federal regulations regarding discrimination and disability, but are usually exempt from teacher certification and union work rules, and design their own policies and curriculum. Charters receive state monies by a formula, and often get less than public schools (the national average is 80%) and frequently are not provided with buildings or buses. They generally must perform state-mandated academic testing. Charters are governed by their own boards, and enjoy significant autonomy to innovate for success (or failure). In some states, Educational Management Organizations (EMOs), which can be for-profit or non-profit, run the lion's share of charter schools; in Michigan and Ohio, it is 70%. Nationally, 30% of charters are conversions of public or private schools and 70% are new schools. Those run by non-profit community and parent groups often rely heavily on volunteers for important labor-intensive committee positions that are performed by paid personnel in public schools. "Founding families" usually have preference in enrollment lotteries. Autonomy is both a strength and a weakness of charter schools, depending on how accountable they are to enrolled families and the larger community.

The first charter school opened in 1991 in Minnesota. As of October 2005, there were over 3600 charter schools in 41 states, enrolling over a million children, or 4 percent of the nation's public school students according to the Center for Education Reform. There are about 90,000 public schools in the U.S., so the charter movement is still relatively small. By comparison, approximately 1 million are home-schooled and 5 million are in private schools. The states with the largest number of charters are California, Arizona, Florida, Texas, Ohio, and

---

3.   "Long-delayed Education Study Casts Doubt on Value of Vouchers," Wall Street Journal, July 15-16, 2006.

4.   "Vouchers in Black and White," Wall Street Journal, November 8, 2006.

Michigan. Colorado is in the middle of the pack with 120, and many states are in the single or double digits. The closure rate for charter schools is about 11% nationally, with financial troubles, mismanagement, or outright fraud being the major causes. There is scant public data on disenrollment rates back to public schools, but nationally, charters are gaining students, and parents appear to be voting with their feet. Surveys on pro-charter web sites report high satisfaction, but this is a select sample. Charter schools in general enjoy widespread public support including Republicans, Democrats and Independents in that order.

Charter Success—or Poor Scores and Segregation?

The original rationale for charter schools, improvement in education through innovation, has not born fruit, and the rationale has morphed into choice and competition, according to the American Federation of Teachers Union 2002 report, "Do Charter Schools Measure Up?"[5] Indeed, the findings of the 2003 National Assessment of Educational Progress Report found that 4th graders in charter schools were 6 months behind public school students in reading and math. Only 25% and 30% proficiency respectively in charters and public schools is "shockingly low," a dismayed charter school supporter, Chester E. Finn, commented.[6] When these results were subjected to re-analysis, public school students still out-scored charter school students, even when adjusted for socioeconomic factors.[7] Neither charters nor public schools are succeeding, and achievement score comparisons between charters and public schools are a mixed bag, most educational observers would probably agree. There is great variation by state, district, school and grade level in charter vs. public school performance. A lengthy review of news items on uscharterschools.org reveals this. In Colorado, for example, charter school elementary students scored slightly better, and high schoolers much worse, than public school students on state testing in 2005.

A six-year study of about 340 charter schools in Colorado, Illinois, Massachusetts, North Carolina and Texas, was done by the University of Rochester for the U.S. Dept. of Education before the passage of the federal No Child Left Behind Act (2001), to get an idea where states stood in regard to this proposed legislation. NCLB requires steady improvement towards academic proficiency in basic

---

5.   Education Review, edrev.asu.edu/reviews/rev/190htm
6.   Voice of Reason, No.4, 2004. Discussion by Columbia Teachers College Professor Wells on 2003 NAEP results.
7.   "Charter Schools Face New Setback Amid Test Review," Wall Street Journal, August 23, 2006. Counterpoint editorial on August 28, 2006.

subjects for all races and socioeconomic classes of children. Previously, lower performance by minorities, poor children and non-English speakers could be buried
in an average for the district or state. This study found charter schools less likely
to meet state performance standards than regular public schools. State performance standards set the initial floor on the acceptable percentage of students proficient in reading or math. For example if a state set it at 85%, and if this was
met, then the state reached 100% of its goal. Over time, the state is expected to
make adequate yearly progress towards these goals under NCLB. Dramatic differences were found in how well these initial standards had been met (charter vs.
public): in Texas, 66% vs. 98%; North Carolina, 88% vs. 100%; Massachusetts,
64% vs. 87%, and in Illinois, 52% vs. 82%. In Colorado, charter and public differences were less marked, 90% vs. 98%. Charters' poor performance has been
attributed to higher numbers of at-risk and minority students in these schools,
and this showed that charters may have difficulty in meeting NCLB standards,
the study concluded.[8]

Of great concern is that state student assessment testing of individual students
is usually less rigorous than National Assessment of Educational Progress (NAEP)
student tests. On average, NAEP scores are about one-third to one-quarter of
state tests! For example, in North Carolina, 88% of 8th graders were proficient in
reading by state testing, but only 27% were proficient by NAEP; in math, it was
84% vs. 32%. How hard is NAEP testing? Fourth graders are proficient in math
if they can add, subtract, multiply, have a conceptual understanding of fractions
and decimals, and use a four function calculator and a ruler. I would have to
agree with Mr. Finn, former chairman of the NAEP board, in his assessment that
we're in bad shape if this is too much to expect.[9]

Failing urban schools were the reason for schools of choice, but how many
charters are serving these students as opposed to suburban and rural students?
The Rochester study noted that charter schools tend to be located in cities, serve
higher percentages of minority youths (27% of charter students are black, compared with 17% of public school students), but have fewer special ed students
(California, Minnesota and Massachusetts are exceptions). Washington DC, for
example, has a 26% charter enrollment rate, and a study by the National Charter
School Research Project at the University of Washington's School of Public

---

8.   "Report: Charter schools' progress lags...," Washington Times National Weekly
      Edition, November 29-December 5, 2005.
9.   "Basic Instincts," by Chester E. Finn and Diane Ravitch, Wall Street Journal, Feb-
      ruary 27, 2006. Discusses NAEP and state testing comparisons.

Affairs also says that charters serve a higher percentage of minority and low-income students than traditional public schools.

According to the Progressive Policy Institute,[10] an arm of the moderate Democratic Leadership Council, Colorado has the highest percentage of suburban charters in the nation at 47% of the state's 120 charter schools. Colorado has the reverse of a national trend towards serving more minority, special ed, and at-risk students. Colorado opened its first charter in 1993, and these schools now are 6% of all public schools with 7% of enrollment (44,000 students), with 25,000 on waiting lists.[11] Two thirds of these charters have opened since 2000, the year after the Columbine tragedy. This is one strand of the Columbine connection to Colorado's atypical suburban charter school growth pattern. (Nationally, charter school openings peaked in the 1999-2000 school year, according to the Center for Educational Reform, reflecting in part the reaction to the late 1990's string of school shootings, in my opinion.) Of 116 charter school descriptions listed on the Colorado League of Charter Schools web site,[12] only 16 appear to have any mission to serve minority or at-risk youth, and 16 (these two groups of 16 overlap but are not the same) are located in Denver.

Charter schools and schools of choice are said to be accelerating "white and middle class flight" to the suburbs, and accentuating divisions along race and class lines, according to a Michigan study, which also noted that niche curriculums which shape clientele contribute to loss of community when neighborhood students attend several different schools.[13] In Lansing, charters have been said to "counsel out" students not felt to be a good match.[14] The American Federation of Teachers study, above, and a Harvard study, below, also have sounded the alarm on increasing racial and ethnic isolation of students in schools of choice, both public magnet schools and charter schools. In New Zealand, which converted all public schools to charters in 1989, there has been dramatic spontaneous resegregation by race and class, with some schools literally shrinking beyond the ability to provide a quality education, and parents who are able, pick schools by published socioeconomic ratings. The New Zealand experience is detailed in the Brookings Institute publication *When Schools Compete: A Cautionary Tale*

---

10.   www.PPIonline.org
11.   "A movement grows up," by Asst. Prof. Korach and PhD. candidate Ramsey, Denver University, in the Rocky Mountain News, August 20, 2006.
12.   www.coloradoleague.org, Gives extensive information on Colorado charter schools.
13.   www.wmich.edu/evalcrt/charter/micharter/.html
14.   Ed-web3.educ.msu.edu/news-briefs/1999/rreview.htm

(2000). This is the ugly side of totally free school choice, and it is beginning to happen here.

Recent data do show that Colorado charters are more segregated by race and income than public schools, but that this picture may be slowly improving.[15] However, some school districts such as Denver and particularly Boulder are showing increasing resegregation in schools, or "white flight," attributed to Colorado's school choice laws,[16] as families who are able appear to group themselves by race, language, and achievement (by going to higher-scoring schools). In the Boulder Valley School District (BVSD) in 1987, no school had more than 50% minority students. Now there are 8 schools with at least 50% minority (one is 80%), and 7 of the 34 elementary schools enroll more than 60% of the district's low income elementary students.[17] Lafayette schools are a perfect example of the resegregation tailspin that can be caused by charter and magnet schools.[18] As middle class whites sought the educational grail promised by Peak to Peak, poor and minority students left behind in neighborhood schools became the majority and school testing scores declined, prompting more middle class flight. One parent who was reasonably satisfied with her child's academic progress nonetheless pulled out, saying her child felt isolated on the playground with Spanish-speaking children. To its credit, BVSD has formed a task force on this issue, but the charter horse is out of the barn and is not under the district's control.

A 2003 report by the Civil Rights Project,[19] a Harvard University study that included Colorado, said that segregation in charters has become a national problem and must be solved with policies addressing everything from admissions criteria to easing transportation barriers. In Colorado, the public interest law firm Children's Voices seeks more adequate and equitable school funding and claims that "Charter schools and schools of choice have substantially contributed to socioeconomic, ethnic and linguistic stratification within and among school districts, resulting in unequal and irrational disparities in educational opportunities and the relative costs of education." This group is partially funded by the teacher's union, the Colorado Education Association, but I agree with this statement 100%.

---

15.   "Charters more diverse," Rocky Mountain News, December 20, 2005.

16.   "'White flight' in Boulder," Rocky Mountain News, December 19, 2005

17.   "Boulder Valley tackles segregation," Daily Camera, August 14, 2005.

18.   "BVSD tackles segregation," Daily Camera, February 6, 2006.

19.   "Still separate, Study: DPS remains divided along ethnic line a decade after end of forced busing," Rocky Mountain News, January 20, 2006.

In Minneapolis, Minnesota, there has been "black flight" from city public schools to charter schools, which are now 91% minority and 84% low income, as compared with 72% and 67%, respectively, for public schools. Many are specialized and cater to particular ethnic communities like the Hmong, Somali, or black students, and some focus on the arts or career preparation.[20] It is only natural that minorities would gravitate to schools where they feel respected and safe. And well-intentioned white school district personnel and the public may support racial identity politics and niche schools. Conservative historian and scholar Victor Davis Hanson has said on this subject, "Unfortunately, abstract deference in white America to racial tribalism often provides psychological cover for an unwillingness to live among, or send one's children to school with, the 'other'."[21] Sensing an ominous return to the past, the NAACP has filed suit to prevent the Omaha, Nebraska school district from splitting into three racially identifiable districts (white, black and Hispanic).[22]

The Michigan experience with one of the most permissive charter school laws in the country is detailed in *What's Public About Charter Schools: Lessons Learned About Choice and Accountability*, by Gary Miron and Christopher Nelson (Corwin Press, 2002). This well-documented and scholarly work frames the charter school debate in terms of public vs. private goods of education, as well as in terms of academic results, parent and teacher satisfaction, and accountability. They explain that public education in a democracy not only serves a private good, the education of your child, but also the public goods of equity and socialization. Charter schools alter this balance by tilting towards the private goods, including the rights of parents to control what their children are exposed to, at the cost of equity of opportunity and a common socialization that benefits communities and the larger society. While school safety was a major stimulus of the state's charter school law (the governor brandished a student's sawed-off shotgun as he lauded school choice in 1993), religious conservatives saw the narrowing of scope in education to private goods as a moral imperative, and a way to create schools more in line with their moral values. The authors also found evidence of social sorting by race, socioeconomic status and ability as a result of charters, stating "The ques-

---

20. "Don't Protest, Just Shop Somewhere Else: The Black Exodus to Charter Schools," Wall Street Journal, March 2, 2006.

21. "France provides wake-up call for the U.S.," The Washington Times National Weekly Edition, November 28, 2005.

22. "NAACP files suit over splitting school district," Rocky Mountain News, May 17, 2006. As of September 2006, the law implementing this split had been blocked by a judge.

tion for policy makers is whether such social sorting, even if driven by the pursuit of educational preferences, is acceptable in public schools." The Michigan experience has been decidedly mixed in all areas studied, with exceptions of generally high parent and teacher satisfaction, and a positive effect on local school district willingness to innovate in order to keep students. A number of recommendations are made, including variation in state funding according to the relative costs of educating different students (for example, special ed and high school students are more costly to educate), strengthening and more public transparency of school district and state oversight processes and findings, and capping the rapid growth of charter schools in the state until problem-solving processes can be put in place. "This is a vision of what a more robust, national movement might look like, with extensive and comparatively unregulated private involvement."

Colorado has a similar unregulated charter school environment, but without the large presence of EMOs as in Michigan. Suburbanites in Colorado are flocking to charter schools, even though suburban Denver school districts are some of the best in the state. And that did include our family, in Boulder Valley. When our son was in the 5th grade, in 2000-2001, I remember being more concerned about academics and atmosphere than school safety. But Columbine and school safety was certainly a big topic among the soccer and Cub Scout set, and with school choice, it was almost like parents were negligent if they didn't put effort into finding the best school for their children. It certainly is no longer like when we were kids: you went to your neighborhood school and that was that.

Peak to Peak Charter School was started by a group of families who left Boulder Valley Schools including Summit Charter Middle School, one of Boulder's first charters. Summit had quickly cherry-picked the best and the brightest students among Boulder's highly educated populace, had the highest test scores in the state, and developed a long waiting list. These families were concerned that a K-12 college prep school was needed to fill this demand, according to Peak to Peak's web site,[23] although they could have asked for expanded grades and enrollment from the district. Why several of these families, some of whom shared fundamentalist Christian religious beliefs and some attended the same church, decided to break away is anyone's guess, and the school adamantly maintains that "The founders were a diverse group of people with an academic, not religious, vision." And from what I have gathered, this may have been true initially, and perhaps evangelicals came to numerically have more "voice" at the school. But there is strong scuttlebutt that this was to be Boulder County's de facto Christian

---

23.   peaktopeak.org

school, and it was duly located in the east county where Lafayette and Erie form its Bible belt, and there are cafe discussion groups on such topics as, "Did the Devil Make Me Do It?" featured in the Lafayette News.[24] The Boulder Valley School Board voted 4-3 on its initial approval, contrasting with its 7-0 renewal vote 5 years later.

Many talented people poured countless hours into every aspect of the school, from finances to curriculum, and pulled off what many charters cannot: a large brand new building built with bond money. Where the money comes from to run a school and pay off bonds on the per-pupil amount of about $6600 minus significant "kickback" to BVSD for various services, is buried in its foundation report, Friends of Peak to Peak. I have been trying for a year to get this financial data without success. On their website, it is stated that about 25% of the $6K is needed for bond debt, and must be replaced with donations through Friends of Peak to Peak. This is $1500 times 1000 students, or $1.5 million. About $250,000 is claimed to be raised in donations each year; where is the rest coming from? Is it ok that a charter school can siphon tax dollars by relying a shadowy foundation to make its survival and continued feeding at the public trough possible? Public schools in wealthier neighborhoods do a form of this also, though, by parent fundraisers and solicitation of corporations for such things as state of the art studios and labs, while poorer schools make do with what the district provides. BVSD has struggled with gifting policies in an attempt to maintain equity between schools, but charters are exempt.[25] The Bill and Melinda Gates Foundation and other charities are trying to rectify this imbalance, but they can't help all schools.

Most of the charter schools in Colorado are parent volunteer run, as opposed to being operated by EMOs, and huge amounts of time are spent by volunteers on tasks that would normally cost lots of money. Parents are strongly encouraged to contribute time and money. This leads to a sense of school ownership by parents, which can be a powerful force for cohesion and good works. But it can also foster a sense of entitlement among those who work the hardest, and favoritism towards their children. A former teacher's aide at Peak to Peak, who was a retired teacher, said it best: "Their children are allowed to run wild," referring to VIP's kids. It seems reasonable to think that the non-certified teachers in charter

---

24. "Far reaching influences," December 29, 2004.
25. "BVSD puts donations to work: Schools use gifts from parents to expand programs," Daily Camera, September 5, 2006. One Boulder elementary school raised $100,000, while a Lafayette school only raised $3000, which was supplemented by a $2000 grant from a 10% "tax" on gifts made to wealthier schools.

schools,[26] who have no training in child development, would be less effective disciplinarians even in the absence of favoritism. While favoritism can happen in a public school, most often towards top athletes, it seems even more unfair when there is no star quality to the students who rule the roost in charters. Private schools may be like this, but public schools should not be.

Favoritism was apparent to us as well as others, I'm sure, when VIP children ran roughshod over other students and even teachers. Teachers, including one I spoke with, were reportedly fired for VIP parent and student complaints, despite good evaluations. The parent-run charter model, combined with poor accountability and at-will hiring of teachers fosters this abusive favoritism. And as we also found out, charter schools do not like parents complaining in public. A group of Florida charter parents were threatened with a lawsuit by their charter school when they created an independent website to discuss problems. The school later backed down and agreed to improve communication with parents.[27] While public school administrations can also be unresponsive and defensive, I have never heard of a public school suing parents for complaining.

Black Box Schools and Accountability

With autonomy and independence from school districts, there is much less oversight, and charter schools can become black boxes in which no one knows what is going on except the insiders, and accountability suffers. Unhappy families leave, but say nothing, since most are too busy to do otherwise. Eventually, poorly performing schools fail, sometimes spectacularly, leaving students in the lurch. Financial mismanagement and poor academic results have brought down most of the failed charters nationally, and Colorado mirrors this with its 9% closure rate. A partial list, primarily from a news log on the pro-charter site uscharterschools.org, and a few from the anti-charter protectourpublicschools.org and local news reports, reveals these typical problems:

* A large chain of charters in California, California Charter Academy, was shut down after a state audit revealed that operators pocketed much of the money. A new law gives county education offices more oversight and audit rights.

* In Indiana, Flanner House Learning Center, a charter school that inflated attendance figures and had low test scores, was shut down.

---

26.   Some other states such as Michigan, do require certification for charter school teachers.

27.   "EMO threatens parents with lawsuit," News-Press, May 6, 2005.

* In Massachusetts, Roxbury Charter School came close to revocation over financial troubles and high staff turnover.

* In Colorado, Pinnacle Charter School escaped closure by firing top administrators who were accused of financial mismanagement and use of school funds for personal travel. The founder of another school, Community Leadership Academy, was investigated for embezzlement, and resigned, confessing to a gambling problem. Brighton Charter School came under scrutiny after two teachers, relatives of the Principal and the Board President, were arrested for sexual assault on students.

* In Florida, one charter for at-risk youth was found to be pocketing state tuition money and wages for kids who picked up roadside trash and only spent one hour a day in classes.

Broward County had to close 4 of 8 charter schools which were found to fail safety guidelines and building inspections. Nearly half of Florida's charters did not meet state and federal accountability standards for the 2003-04 school year. In Palm Beach, the school district tightened guidelines for charter school approval after seven charters received grades of D or F in state assessments. Many districts are spending more time investigating charter applications, previously having relied on the honesty of applicants.

* One third of charters in Minnesota have failed to submit timely audits or comply with Open Records requirements. One of the state's earliest charter school operators was indicted for diverting school funds to vacations and second homes.

* In Texas, education officials recently enacted new rules to give the state more power to close poorly performing charters after a wave of high-profile financial scandals and poor academic results in charters granted since 1998, and enacted new rules to close academically underperforming schools.

* Washington DC has closed nine charter schools for failure to collect data needed to monitor student achievement, and other problems.

* In Ohio, new rules for accountability allow shutdown of poorly performing schools and restrict charter sponsors to nonprofit organizations with at least five years of educational experience. Half of southwest Ohio's charters had been found to be in "academic emergency." A school superintendent of one county was being investigated for singularly approving contracts with 78 charter schools.

* The Chicago Public Schools have taken a "slow growth, high-quality" more cautious approach to chartering, with better academic results, according to the previously mentioned Progressive Policy Institute.

* In Arizona, the State Board for Charter Schools decided in 2005 to begin using test scores in its decision-making on closing poorly performing schools.

* In Missouri, state auditors have found that charter schools have repeatedly violated state law without financial penalty or revocation.

* In South Carolina, a criminal investigation was initiated against a Charleston charter school that spent over $360K that it should not have received from the state.

* In Denver, Colorado, the first forced charter school conversion, run by an EMO, had a rough start, with three principals in the first year and conflict over who would pay for Spanish translators at community meetings at the heavily Hispanic school.[28]

The pro-charter Center for Educational Reform claims that the teachers unions and school districts have caused other charters to fail, but gives no details. News reports on their website do document a pitched battle between charter proponents and school districts/teacher's unions, with state legislatures and education boards trying to do a balancing act. The Economic Policy Institute commented in a 2005 study that "Freedom from bureaucratic rules permits some charter schools to be unusually creative and others to be corrupt or inefficient." Charter supporters say this group was influenced by money from the American Federation of Teachers Union. I would say that several large states' experience supports the Institute's opinion.

Accountability was big problem for us at Peak to Peak as we tried to work with the school to stop the religious bullying of our son, and were treated with indifference even by the board of the charter school. The school district, even after becoming aware of the problem with our Public Complaint, did not seem to want to step on toes to interfere with the school's autonomy. Appropriately, the district, after seeing that ours was not an isolated complaint, inserted a clause in the school's new contract to improve accountability, and the school has formed an accountability committee to liaison with the school district. Colorado as a whole has taken the opposite tack of some other states, however, and seeks to give charters even more autonomy through the State Charter School Institute. This unelected pro-charter school body can authorize charter schools that have been denied by "unfriendly" school districts who have been so labeled on flimsy grounds by the State Board of Education. Several districts including Boulder Val-

28. "Critical eye cast at first school takeover," Rocky Mountain News, September 13, 2006. Recommendations for avoiding pitfalls were made in a Piton Foundation report, "Opening Closed Doors: Lessons from Colorado's First Independent Charter School," at www.piton.org, click on publications.

ley have had to grovel to their charter schools and the Board of Ed in a bruising fight to regain control, of which my son, Johanna and others could be considered collateral casualties. The districts have dusted themselves off, and are now pursuing a lawsuit over state constitutionally-mandated local control of schools.[29]

Overall, performance by charter schools appears to be uneven by any standard, whether it be by academic, financial, stability, or accountability standards. There is no clear national trend to suggest this experiment is yet succeeding. Perhaps when the shake-out of underperformers and scammers is finished, certain charter school models will be shown to be superior with different populations of students? Only time will tell. I wonder how many other families feel like guinea pigs, and I worry about the Balkanization our schools.

Clearly, the meteoric growth of the charter school movement has fostered problems that have given ammunition to anti-charter forces, and self-policing by charter support organizations is just now beginning. Accountability is the big watchword, even according to the pro-charter National Alliance for Public Charter Schools, which has released a report[30] encouraging state policymakers to focus on more scrutiny of applications and stronger oversight of school operations instead of caps on charter school numbers and size. This group recently received an $80 million grant from the Bill and Melinda Gates Foundation to improve quality and accountability in charter schools.

The Elephant in the Classroom–School Culture

Culture is the driving force behind all good organizations, and schools are no exception. This brings us to charter schools with a hidden religious agenda, which are found in Colorado and other states. This is the other strand of the Columbine connection to charter schools. Columbine victims Cassie Bernall and Rachel Scott were portrayed in popular books as martyrs for their Christian faith, and, without meaning any disrespect, this contributed to the fears that others would likewise be targeted in public schools. I believe that understandable safety concerns after Columbine, even if overblown when seen in the harsh light of statistics, fed the growth of charter schools in one strand, and specifically Christian fears have increased community acceptance, if not outright support, for quasi-Christian charter schools, in the second strand. One telling trend is the admission

---

29. "Charter agency in jeopardy," Rocky Mountain News, July 5, 2006. Also, Striking back, Daily Camera Editorial, January 14, 2005.
30. "Renewing the Compact," National Alliance for Public Charter Schools, released August 8, 2005.

of religious science fair projects to regional and state competitions, such as an 8 year-old's rock age experiment "supporting that the earth is only 6000 years old" in the Northwest Louisiana Regional Science Fair in the spring of 2006.[31] Another worrisome development is a 2004 Eighth Circuit Court of Appeals decision that teachers in a public school could go directly from the classroom to lead after-school Bible clubs.[32] I agree with one superintendent's concern about the ability of elementary school children to separate this mixed message from their teacher. Even with "student-organized" clubs, the Freedom from Religion Foundation (Madison, Wisconsin) has said, "A chronic complaint has been Christian kids who flaunt their religion.... going to class with Bibles under their arms, trying to convert classmates." This concern is echoed by Americans United for Separation of Church and State: "These Bible clubs coming into schools present a great danger.... (some groups) want to train kids to evangelize others."

There are at least four other charter schools in Colorado that, like Peak to Peak, seek to push the envelope on what is permissible and it is hard to prove that what they are doing is illegal, that is, failing to maintain neutrality towards all religions or no religion. According to State Board of Education member Hudak, one school board, after receiving multiple parent complaints about a religious agenda, forced a metro area charter school to change its board and principal, solving the problem. The Classical Academy in Colorado Springs openly introduces Intelligent Design alongside evolution. One of its students recently said in a news article,[33] "The Classical Academy is kind of a circle of believers. We have mostly people who believe in the same religion. We're all pretty tight with each other." She voiced skepticism in her evolution lessons, and her father expressed feeling sorry for students who were shocked at arguments against evolution. My husband Mark is aware of another area charter school that has "similar problems" which cannot be detailed due to confidentiality constraints.

The most well-known case in Colorado is instructive. In 2004, The Anti-Defamation League received complaints about the promotion of a strongly Christian agenda at another suburban Denver charter school, Elbert County Charter School.[34] These complaints included a principal's remarks about his personal religious beliefs and quotes from the Bible at a holiday concert, trivia game questions for students about the New Testament, the routine playing of Christian music in

---

31. Wall Street Journal, February 18, 2006.

32. "Saving Souls at School," Wall Street Journal, May 20-21, 2006.

33. "School evolves to teach intelligent design," Rocky Mountain News, March 1, 2006.

34. Extensive national and local reporting in December 2004; personal communications, Mountain States ADL.

the school office, and the showing of a creationism video in science class which stated "The only way to be saved from the next flood is to accept Jesus Christ as your savior." When parents met with the principal to start planning for a more inclusive holiday concert, the children came home with a list of songs being rehearsed that was overwhelmingly Christian religious carols. The principal was only willing to add a Hannukah song because Jesus was Jewish. When the ADL and ACLU contacted the school, the school's attorney (from the Alliance Defense Fund, a group of lawyers founded by Focus on the Family to "keep the door open to the Gospel in America") went on a national public relations campaign that falsely accused them of demanding that even Jingle Bells and Frosty the Snowman be removed from the program, and condemning them for trying to censor Christmas. The ADL and the ACLU were properly interpreting a long line of Supreme Court decisions which prohibit public schools from giving students the impression that it prefers or sanctions a particular religion, or religion in general. The complaining families ended up leaving the school. The resolution of the problem only came when the principal left the school for unrelated reasons. According to the ADL, problems of this type are very dependent on school culture, and if someone in power, like the principal or board members, has a religious agenda, abuses can happen.

The Mountain States chapter of the ADL in Denver annually receives approximately 20 calls about religious harassment or other related complaints about schools, with 1 or 2 of these from charter schools, according to their director, who pointed out that public schools are not immune from these problems. Indeed, anti-Semitic and other religious harassment by Christians at Columbine High School was noted by Brooks Brown, a former friend of the killers, in his book *No Easy Answers, The Truth Behind Death at Columbine*. How sad it is to note that Dylan Klebold's mother is Jewish (according to *Chain Reaction*, a book by Columbine victim Rachel Scott's father), and his apparent turning on part of himself as he made Heil Hitler jokes as if to say "I'm not Jewish." Other public school students have been subject to similar harassment, e.g., goose-stepping and oven jokes in proximity to Jewish students, according to one father who wrote in recently to the Denver Post, disgusted that the school would not do anything about the harassment of his son.[35] To me, it is ironic that the very behavior that precipitated the Columbine tragedy, that is, intolerance of those who are different, is now being distilled and perfected in schools formed to escape the evil of

---

35.   Dear Abby, Denver Post July 16, 2006. Also, Letter to Denver Post, "Other types of racism," by Steve Feld, March 2005.

Columbine. This is the dark heart of the Columbine connection to charter schools.

The evidence for a charter school "stealth agenda," i.e., the purposeful creation of charter schools to promote a religious agenda and escape heathen classmates and secular influences, is shadowy and anecdotal. This was warned against early on in the charter school movement by the Harvard Educational Letter, which recommended "Community vigilance in regard to charters and magnets … parents make choices based on religious, class or racial-ethnic grounds, so parents creating charters could make similar choices, which could damage the public character of these schools."[36] In 1997, the North Central Regional Educational Lab voiced "concern that homeschooling charters use public money to teach religion." And a 1999 School Administrator article also expressed the opinion that "charter schools (are) an opportunity to use public money to subsidize the efforts of the Catholic Archdiocese."[37] These concerns may now have come to fruition.

This "stealth agenda" has been referred to by at least two local newspaper columnists, Mike Littwin of the Rocky Mountain News, and Clay Evans of the Boulder Daily Camera, the latter of whom said "A subset of believers does see charter schools as a surreptitious way to create a quasi-religious schools on the taxpayer's dime, and there does seem to be a faith-based subcurrent at Peak to Peak."[38] (Neither of these two columnists returned calls asking for elaboration.) No charter school is going to post their religious agenda on their web site, of course. There are now numerous legal and school support organizations available to guide these charters in skirting the intent if not the letter of the law. Many proponents are determined to see Christian religious influence in schools grow, which they see as a freedom of religion issue, and not at all a "stealth agenda," but a matter of rights and fairness and honoring the Judeo-Christian heritage of our country. Should they be able to use tax dollars on quasi-religious schools? After all, they pay taxes too. Should a church be able to start a charter school? In Colorado, there is no prohibition against it, as long as the school is nonsectarian. In Michigan, religious organizations may not organize or affiliate with charters, but this appears to be not held to firmly, and there are two Muslim charters in Detroit, Christian private school conversions, as well as large numbers of students switching from Christian private schools. National Heritage Academies, one of the largest EMOs in Michigan, "see their schools as quasi-Christian," according

36.   National Council of Churches 1998 General Assembly Policy Statement, "The Churches and the Public Schools at the Close of the Twentieth Century.

37.   Bernstein, Marc, School Administrator, Vol. 56, August 1999.

38.   "God doesn't need bullies," Boulder Daily Camera, December 19, 2004.

to one private Christian school representative. In Fresno, California, a charter school was started by Muslim group (its charter was revoked for mismanagement and other improprieties).[39] In Washington state, one of nine states without a charter school law, a failed 2000 proposal (I-729) to introduce charters schools in the state specifically excluded religious group donations or financing.

"Exodus 2000,"[40] started in South Carolina by conservative Christian Ray Moore, and supported by James Kennedy, Tim LaHaye and other prominent evangelicals, is a movement to convince Christian parents to pull their children out of public schools because of safety issues raised by Columbine, and secular humanism in schools. Paul Weyrich, considered the architect of the religious right, also advised abandonment of public schools for homeschooling and Christian schools. Rev. Jerry Falwell has said, "I hope I will live to see the day when, as in the early days of our country, we won't have any public schools. The churches will have taken them over again." In 2004, the National Association of Evangelicals, formerly led by Colorado Springs pastor Ted Haggard, issued *For the Health of the Nation: An Evangelical Call to Civic Responsibility*, a document urging more Christian involvement in education and other areas, not just in the traditional issues such as abortion and gay marriage.[41] These leaders have given the clarion call to conservative Christians, who have risen to the challenge by homeschooling, private schooling and charter schools as well as supporting legal action in school religious rights suits. In 2006, this exit strategy has now been rejected by the Southern Baptist Convention in favor of calling on its members to "engage the culture of our public school system" by exerting "godly influence," including running for election to school boards.[42] This I find even more concerning!

In California, about a third of charters are homeschool hybrids. According to J. Shelton Baxter of the National Center for the Study of Privatization in Education at the Teachers College, Columbia University,[43] these charters appear ripe for judicial review of some practices which may be violating California charter school law. These practices include continuation of religious activities in the school setting that were previously done at home, use of religious facilities for schooling, use of school facilities by religious groups (presumably free of charge as

39. Jewish News Weekly, January 2001.
40. Multiple sources online, including www.cuttingedge.org/news/n1142.cfm and www.rethinkingschools.org/archive/13_01/rescure.shtml
41. "A wider outreach for evangelicals," Denver Post, October 30, 2004.
42. "Southern Baptists won't 'exit' schools," Rocky Mountain News, June 15, 2006.
43. "A Constitutional Right to Operate Sectarian Public Charter Schools?", February 2005.

opposed to other paying community groups), and student religious publications. In many states, homeschool hybrids are not allowed, including Colorado. Home-schooling originated primarily with religious families. In a 2006 Harris Interactive Poll on parent reasons for homeschooling, the top three were: academics (65%), the desire to provide religious or moral training (60%), and public school safety concerns (53%). Many homeschoolers appear to be doing an excellent job, judging by spelling bee winners. There is a vigorous debate going on among conservative Christian homeschoolers as to whether charter schools could provide free textbooks, support, and relief for parents. The answer appears to be that it depends on the school: those with a Christian emphasis or friendliness to Christian expression are acceptable. John M. Frame, in *Christians and Charter Schools*, writes that "… charters schools can be of great benefit to some Christian families … when a charter school is formed under Christian influence, seeking to limit the influence of non-Christian ideas …" but warns that "Some charter schools have gotten into trouble trying to use state funds to buy Christian texts."[44] The Alliance for Separation of School and State, an organization that seeks to abolish government run schools, held a Christian Education Symposium on the dangers of vouchers and charter schools. Cathy Duffy, a participant and author of the *Christian Home Educators Curriculum Manual*, stated "The more insidious problem with charter schools is that some schools and parents are disobeying state law and using Christian materials for curriculum."[45] You heard it right from those in the know!

During my web research, I have run across corroborating comments from charter school parents such as:[46]

St. Helens, Oregon parent—"One drawback is that no spiritual training can be counted as seat time. Because this is a publicly funded school, all curriculum must be secular. I still feel confident that I will be able to share our views with the kids and it won't be hard to bring the gospel into the discussions as we study together … I have been hesitant to tackle homeschooling with six kids …"

California, Dehesa Charter School Director—"A large percentage of our student population is LDS [Mormon]." This school's web site states that religious training during lessons can be done by the parent but not the mentor in this charter school that supports homeschoolers.

---

44.   www.frame-polythres.org/frame_articles/2002charterschools.htm
45.   www.homeschoolchristian.com/ChristianEd/DuffyVouchers.html
46.   Meridian Magazine, Education Series, Part 7, 2004.

Peak to Peak parent who previously homeschooled—"In a few days all four of my children will be attending Peak to Peak Charter School and I will be happily at home taking care of our one year old ... our school district is the most liberal in all of Colorado and the gay curriculums will be expanded once again, not too much of this stuff is going on in our charter school however." Surprisingly, she adds, "A charter school is no guarantee that a child will be taught phonics ..."

California, Redding School of the Arts parent—"Although they don't teach religion, the majority of the children and parents involved in the school are conservative Christians (including the directors) ... It has very few of the problems that public schools have, and operates much as a large family. There are quite a few of these type charter schools in our area and I think they are a great solution ..."

Other Christian groups, such as the liberal National Council of Churches, have taken an anti-voucher stand, and echo the concerns of the above-quoted Harvard Educational Letter about charter schools. Catholic schools have of course been pro-voucher, but at the same time have a long history of serving the urban poor and minority population, and it is hard not to sympathize with this mission. Conservative Christian writer David Goetz, in describing his book *Death by Suburb: How to Keep the Suburbs from Killing Your Soul,* says "Many suburban Christians are looking for safe places, so we send our children to Christian schools ... the segregation allows us to feel safer ... to me, the gospel is about losing the anxiety of being around people who are different than you are." He notes a trend away from the isolationism of self-contained large Protestant churches with schools, gyms, and extensive social activities for their members. I believe charter schools also serve this impulse to self-segregation and safety, which is natural and understandable, but may not be in the long term best interests of either our kids or society.

The First Amendment and Schools

The Bush administration's Faith-Based Initiatives includes the Department of Education which encourages churches to become involved in education, and as a result, in several areas around the country religious groups have been involved in developing charter schools.[47] The Department of Education has given millions of dollars to states to develop charter schools, including a push to replace public

---

47.   www.ed.gov/policy/fund/reg/fbci-teg/html

schools damaged by Hurricane Katrina.[48] These guidelines were issued by the Department as a caution, however, to religious groups:

"It is not appropriate for members of faith communities to use their involvement in public schools as an occasion to endorse religious activity or to encourage participation in a religious act. Adults who choose to volunteer in public schools must respect both the rules established by the school and the strong constitutional protections that children have from becoming a captive audience."

Readers are likely familiar with the well-publicized case of religious harassment of non-Christians at the Air Force Academy in Colorado Springs. These college airmen and women are also in a somewhat "captive" situation, as are adults in the workplace, and should be protected from harassment and unwanted proselytism. (The reforms enacted at the AFA unfortunately are being quietly peeled back, according to recent news reports.[49]) It is even more important to protect children in public schools from religious pressure, indoctrination, and harassment.

Just what are the legal issues involved with religion in schools and the separation of church and state? Here's a synopsis, according to legal scholar Charles Haynes of the First Amendment Center in Arlington, Virginia.[50]

The first ten words of the First Amendment prohibit our government from establishing an official state religion (e.g., historically, the Church of England or the Catholic church in France; modern examples of countries with official state religions are democratic Israel and totalitarian Iran). The next six words prohibit government from interfering with the free exercise of religion.

"Congress shall make no law regarding an establishment of religion, or prohibiting the free exercise thereof; or abridging the freedom of speech, or of the press; or of the right of the people to peaceably assemble, and to petition the Government for a redress of grievances."

How does a judge decide whether a governmental body such as a school is "establishing" religion or prohibiting the free exercise of religion?

1. The concept of neutrality is the guiding principle for the government's relationship to religion. In the landmark case of Everson vs. the Board of Education

---

48.   "Charting a New Course," Wall Street Journal, August 24, 2006. Louisiana state officials took control of New Orleans schools, and now half of schools preparing to open in the fall are charters.

49.   "Reviews mixed on A.F. religion rules," Rocky Mountain News, February 10, 2006.

50.   Religious Liberty in the Public Schools: When children are involved, the battle between church and state intensifies, FACSNET, February 16, 2006.

(1946), Justice Hugo Black said, "The First Amendment requires the state to be neutral in its relations with groups of religious believers and non-believers; it does not require the state to be their adversary. State power is no more to be used to handicap religions than it is to favor them."

The Supreme Court has applied a more stringent test of neutrality to the public schools because young people are more impressionable than adults, and students are a captive audience in a compulsory school system. Several subsequent cases have devised tests for neutrality, such as the Lemon test—is religion being accommodated, or is it being promoted? The posting of Bible Study advertisements in school hallways by adult volunteers fails this test, as does a teacher reading religious material in a health class. Indifference to student on student religious harassment also violates this principle. Another test is the coercion test—are people being coerced to support or participate in religion? School-sanctioned prayers and invocations, use of religion in discipline, and musical proselytism by staff fit this coercion category. Classes may study religion and its impact on society and history as long as they don't practice it, promote it, or denigrate it.

2. Free exercise of religious expression in the schools was established by the 1969 Tinker case. Justice Abe Fortas said: "It can hardly be argued that either students or teachers shed their constitutional rights to freedom of speech or expression at the schoolhouse gate."

But because the school is a special case of a captive audience and not the public square, there are limits. As agents of the state, staff may not lead a prayer, but moments of silence are allowed if its purpose is not to promote prayer. Students and teachers may pray privately before lunch, or students may meet "at the flagpole," or in before/after school prayer groups or Bible clubs, if not led by staff (but as noted previously, the 2004 Eighth Circuit decision now allows staff to lead religious groups at school, and this ruling will likely spread). In schools with uniforms, students may still wear religious headwear and jewelry that is not disruptive; in non-uniform schools, there is wide latitude to enforce dress codes, but nondisruptive religious T-shirts would be upheld by courts. Teachers may wear non-obtrusive religious jewelry but not any clothing that advertises their religion, like a printed T-shirt. Students may express religious views and invite others to their church, but cannot be disruptive or disrespectful, e.g., "You're going to hell." Religious flyers, when given to selected classmates between classes, are usually held by courts to be within this guideline, but when given with staff assistance to all students is held to be promotion of religion. Some court decisions have supported schools in banning all literature given out by students, to maintain neutrality. After school student-led Bible Clubs and limited posters advertising them are usually permissible. Students may not use oral reports to sermonize or proselytize in the classroom, which violates the rights of other students in the captive audience. Written assignments may be religious in nature only if it fits the assignment.

One fairly recent First Amendment public school speech case is concerning for the future of bullying control. In 2001, the entire anti-harassment speech code of a Pennsylvania school district was invalidated, and the decision was written by now-Supreme Court Justice Samuel Alito.[51]

Evolution and creationism, including Intelligent Design, remains a highly contentious and an unsettled area of law, continuous back to the infamous 1925 "Scopes Monkey Trial," in which a biology teacher was prosecuted for teaching evolution. The teaching of creationism (the world is 6000 years old, a literal interpretation of Genesis) or Intelligent Design (the universe is too complex to have happened by chance and one explanation for this is a Creator) is currently being decided at the state level; it was struck down in Georgia and Pennsylvania, but upheld in Kansas as of 2006. Disruption of science classes appears to be the latest tactic of creationist students, using false cover of free expression, and students are reportedly being taught how to do it by parents and churches (e.g., Ken Ham, Answers in Genesis[52]). It is probably just a matter of time until a charter school that steps over the line is brought into court for allowing teaching, discussions, or debates of creationism or Intelligent Design in science classes.

Similarly to the evolution-creationism front, other school culture war battles are being fought over what some religious parents see as an effort by schools to push secular humanism, pro-gay health classes, new age practices (such as Waldorf philosophy and Yoga), and fantasy literature with magical elements (eg, Harry Potter). Some schools, such as Peak to Peak, do not have Halloween parties, "out of respect for religious beliefs of some students"[53] (Many Christian fundamentalists think it's devil worship). The now-perennial battles over winter holiday concerts have of course become iconic of the clash. The previously mentioned rural Colorado teacher who was put on leave over the Faust flap had earlier refused to include religious Christmas songs in the school's winter holiday

---

51.   Saxe vs. State College Area School District, U.S. Court of Appeals for the Third Circuit.

52.   www.answersingenesis.org/cec/courses/101.asp–APO101:Foundations in Creation Apologetics.

53.   This was policy when our son attended, and continues, according to a parent testimonial in the February 2005 Peak to Peak Press Release.

concert, according to the town's mayor. Both the teacher and the mayor resigned, and the school won this skirmish.[54]

Summary

I have much sympathy for families struggling with failing and unsafe public schools, and even with those upset about heavy-handed social agendas that seem to intrude on parental prerogatives. I understand the efforts by parent groups to do something about it by starting charter schools. And there is no question that some states and districts have taken this as a big wake-up call to improve. For example, east Boulder County schools in Lafayette are now being fortified with International Baccalaureate programs, and math and science programs in response to Peak to Peak's drawing away large numbers of students. And this response to competition is happening elsewhere as well, such as Florida, where three studies concluded that the threat of vouchers (before the court struck them down) stimulated improvement in failing schools. Some observers, including Nobel Laureate economist John Heckman, point to evidence that early childhood intervention at the preschool level to improve cognitive and non-cognitive skills, and not the current school choice battle, is where the money is in improving achievement and investing in the next generation of citizens.[55] In my opinion, we need to improve both early childhood opportunities and our elementary and secondary schools. Charters schools and voucher programs have performed a necessary service to get the ball rolling.

But the private and public goods of education must be balanced using common sense. And there is the ugly side of school choice: resegregation, overspecialization, non-inclusive culture, favoritism, non-accountability and hidden religious agendas. It appears that some charter schools are coming right up to or crossing the lines of religious neutrality, and it can be a slippery slope which in the absence of accountability can lead to disasters such as ours. The slippery slope we experienced looks like this: Changing of school religious use policy to accommodate churches, and bending policies and teaching to accommodate Christian religious expression in the classroom. OK, not so bad? But what does it mean

---

54.   "Teacher seeks new job after 'Faust' flap," Rocky Mountain News, March 2006.

55.   "Catch 'em Young," by James J. Heckman, Professor at University of Chicago; Wall Street Journal, January 10, 2006. This view is supported by the National Institute for Early Education Research at Rutgers University. Others such as Shikha Dalmia and Lisa Snell of the Reason Foundation, dispute the value of universal preschool, because ten states with these programs, including those with programs started over a decade ago, show no better NAEP scores.

when a parent must go to a church to pick up paperwork or attend a meeting,[56] but that parent is not Christian and feels uncomfortable? Should they be more open-minded? What if you don't bow your head during an invocation? What does it mean when your child is told by the health teacher that prayer can cure anorexia, and his science class often gets off track from science? Or hears classroom sermonizing that Jesus is my hero, why isn't he yours? Or asked why he isn't he going to the church overnight activity? Should the parent just tell the child, "Those are not our beliefs"? What about when your 12 year old comes home upset because he's been tripped and shoved and told he's the child of Satan? And the principal says he's paranoid? Or the Dean asks students, "What would Jesus do?" Then what to do, when the school and the police say that your daughter being told she's going to burn in hell is "a difference of opinion between students"? And as I found out, others experienced a racial second class status, sexual orientation harassment, or an elitism that subtly puts down those who aren't high achievers or award-winners. Many of us were told in so many ways, "You don't belong here."

Is this sort of experience also collateral damage in the school battlefield of American culture wars? Is this trampling of innocents just another bump in the road to absolutely imperative school reform? To me, it's all part of new Victorian Age whose impulse is understandable, but now due for moderation, and America needs to begin making that moderation a reality.

---

56.   For the first two years, Peak to Peak Board meetings were held at a church, some of whose members helped found the school, and in the first year, some of the paperwork and copying was done at this church.

10

Bullying: Where Are We Seven Years After Columbine?

"... the deadly thing was that school life was a life almost wholly dominated by the social struggle ..." from C.S. Lewis' autobiography

A Dangerous Rite of Passage

Growing up, almost all of us were at least teased or mildly bullied by peers. Many of us, up to a quarter, experienced serious bullying during our school careers, and we survived it and may even feel that we were strengthened by it. A good portion of us, about 10-20%, were bullies, and recall with dismay or shame some of the mean and even cruel things we did to others until we grew out of it. Some of us were both victims and bullies.[1] A few of us, maybe 5%, still are bullies in our workplaces, families and in the checkout line at the supermarket. Is this just life, and all this fuss over bullying just a further attempt to over-control children in an extension of the government nanny-state?

But the fact is, some of us did not survive and committed suicide. Many more of us ran away, were chronically truant, frequently stayed home sick,[2] or left school at the earliest opportunity to escape persistent bullying. These lives were lost or denied their fullest potential. Many of us who were child bullies are now

---

1. Extensive bullying data available from the National School Safety Center and many other sources.

2. 160,000 kids stay home each school day due to fear of bullying, according to Prevent Child Abuse America, www.preventchildabuse.org. Bullying is the most common cause of school refusal behavior in pre-teens and teens, according to a Jane Brody Well Being column of September 5, 2006. Reviews findings of psychologist Christopher Kearney in the August 2006 issue of The Journal of Family Practice. Serious academic, social and legal consequences can result from unaddressed school refusal behavior.

151

incarcerated adults, never having been steered away from this path. In an earlier day, this loss was against the background of a tougher life of more frequent set-backs, hardships and deaths than the middle class is accustomed to in the 21st century. Since a good education is now critical to life success, as mentioned in the last chapter, students must be given every chance to succeed in school, academi-cally and socially. And children know this. They are not stupid, and pick up quickly that social and academic failure are a sentence to life failure. This leads to frustration, oppositional and aggressive behaviors, anxiety and depression, early sexual activity, and substance abuse. The epidemic of medicated children, espe-cially of fidgety and aggressive boys diagnosed with Attention Deficit Disorder, and boys' dramatically higher rate of expulsion (even in kindergarten![3]) are symp-tomatic of this dire situation. I also believe the fad in diagnosis of adolescent Bipolar Disorder in both boys and girls reflects pressure to conform and succeed.

Suicide is the third leading cause of death among children and adolescents aged 10 to 19 years, after accidents and homicide.[4] Every year approximately 2000 youths, or about 5 out of every 100,000, kill themselves. The teen suicide rate tripled from about 1960 to 1990, probably due to the increase in social stres-sors that have affected families, neighborhoods and schools that was referred to at the beginning of Chapter 9. Some of the rise in the suicide rate may be more accurate reporting, as suicide and mental illness carried a heavier social stigma for families in the past than today. Authorities believe teen suicide is still underre-ported, because sometimes the circumstances of a death in the absence of a sui-cide note, evidence of stress or depression, or tips such as giving away belongings, do not point to suicide. Even so, it is believed that the true teen suicide rate rose, and is now declining in the last decade due to better recognition and treatment of the problem. Attempted suicide is many times more prevalent; an alarming 1 out of 13 high school students in the U.S. report making a suicide attempt in an aver-age year. Colorado has about 50 teen suicides annually, much higher than the national average, for unclear reasons. We have a highly educated populace, and pressure for success may be higher here. Nationwide, gay and lesbian teens are at higher risk of suicide.

Anxiety, depression, social withdrawal and aggressive behavior are all risk fac-tors for suicide. It has been said that "girls get sad (turn their anger inward) and

---

3.   "You've Got Male!" by Lionel Tiger, Wall Street Journal, December 17, 2005. Tiger is a professor at Rutgers University, and the author of *The Decline of Males* (St. Mar-tin's, 1999).

4.   Methods of Suicide Among Persons Aged 10-19 Years—United States, 1992-2001. Journal of the American Medical Association, July 28, 2004, Vol.292, No. 4.

boys get mad (turn their anger outward)," in response to severe stress including bullying. Particularly for boys, suicide is often a complete shock to the family and teachers. Girls let their feelings show more, and make more unsuccessful attempts because they use less lethal methods such as pills and knives. Boys hang, suffocate, and shoot themselves with finality. Some, such as the bullied Florida boy who waved a pellet gun around at his school,[5] commit suicide by cop. Also, a Washington teen was killed by police after he brought a gun to school and raised it when confronted; a suicide note made clear this was his goal.[6]

"Bullycide" is the term coined by Marr and Field to describe suicide due to unrelieved bullying. The most publicized case of bullycide is of the Connecticut 12 year old, D.S., who hung himself in his closet with the tie he had just received for Christmas from his mother. His single mom struggled with two jobs, leaving the house unkempt and the laundry undone. D.S. was picked on for his mismatched clothes and poor hygiene, shoved into desks, had his belongings stolen, and almost had his neck broken. When he fought back, he was suspended for fighting. He refused the aid of his older sister and mother against the bullies, telling them that it would only make things worse. Teachers said the boy, who had a high IQ, wet himself and baby talked in class. Guidance counselors documented problems and gave the mom lists of community resources. Someone did call social services; they found the home to be adequate and closed the case six days before his death. After he died, the blaming began. The school blamed D.S. for bringing all his troubles on himself. The mother blamed the school, and filed suit. Police blamed the mother, who was convicted of contributing to his suicide because the three-bedroom apartment was cluttered and dirty. A group of supporters rallied outside the courtroom to protest with signs reading, "Punish the bullies, not the grieving mother." She received 5 years probation, and lost both of her jobs due to the conviction. A 41-page report by a child advocate reserved most of the fault with the school and social services system which had both failed a child at risk. The parents at the school knew that failure to address bullying was the root cause, and formed an anti-bullying organization. The legislature passed laws mandating schools to report bullies to authorities, a sad commentary on the distrust that the school system would do anything substantive on its own. The Connecticut Supreme Court later overturned the mother's conviction, and the

---

5.   "Kin of slain teenager tried to warn police," Associated Press, unknown date, story out of Longwood, Florida.

6.   "School shooter may have sought death by police," Associated Press, unknown date, story out of Spokane, Washington.

opinion notes that social services inspected the boy's home days before the suicide and suggested he be kept home until transferred to another school.[7]

Here are the moving final diary pages of a 13 year old victim of bullycide:

I shall remember forever and will never forget
Monday: my money was taken
Tuesday: names called
Wednesday: my uniform torn
Thursday: my body pouring with blood
Friday: it's ended
Saturday: freedom
(from *Bullycide, Death at Playtime: An Expose of Child Suicide Caused by Bullying*, by Neil Marr and Tim Field)

Barbara Coloroso's book, *The Bully, the Bullied, and the Bystander,* gives a list of other child and adolescent suicides due to bullying, nearly as long as my list of arrested and suspended children in Chapter 8. While it is difficult to know what proportion of all youth suicides are due to bullying, it appears significant and is an international problem. In the United Kingdom, a smaller nation of 60 million, it is estimated that there are 16 bullycides annually.

Bullycides are preventable deaths. The terrible fact is that it often takes a death to mobilize a community against bullying.

The Columbine tragedy brought the bullying problem in our nation's schools into sharp focus after two boys with young lifetimes of daily abuse at the hands of their peers exacted revenge in the process of their bullycide. They were quoted in one of the "basement tapes" done prior to the massacre, "We're gonna kickstart a revolution!" Indeed they did. It took the deaths many innocents at once to get the whole nation's attention to the high cost of emotional violence in our schools. Prior to this, youth suicides were judged random, fully attributable to mental illness and dysfunctional families. And homicide was just that unpredictable human murderous passion that has been with us from the dawn of time. Bullying was a rite of passage. These things just happened, and were not connected.

Columbine has been dissected in detail, and provided a concentrated case study of all the factors, errors upon errors, that contribute to these catastrophic events, and gave lessons for the future. From the large, impersonal school, to inat-

---

7.   Extensive national reporting; see Associated Press, "The legacy of boy's suicide," January 17, 2004, and AP, "Court: Can't blame mother for suicide", August 29, 2006.

tentive teachers and administrators, to complicity with athlete-hero-bullies in maintaining school status quo and scapegoating misfits, to allowing social hierarchies to rule, and to student bystanders who felt powerless or contributed to this toxic environment, everything that could go wrong did go wrong in a horrific way. Even before the police response went wrong in its myriad ways. Studies of other school shootings such as in West Paducah, Kentucky and Pearl, Mississippi, show that smaller schools and communities also can have similar "not my job, none of my business, there's nothing to be done" attitudes toward troubled youth. As previously mentioned, in 75% of school shootings since 1974, according to a Secret Service study, someone knew trouble was brewing, but did not say anything or take action, thinking or hoping it was not serious. Furthermore, according to the study, "Three-quarters of school attackers felt bullied, threatened or injured by others prior to the incident. While bullying was not a factor in every case, nevertheless, in a number of incidents of school violence studied, attackers described being bullied in terms that suggested these experiences approached torment."[8]

Brooks Brown, in *No Easy Answers, the Truth Behind Death at Columbine*, describes his former friends' almost psychotic transformation. The more abuse, humiliation and ridicule were heaped upon them, the more angry, alienated and weird they became, "inviting" more of the same in a downward spiral. And they mostly kept it from their parents, who saw them successfully complete juvenile diversion programs for misdemeanor offenses, and who helped Klebold plan for college, and got psychological help for a depressed Harris, whose therapist was later as shocked as anyone. Teachers saw the anger in writings and videos and some had awareness of the bullying, and the police were directed by Brown's father to Harris' angry web site. All of this screamed "Help!" But no one dreamed of what was being planned, and no one saw it as their job to intervene. The former head of technology at Columbine was recently quoted after the summer 2006 release of much Columbine material, as saying he worked with the two boys closely for their first two years at the school, and saw them change from bright-eyed freshmen to teens with darker attitudes.[9] Many noticed, but few did anything, it appears.

The wounds of Columbine were reopened earlier in 2006 when a free computer download game called Super Columbine Massacre was described in the newspapers. The creator, a young man who was severely bullied in another Colo-

8.   www.edu.gov/bullying
9.   "Attack plan on school server," Rocky Mountain News, July 8, 2006.

rado high school in 1999, decided to go public with his rationale for the game, whose graphics are rudimentary, in order to help the public understand how extreme abuse can warp reality. He said, "When you get pushed every day, when you are ostracized not once or twice, but years in and out, your perception of reality is distorted. These things really do warp your understanding and your perception of humanity in some almost irrevocable way." When he saw what the killers did, it turned him away from the wrong path that he could see himself on, and he sought help in therapy and learned martial arts.[10] The latest entry in this new and controversial genre is "Bully," by Rockstar Games: "As a troublesome schoolboy, you'll laugh and cringe as you stand up to bullies, get picked on by teachers, play pranks on malicious kids ..."[11] These games do not get a following without hitting a chord among disaffected youth.

In Columbine's aftermath, schools, communities and states began to tackle bullying head on, forming task forces such as Colorado's Safe Schools Coalition. Many books were written and anti-bullying strategies revamped. We still don't really know which bullied children will turn angry fantasy into murderous reality, similar to the situation with aggrieved adults in workplace rampages that surprise co-workers and neighbors. Profiling is not much help given the rarity of violent events in comparison to the large number of students fitting these profiles. In one study done by New York's Alfred University, as many as 20 students in a school of 800 could be considered at high risk of shooting others at school, based on questionnaires. And widely published lists of youth risk factors for violence (by Gavin de Becker and the National School Safety Center) appear to apply to vastly more students than ever commit these acts. Appropriately, student distress signals are now taken more seriously, even though the response is often over-reactive and dysfunctional, as we saw in Chapter 8. Most problematic, school efforts to correct bullying are uneven and often counterproductive. What do we know in 2006 about anti-bullying theory?

Why Bullies and Bullying Targets?

Why are some children bullies, and some targets of bullying? Why does the problem appear in school age children, peak in middle school, and ease by the end of high school? Although the latest thinking on bullying has gotten away from the why, and more towards the what-to-do, it is nevertheless a common question. It

---

10.   "Gamer was on deadly road," Rocky Mountain News, May 24, 2006.
11.   "Evolution or Exploitation? 'Bully' fuels latest generational clash: gamers vs.mainstream," Rocky Mountain News, August 12, 2006.

is important to note at this point that not all peer to peer negative interactions are bullying episodes, 70% of which are verbal, less than a third are physical, the remainder being exclusion. Teasing banter and more serious disputes between students are different in that there is no power differential, and it is usually worked out between them with or without adult help. Teasing is not meant to be hurtful, and usually tossed back and forth between equals in a light-hearted fashion. Bullying is the ongoing purposeful emotional and physical abuse of a student with less social power, by students with more social power. Verbal abuse is often in the form of thinly disguised jokes that are humiliating, cruel or bigoted. Serious, bigoted bullying is a hate crime in some states. Disputes between rivals do not have this one-sided quality and usually focus on the issue, e.g., a girlfriend. No one on either side of it, whether it be a dispute, teasing or bullying, usually has any doubt as to which it is. Coloroso gives a helpful list characteristics of teasing and taunting in her book. Cliques commonly form to protect their members in an attempt to equalize social power that may or may not be successful. Those without the social skills to form these bonds are at the most risk of poor outcomes such as drop-out, depression and suicide. The bullying problem may appear to the public as one of privileged suburban kids, but it could be that we just hear more about it, while inner city kids are used to the fact that those in authority don't help so they just take care of things themselves the old-fashioned way.

Characteristics of bullied children has long been focused on—what are they doing to "invite" attacks by their peers. The standard answer has been that these children are in some way different physically, socially, or emotionally from others. Fat, skinny, tall, short, plain, bad skin, uncool clothes or grooming, low socioeconomic status, early developing girls, late developing boys, quiet, sensitive, stupid, smart, disabled, clumsy, minority ethnicity or religion, actual or perceived homosexual orientation, etc.; anything different. Even being beautiful and smart, but not "knowing your place" socially because you are black, was a risk factor for Erica Harrold, a Miss America winner who dedicated her tenure to eradicating bullying. A small group of so-called provocative targets are said to arouse irritation in their peers with annoying or exasperating behaviors. These kids may have poor social skills and some of them may be disabled (e.g., mild autism), but do not deserve to be labeled provocative, which indicates that their classmates' response was justified. Even many kids who appear in no way different feel ill at ease in their schools; in a local school district survey, whopping 40% of students reported that feel like they "do not fit in" at their schools.[12] Consider what Dylan

---

12.   "Few BVSD students say they feel trusted," *Daily Camera*, September 24, 2003.

Klebold wrote in his journal two years before the Columbine massacre: "I don't fit in here. Thinking of suicide gives me hope, that I'll be in my place wherever I go after this life–that finally I'll not be at war with myself, the world, the universe–my mind, my body, everywhere, everything at PEACE."[13]

Depression or anxiety can develop as a result of bullying, and depressed and/or anxious children are more likely to be bullied, according to a carefully designed Netherlands study recently published in the Journal Pediatrics. At the beginning of the study, kids without depression or anxiety who were bullied developed these symptoms by the end of the school year, and kids who already had such symptoms experienced more bullying than their asymptomatic peers.[14] Not earth-shattering news, and this is just common sense.

Is bullying a form of vestigial natural selection, acting to weed out the "unfit"? Many animal species attack or abandon those of their own kind that are not perfect specimens, are injured, or behave out of norms. Primitive humans did the same, and practiced infanticide and abandonment of those who could not be functioning members of the tribe; it was a group survival issue. Social ostracism remains a powerful tool for group cohesion and maintenance of social norms, usually having a positive effect, sometimes crushing human spirit and innovation. Researchers have recently discovered that the distress of exclusion or rejection registers in the same part of the human brain as physical pain. The need for social inclusion is a deep-seated part of what it means to be human, they concluded.[15] Feeling pain from social exclusion or rejection does not mean a child is a sissy, but a normal human being. Humans have a wide normal range of many types of characteristics; sensitivity is just one of these characteristics of which some of us have more, and some less, and it makes for a more interesting and productive world of both artisans and warriors, and everything in between. Resiliency is a characteristic that researchers, using preliminary primate models, believe may have both genetic and environmental contributions.[16] Intelligence is primarily genetic, but needs proper early stimulation to reach its potential. Brain growth in

---

13.   "Writings offer new glimpse of killers," Rocky Mountain News, July 7, 2006. Extensive article on released Columbine documents.

14.   Discussed in "Depressed Kids Make Prime Targets for Bullies," Newsmax, July 2006.

15.   "Exclusion shown to cause pain," AP and Rocky Mountain News, October 10, 2003. Summarizes UCLA study published in Science on same date, by researcher Naomi Eisenberger.

16.   "Researchers Seek Roots of Resilience in Children," by Tracy Hampton, Ph.D., Journal of the American Medical Association, April 19, 2006, Vol. 295, No. 15.

smart children has been recently shown to be slower than in average children;[17] is this somehow a source of these kids frequently being bully targets? While it is interesting to speculate on all this, the important thing is to develop and implement effective ways of correcting the bullying problem.

The Cost of Ineffective Anti-Bullying Efforts

Way back in my baby boomer youth, boys and girls mostly behaved in the classroom where iron-fisted teachers kept control and did their share of bullying, hall monitors brandished rulers, and principals glowered and paddled. At my high school, girls were sent home for too-short skirts and boys were dragged by the collar to the barber by the principal for too-long hair! But bullies were in charge in the locker rooms, bathrooms, and under stairwells—and still are today. Boys engaged more in physical bullying, and girls more in relational bullying, i.e., shunning and rumor-mongering. Bullying victims generally did their score-settling in the alleys and neighborhoods after school, engaging the help of older siblings and sometimes parents. Sometimes it helped, sometimes not. It was rough and tumble, and children got teeth knocked out and black eyes, and had money and belongings stolen and extorted. This free-wheeling, do-it-yourself justice is no longer allowed, and this is to the disadvantage of victims, who are more likely to truth-tell and follow rules than hot-headed, impulsive bullies. Unthinking zero tolerance discipline often re-victimizes youngsters such as D.S., suspended for fighting back. A good defensive punch in the nose will get a kid arrested these days.

More recently, parents were told by the experts to help their kids fit in by addressing those characteristics inviting abuse. Buy her the right clothes, get him acne treatment and sports lessons, develop their social skills and host parties, tell them to be tough and ignore the abuse and stuff down feelings, don't make waves. I read books like this as recently as 2002. The next set of anti-bullying recommendations was: Don't fight back, because you're stooping to their level, also, you'll get in trouble too. Instead, use these tips:

* get **Help** from friends and teachers. (but risk being called a tattle or liar, and make the disheartening discovery that most teachers don't do anything)
* **Assert** yourself with firm statements objecting to the bullying. (this often stimulates more derision)

---

17. "Smart children's brains grow more slowly," Daily Camera, March 30, 2006. Details National Institutes of Health study published on same day in the journal Nature.

* **Humor**—make a joke about the situation. (very difficult to do under stress)
* **Avoid** the bully. (this also stimulates derision)
* **Self-talk**—ignore it and tell yourself the bully is just having a bad day. (but the bully is actually having a great day bullying you)
* **Own** it by agreeing with the bully—e.g., yes, this is an ugly dress, my mother made me wear it. (participate in your own bullying)

This widely used strategy, known as "HA-HA-SO", used at Peak to Peak, and reportedly at Columbine after the tragedy, is still touted today in local Newspaper in Education programs[18] and Family Helpline columns.[19] Targets find out quickly that these strategies are worse than ineffective; they are counterproductive. Kids then either fight back, or take it, which often leads to more problems, so painfully demonstrated in Jeff's and Johanna's situations. Families are told: Don't rescue your kid, they need to learn and use the anti-bullying strategies, because adults can't be there all the time to intervene. While there is the notion of bystander empowerment, because of the imbalance of power in the dynamics of bullying, this is less effective when adult correction of the bully is not part of the strategy.

Bullies are still heroes in our society, and parents are still proud of them; witness the dueling bumper stickers "My kid beat up your honor student" vs. "Honor Student at X School." Historically, aggressive men were more valuable to societies than quiet thinkers until modern times. And socially aggressive women have wielded power behind the scenes from time immemorial. Modern analysis of bullies at first excused their behavior as springing from poor self-esteem due to deep insecurities, dysfunctional or abusive families, behavioral disorders such as ADD, having been bullied as younger children, or having poor social skills and/ or low intelligence. While this may still apply to some bullies, it has been discovered that most bullies have average or above average self-esteem, and are overconfident, socially adept, witty, popular with other students and teachers, even charismatic. They tend to be hot-headed, impulsive and have little empathy for their victims, who "deserve it," and use their social power to draw in willing

18.   Program offered February 12—March 31, 2006 via Post-News Educational Services, www.PostNewsEducation.com, www.teenhealthcentre.com/articles/publish/article_138.shtml

19.   Family Helpline, by Beth Pfalmer, Rocky Mountain News, November 28, 2005. In response to a parent question on his boys' harassment at school, "You need the help of school officials to identify the reasons your sons are targets and to learn how to help them."

henchmen or silent accomplices. These bullies often had a mean streak as younger children which blossomed in middle school as adolescent acceleration-over-brakes brain development took off.[20] Typically, bullying behavior tempers as the brain matures in late adolescence.

Perhaps a quarter to a third of childhood bullies are budding sociopaths. This condition is now called Anti-social Personality Disorder, and is only diagnosed in adults; most children who become sociopathic had more severe behavior problems and lack of empathy, formally known as Conduct Disorder. Sociopathic adults continue to victimize, control, and manipulate others throughout their lives. Some of the smarter ones can be found in corporate boardrooms and the not so smart in prisons, and some are professional assassins. About 1 in 25 of us, in fact, are sociopaths, and it is not known why certain people are this way, whether it is inborn, or partly inborn and partly upbringing.[21] In an evolutionary sense, being selfish and manipulative had some individual survival benefit and so this trait persisted in our genes, but the group cannot survive if we're all like that, so it is not common.

No matter how you came to be that way, being a childhood bully is not without cost. Bullies are more likely than their peers to be injured in fights, engage in vandalism or theft, and to smoke and drink alcohol. Studies show that being a childhood bully brings a dramatically increased risk of young adult criminal behavior and incarceration, that is four times that of non-bullying peers! Nearly 60% of boys who were bullies in middle school had at least one criminal conviction by age 24, and 40% had at least 3 convictions, according to a study done by the advocacy group Fight Crime: Invest in Kids. Add abusive relationships, failed marriages and lost jobs to this life derailment, and you can see that failure to correct child bullies is an adult responsibility that must not be shirked.

Neither does the bystander escape negative consequences, because they are drawn in by bullies to be henchmen, or feel guilty for not coming to the aid of victims for fear of becoming victims themselves, or say inside, "This is none of my business," or "If I get involved, I will be punished, too." In local school student surveys, "Other students help when they see bullying," is one of the lowest scores, in the 20% range! There are many of us who can recall such situations in which we felt powerless to do the right thing, and were ashamed. It is easier and safer to remain silent, turn away, and not get involved, even for adults. Tragically, the innocents murdered at Columbine, some of whom who did not even know

---

20. Dr. Ken Winters, BVSD Seminar on Teen Brain Development, January 17, 2006.
21. *The Sociopath Next Door,* by Martha Stout, Ph.D.(Broadway Books, 2005).

the killers, received the payback for all the bystanders at the school who saw wrong and did nothing. There are no innocent bystanders, according to author William Burroughs and bullying researcher Dan Olweus.

Is being bullied character-building? Does it prepare you for the adult world? Some Colorado legislators think so, and only narrowly approved a No Name-Calling Week in schools in 2005. One opposing Representative said childhood teasing, such as his being called "a red-headed woodpecker," helps develop problem solving skills.[22] But such light teasing is different from bullying, and being called a "dumb-ass," "ugly," or "freak." And being bullied is only character building if you are able to get resolution, and the bullying stops. Unfortunately, once a child becomes an identified victim that schoolmates or adults have not stepped in to defend, the pack mentality that thrives on having a scapegoat makes the abuse hard to stop. It is not a virtue to be able to take abuse that you don't deserve, day after day, and only trains you to knuckle under. It is not self-esteem building to have to become the class clown to get through the school day, only letting down your guard in the quiet behind your bedroom door. Joining a clique of outcasts for protection, or becoming a caricature of yourself to shout "I'm OK the way I am," is wearing and constraining on the psyche. Hiding your essential nature or family heritage is self-denial. It is not healthy to become mean, like a dog in a cage constantly poked with sticks. Children need love, caring, acceptance, respect and adult guidance to grow up into strong, compassionate individuals who can deal with adult setbacks. This does not mean they are to be totally cocooned from adversity, but this is impossible anyway. The character argument just doesn't wash.

Bully, target, or bystander: we're all human and need to get along and grow up healthy. This is the practical bottom line. Lost human potential from this common source of childhood conflict is no longer acceptable. Kids have a right to an education free of emotional and physical violence, and one which guides them into being responsible and productive citizens. Analyzing and categorizing bullies and targets, or what our families did or did not do to make us this way is not worth the effort, because most are just normal kids and families with typical life stressors. Of course, there are exceptions in cases of mental illness or child abuse that can be picked up by attentive, involved counselors. But typical life stressors or diagnosable conditions should be no excuse for adults failing to take effective action against bullying.

---

22.   "House takes on school bullying," Rocky Mountain News, January 25, 2005.

One way for adults to relate to these new rights in education is to make the analogy to the workplace. Schoolchildren are being asked to put up with verbal, sexual and physical harassment that adults in the workplace would not put up with for one instant. A landmark case making schools liable for known peer to peer sexual harassment (under Title IX) is a step in the right direction, and needs to be extended to other types of serious harassment. Employment used to be the same as schools are now: if you don't like it, too bad, go somewhere else. Adults are now protected by a host of laws that have made the workplace a lot more civilized. Some complaints may appear overblown, but the overall effect has been salutary.

Likewise, domestic violence used to be societally accepted, even enshrined in literature and plays such as My Fair Lady. Then more recently it was hidden from view and not the topic of polite conversation. Women were told they deserved it, and they believed this. Now domestic violence is unacceptable and illegal, and there are support programs for victims and corrective programs for abusers. While the approach needs fine-tuning to address sometimes overly harsh and inflexible police and court responses, a new paradigm was long overdue.

The new paradigm in school bullying is no longer to blame, change, or saddle the child with the entire responsibility for stopping the bullying. It is to believe, support and protect the bullied child, correct and counsel the bully, and empower the bystander to be a witness and get involved.

But before we get into the details of this new way of thinking about and dealing with bullying, it is important to discuss school systemic contributions to the problem. It is not just the children who are the only ones involved in the conflict.

The School System's Role in Bullying

Most of us can recall at least one teacher who was just plain mean, and picked on particular students unmercifully, for example my 6th grade teacher who singled out the pig farmer's son for abuse although the kid did nothing to deserve it. Unfortunately, some people gravitate to teaching for the control they can exert over their young charges, deny any accusations made against them, and are protected by the union work rules from dismissal. Bullying by the teacher in the classroom is not common, but does happen and can make for a miserable year for the target. And beware of complaining without being prepared to move your kid, because "No one does passive aggressive like teachers," as one union president was recently quoted as saying in regards to a negotiation.[23] Ouch! I also remember a teacher's letter to the editor after a publicized peer bullying story in Denver. This teacher said, "The dirty little secret is that many teachers agree with the bully and say that the victim deserved it because he's such a dork."[24] This attitude is more of a problem than a few mean teachers, or coaches who manhandle unruly boys.

The elephant lumbering about the school that is beginning to get more attention is again culture. James Gabarino's book, *And Words Can Hurt Forever: How to Protect Adolescents from Bullying, Harassment, and Emotional Violence* (2003), attacks this issue head on. Administrators and the school culture they foster are complicit in bullying. One way this is done is by neglect and the learned helplessness of professional school bureaucrats in large schools: "There's nothing we can do about it," or "It's not our job to police every student social interaction, we have enough to do." One local principal acknowledges this and said that some of his teachers "flat out ignore it and say it's not my job," to counter anti-gay slurs in the hallways, for example.[25] Other news stories, letters to the editor, and teen focus groups I have attended confirm that many teachers ignore racial, gay and religious slurs, and bullying in general. In local school confidential student surveys, "Teachers help when they see bullying" is in the 50% range.

A second way that school culture is actively complicit in bullying is through the support of the hierarchy of cliques in the school, to maintain social order and weed out misfits. The dominant cliques often perpetrate the worst bullying in order to maintain their power. The classic and most common example is jock culture, in which star athletes rule the roost and abuse nerds and misfits, and are excused and supported by administration personnel who themselves may have been products of such school cultures. It's a human group dynamic; families, workplaces, the military, and institutions of higher learning (including medical residency training!) exhibit this age-old pattern of passing on abusive power traditions. This tradition says, "I survived it, you will too."

Scapegoating nonconformists, misfits and minorities to consolidate group unity is also a human social dynamic that plays out in the culture of these organizations. For example, after her mother went public, Johanna was e-mailed and phoned by students who told her "You're ruining our school!" A student letter to the editor said "Her pain cannot be blamed on our school." Another typical

23.   "More Districts Pay Teachers for Performance," Wall Street Journal, March 23, 2005.

24.   The Open Forum, "How schools deal with bullying," by Elaine Zupaniec, Denver Post, January 18, 2005.

25.   "Sports focus of Safe Schools Coalition: Boulder Valley teams encouraged to be more open to gay, lesbian students," Daily Camera, by Amy Bounds for the Enterprise.

dynamic in blame deflection is to use mental illness, whether truly present or not, as the root cause of the victim's problems. A noteworthy adult episode of blame-shifting involves the highly publicized bulldozer rampage of a Granby, Colorado man, who destroyed a small town and then killed himself. He was portrayed as mentally ill, but what is less known is that this small business owner had apparently been relentlessly targeted by town officials who essentially zoned him out of business and then made his property unsalable.

Norm enforcement by cliques and scapegoating of misfits is apparently what was occurring at Columbine. After the tragedy, an athlete was widely quoted as saying, "Columbine is a good clean place except for those rejects ... the whole school is disgusted with them ... if you want to get rid of someone, usually you tease 'em. So the whole school would call them homos ..." The principal, a former coach, professed not to be aware of this chronic situation, saying that Klebold and Harris should have come to him if they were having problems, displacing all responsibility onto the students. About this same time, a Columbine athlete who was charged with stalking a girl had no school restrictions placed on him despite a restraining order, while the girl was told, to solve the problem, she could leave the school early and still graduate. It is the misfit's problem to take it or leave. This is a cultural problem.

Another jock culture tragedy happened in a small Colorado farming community where football is king. There, a 14 year old girl was raped by a 16 year old star athlete, who was given probation. The community rallied to his defense, the school allowed the boy to ignore the restraining order, and students vilified the girl and called her a whore. The family was forced to move in order to transfer her to another school. Emotionally devastated by the family upheaval and loss of friends, she then committed suicide. The boy, who was done no favors by the lenient treatment, was later convicted of a second rape.

Hazing is also used in college and high school athletics and clubs to maintain the power relationships of social groups, and although it is illegal, it still goes on in locker rooms and off-campus locations, protected by the code of silence. The University of Colorado Football team, which allegedly enticed recruits with raunchy off-campus parties was also protected by this code of silence for years until sexual assault victims spoke up. Coaches sometimes turn a blind eye to on and off campus hazing rituals, in the furtherance of group cohesion via enforcement of the social hierarchy that masquerades as tradition. When strict no-hazing and anti-bullying policies are put into effect, those disempowered have complained of upsetting this tradition, of course. At the Air Force Academy, new prohibitions against unwanted proselytism and hazing that were instituted to address abusive practices are quietly being peeled back.[26] Traditions that support power relation-ships are hard to eradicate. In private schools, it is students with the most impor-tant parents and fanciest cars who wield power, and administration personnel pay obeisance. In some urban schools, gangs enforce submission in the hallways while adults cower in classrooms and offices. And as mentioned, charter schools can have their own variations on favoritism that foster abuse. It is a widespread school culture problem.

When administrators and teachers abdicate their adult leadership responsibili-ties or allow student cliques to enforce social norms for them, school culture does not support the educational rights of any students, whether they are bullies, vic-tims or bystanders. Strong school principals must develop a positive and inclusive school culture, and teachers and students must all have buy-in on it. How is this done?

Steps to School Culture Change

Fortunately, not all schools have culture problems as serious as did Peak to Peak or Columbine. But it is common enough, and is now known to be correctable. Recognition of a problem at a particular school must occur first. If you or your student think you have a great school "except for those dirtballs," think again. Warning signs of a school in trouble include statements by your bystander stu-dent such as "Teachers know about bullying but don't do anything," or "There's a lot of bullying, but there's nothing that can be done about it." If you have a bul-lied student, he or she is the canary in the mine of a toxic culture, and unlikely to be the only one affected. School culture will not change on its own, and parents must step up to the plate. It is difficult to go it alone because lone voices are easily dismissed, but a small group of determined individuals can make a difference, and is the only thing that ever has, according to famed anthropologist Margaret Mead. Get support from sympathetic teachers, parents of your child's friends, and community leaders, and go to PTO meetings and school forums. If your child is a teenager still at the school, he must be brought on board that in order to change things, it may get tougher for a while but it is the right thing to do. She may want to speak out too; she has a right to an education without hostility. Some kids will need to leave the school if parents plan on becoming vocal, because of strong cultural support for bullies; this is an individualized decision. Bystander families need to give support to those who are vocal by letting them

---

26.   "'Recognition' returns to AFA," Rocky Mountain News, March 15, 2006.

know your appreciation and writing letters and emails to school and school board personnel.

Second, school leadership must have the will and stomach to challenge the status quo, and the people skills to bring all staff on board. Some principals are nearing retirement, unmotivated or even out of their depth running a school, and will not be up to the task. It is also an unfortunate reality that school leadership and culture problems often go hand in hand, and that leadership change may be the difficult, but only solution. The good news is that many principals are dedicated professionals willing to work hard to implement what is best for their students, but just need school district and community support. Go to the school board with other parents to express your concerns in a calm, reasonable fashion. A helpful spur is going to the local press to start a community discussion of the issues. The threat of legal action can be an effective way to get the attention of a sluggish school board, but it should be a last resort because it stifles free communication. It is also costly unless advocacy groups or pro bono attorneys are willing to help. When there has been no responsiveness or communication, this is the time to use this tool.

Third, school culture must be assessed via confidential student surveys that assess all aspects of how students feel about their school. School districts need data in addition to anecdotal parent complaints. Problems are usually more widespread than the small number of vocal parents would indicate, as was the case at Peak to Peak. The 64 question annual Climate Survey is just such a tool, implemented by the Boulder Valley School District in 2002. It has questions about safety, bullying and bystander and teacher response, teacher attitudes and helpfulness, discrimination and harassment, etc. Make sure surveys are truly anonymous, and there is no coaching from survey administrators, usually teachers, to make the school look good. Parents also must be surveyed for their opinions on these issues as well as school quality and responsiveness. Survey results are public information and should be easily obtainable. These should really be called culture surveys, not climate surveys, because culture is under human control, while climate is a euphemism that indicates it is not under human control, like the weather.

Fourth, complaints and survey results must be acted on, and not sit on a shelf waiting for the next incident to be dusted off. School leaders must change their attitudes, and come to believe that there is something than can be done about it, and in fact have their feet held to the fire if need be. School Improvement Committees, PTO's and community input are important, but many parents are too busy to go to a lot of meetings, so input must be gathered via email, phone and snail-mail. Information should be sought from other school districts, outside experts and centers such as those mentioned in Chapter 8 and the end of this chapter. Look for proven newer programs that place the major change responsibility on adults, not children. This is much easier to do in the internet age. I highly recommend the Anti-Defamation League's World of Difference and Positive Impact school programs for developing a culture of tolerance. The ADL is now focusing on all forms of intolerance, not just anti-Semitism. Student groups, not just the student council types, but the nerds, goths and outcasts must be included in decision making for culture change. The school must really want their input, and be innovative in seeking it, and not just put up posters, and then say "oh well" when they don't show up. In short, everyone must work hard and be invested in the process.

Fifth, there must be ongoing monitoring and continuous quality improvement, to borrow a phrase from business. Make sure that changes are not just window-dressing. The tendency to let things slip and revert to old ways is natural, and must be watched for. In the age of school choice and academic accountability, this entire process can be promoted as paying big long term dividends in higher enrollments and improved student academic scores. There is money for schools to initiate anti-bullying and other programs to improve school culture; in Colorado, the Colorado Trust handed out $8.6 million in 2005 for this purpose.[27]

What are the goals for a positive and inclusive school culture? Some schools, such as Peak to Peak, claim to be places "where every student is known and valued." This is indeed the most critical goal, where there are no outcasts, there is no favoritism, and staff truly care about students as reflected in open door policies and willingness to get involved. These outcomes are measurable. Just ask the students. And believe them.

What is the State of the Art in Anti-Bullying Theory?

First, let's talk about an anti-bullying policy that does not work, but is being widely used in schools today. You guessed it, zero tolerance.[28] Many schools and school districts have adopted zero tolerance policies for bullying, which may or may not be equitably enforced. Similarly with peer conflict and school threat problems, severe punishments such as suspension or expulsion may actually dis-

---

27. "Grants to help combat bullying," Rocky Mountain News, April 15, 2005.

28. Both the Stop Bullying Now program and author Barbara Coloroso agree that "Zero tolerance is zero thinking" in regards to anti-bullying efforts.

courage children from reporting bullying they observe or experience, for fear of being socially punished for the misfortune of the bully. While school exclusion may be necessary in small numbers of cases for safety, it is not recommended as a broad policy.

Students cannot thrive in a prison-like school environment, and we have all heard horror stories of innocent actions of young children being misinterpreted by adults, such as the 6 year old harshly punished for kissing a girl. Tag and dodgeball are out. A colleague of mine relayed sadly how her 8 year old exuberant son now cries on Sunday night, fearful of the school week, because students are not allowed to chase or touch each other on the playground! He was given detention for playing king of the hill on a small mound of dirt with three or four other boys, none of whom were pushed down or excluded from playing. What has happened to common sense and in-loco-parentis discipline? Teasing and bullying at the elementary school level are not hard to tell apart, and more eyes on the hall and playground provide essential opportunities for effective teachable moments. Smiling, laughing children look different from frowning, crying children who are playing or being chased. Children's versions of events can be taken, and individualized consequences can be meted out, based on taught behavior standards and consequences. Targets are believed; they are usually upset and crying. Bullies may admit what they did, be remorseful, and just need gentle correction. Bullies who lie are usually calm, cool, and make excuses, or blame the victim for deserving it, provoking it or being the real bully. They need to be firmly disciplined. All are treated as the "humans under construction" they are, and given the individualized support, guidance and discipline they need. Witnesses and those who intervene to stop bullying are rewarded with praise, not punished equally along with the bullies. It is often helpful if parents can be involved in the process. Experts such as Coloroso advise against working with parents of the bully outside the school system, but I disagree. If you can be cool-headed, call a parent and get a good response, you are ahead; if not, it is probably best to work through the school. I recall an episode in preschool when a classmate who was climbing a jungle gym kicked Jeff in the face to keep him off, causing a bruise near the eye. The staff avoided dealing with the issue other than to notify us. Taking a page from Mark's childhood playbook, we called the parents, arranged a face to face session for an apology, and the boys have been close friends to this day.

Yes, some children are more sensitive to ordinary teasing than others, and rough, brash children need to learn this, and learn a little sensitivity themselves. Those whose feelings are easily hurt can be taught to accept apologies gracefully and see that the other kid is really not so bad. "Peace Places" in elementary school classrooms, while they sound touchy-feely, actually are a step in the right direction for teasing and low-level bullying. I recall a boy in my son's elementary school who was very sensitive, clumsy and had poor social skills. He started to cry once after I told him that his shoelace was untied; boy, did I feel awful. I can just imagine the pranks that were played on him. His mom felt the need to be constantly in the classroom to protect him, and he was allowed to get away with tantrums. She was mean to the other children, which built resentment against her son. It is a sad commentary that the school couldn't find a way to reassure this mother and teach the other children how to interact with him. We need to learn as children that we're all a little different, but all want to be treated as human beings.

Bullied children need:

* Recognition by adults that there is a problem, because often the child will not spontaneously complain. There are many lists of warning signs available, eg, Coloroso, and the Stop Bullying Now website.

* Encouragement and support to tell and be taken seriously.

* Protection from continued bullying through adult supervision and effective consequences for bullies.

* Support in not blaming themselves, and for post-traumatic stress symptoms in some cases.

* Sometimes, help in developing social skills.

* Not to be totally responsible for preventing the bullying themselves, or be told to use ineffective techniques.

* Parent and educator respect and support: he is not a "sissy."

Bullies need:

* Consistent, fair, non-hostile, escalating consequences.

* To be held fully accountable for her behavior, and help exploring other behavioral options.

* Positive outlets for energy and talent, such as sports, debate club, student council.

* Sometimes, help in developing social skills and impulse control.

* Parent and educator support in recognizing and changing poor behavior.

What else is not recommended by the experts? In middle school and high school, peer mediation and peer conflict resolution programs are becoming more common strategies for peer to peer disputes, as mentioned in Chapter 8. However, this is not recommended in cases that are clearly serious bullying, because as noted before, this can lead to re-victimization, especially when facilitators are young or inexperienced. Bullying is a form of peer victimization, not peer to peer conflict. It is up to adults to make this determination by listening to both sides in-loco-parentis. Mediation can give bullies the inappropriate message that this was at least partly the target's fault. The right message to the bullied student is, "No one deserves to be bullied, and adults are going to do everything to stop it," while the message to the bully is, "Your behavior is inappropriate and must be stopped." Group treatment for bullies is not recommended, including anger-management groups, because members tend to serve as role models and reinforcers for each others' antisocial and bullying behavior. It is also important to not treat either bullies or targets as time bombs at imminent risk of school threat-type aggression unless there are clear indications of such risk.

Middle and high school in-loco-parentis discipline for bullying is more challenging, especially in the age of so-called no bullying, because kids have become necessarily more secretive and inventive in the cruelties they come up with for their prey. Insults are whispered out of adult earshot, and targets are isolated and surrounded in locker alcoves and threatened, and elaborate, humiliating pranks are devised. In hallways, shoulder checks, tripping, and ripped clothing, as well as roughness in PE, are "accidents." Stolen belongings, sabotaged assignments, sexual rumors, exclusion, false reports of misbehavior or illegal activity via anonymous tip boxes. All of these are on the menu today more so than the past. These behaviors are more difficult for adults to directly witness, and when confronted with complaints, staff find it easy to say "We don't know who to believe," or "She must have done something to provoke it," and wash their hands of it. An older brother of one of Jeff's friends was bullied throughout his three years at a local middle school, including having had his locker repeatedly broken into and winter jackets stolen. The best school officials could come up with was recommending that he enroll in a different high school than his tormentors!

Anti-bullying strategies that may be effective in elementary school are not effective with teenagers, and true culture change at the whole school level is required, according to Gabarino. Older solutions of letting teens work things out on their own may escalate conflict; for example, formation of outcast cliques or gangs for protection against bullying. Some kids don't have the physical size or strength, or are down so far emotionally in a non-inclusive school culture that the playing field is far from level. Even kids with normal resiliency can be overwhelmed. In retrospect, this is exactly what happened to our son Jeff. Anti-bullying strategies were ineffective or backfired, school culture supported bullies, and staff did not take his complaints seriously enough, which only encouraged the bullies. When we then told him to use old-fashioned techniques of giving it right back, it was bound to fail.

Teachers and parents must educate themselves to read between the lines for warning signs of declining grades, social withdrawal, personality changes, etc. Teenagers give fewer facial and behavioral clues for teacher hallway intervention, but they can be encouraged to come forward, which they will do if they are believed and supported, and visible, fair consequences are meted out to bullies. In-loco-parentis school discipline is common sense, not a court of law requiring evidence beyond a reasonable doubt. Parents have a nose for who is telling the truth, taking past behavior into account. So do seasoned teachers and principals, but they often seem to refuse to take this responsibility. Bullies should be given firm consequences that escalate for repeat offenses, whole cliques may also need to be disciplined, and retribution towards targets and witnesses must not be tolerated. Social hierarchies must not be covertly supported. Unfortunately, direct parent involvement in curbing bullies is usually less effective with teenagers, and in fact can be counterproductive in that they may support or excuse the bully's behavior, and stimulate retaliation. Bullied teenagers are usually mortified to have their parents contact school officials, but it may be necessary. Teenagers in general need the same interventions listed above for targets and bullies.

The few teen bullies who will become true sociopaths can't feel empathy and don't usually act out of impulse or anger, but are able to calculate and respond to structured, no-excuses discipline to avoid negative consequences, and can be helped to direct their aggressive energies into positive pursuits. Some harassment and assault offenses do require legal intervention and restraining orders, but it is more avoidable when the school initiates early, escalating discipline. Bullies are done no favors by lenient treatment and may finally land in legal hot water.

The best reference for the state of the art in anti-bullying theory, and the source of much of this section, is found at the Stop Bullying Now website, at www.stopbullyingnow.hrsa.gov. At this source, sponsored by U.S. Dept. of Health and Human Services, there is extensive but concise and readable information and resources for parents, kids, schools and mental health professionals.

What do Students Say Will Help?

Students consistently say they want more, not less, adult supervision in hallways, locker rooms and even bathrooms via walk-in checks and staff use. Some kids just hold it all day for fear of physical abuse or nasty personalized graffiti, and race for the bathroom once home. Kids want caring adult supervision, meaning an adult who won't turn and walk away or pretend not to see a problem. This is hard to believe, but as noted above, students consistently report this as common, even when there is a physical attack, and anonymous surveys back this up. Recently, a girl returned to her old high school in Boulder to talk about abusive relationships, and relayed how seven years earlier, a teacher kept right on walking after seeing her get slapped by her boyfriend, and when she asked for help from a counselor, was only advised not to get pregnant.[29]

It must be every staff member's job to intervene when seeing a student in trouble, and call for help if necessary. Teachers must not cloister themselves in the classroom, and more hall, cafeteria and grounds monitors, which can be trained volunteers, must provide caring adult presence. Custodians, who are usually men, can be valuable additions to the team. School Resource Officers are in many schools now as a friendly bridge to the youth community, and can educate kids on legally risky behaviors, and provide physical force if needed. Principals should manage by walking around, as did the principal at Jeff's elementary school, and he knew almost every student, no small feat in a school of 700. Being a caring adult takes effort. Every student needs an assigned counselor whom he or she has at least met once and chatted briefly with, and the door to her office is open. Johanna, on the day of her suicide attempt, was turned away from the counseling office. Later it was said to be her fault that she did not let them know how serious it was, by picking a low number in the self-triage system then in use. Students in crisis should not be doing their own triage when the counseling office gets busy! This is like telling the man who presents to the emergency room with chest pain to decide for himself whether it's a heart attack or not.

Almost all schools have dark, unmonitored corners and grounds that need to be closed off, or have regular walk-throughs by staff and perhaps have security cameras. There may be some value in eliminating hidden alcoves and attention to design in new schools. Some technology does have a place, but it cannot replace positive and inclusive school culture and caring adults as a solution. In my work world, the nursing home, "He who sees it deals with it." No one walks by a problem without at least notifying the one who usually takes care of that problem, and safety issues are dealt with immediately by all, including administrators and doctors. This is the way caring, responsive organizations work, and how schools should work. Students prefer smaller schools because getting to know other students helps them predict their behavior, and it is not as difficult to be chosen for

---

29. "Woman shares pain to help teens in abusive relationships," Rocky Mountain News, November 15, 2005.

competitive roles in sports and the arts and sciences. As mentioned in Chapter 8, small schools need all their students to participate, even the nerds and misfits. But in the absence of inclusive school culture, small schools are not the panacea. The middle and high school was about 500 students when we left our former charter school. The lesson is that culture trumps size.

Your Part in the New Paradigm

Most families of school-age children will find themselves in this chapter as bystanders—their kids are not experiencing serious problems, but may tell of others who are. Families are busy keeping their own lives together and it is natural to avoid getting involved in problems that do not directly affect them. But the culture at your child's school is also your responsibility, and will affect your child either positively or negatively. Ask your child about bullying at his school, and inquire further if he brings up what is happening to another kid. Encourage them to stand up for kids they see being bullied, because doing the right thing is as contagious as doing the wrong thing, and it may take just one student's voice to encourage others to withhold bully approval and give support to the target. Be a good role model for your kids in your daily life, and get involved in the school and assist the vocal parents as much as you can, like those who attended and spoke at Peak to Peak's forum after Johanna's near-tragedy.

Families faced with the fact by school officials or other parents that their child is a bully are often very defensive. I say to you: get over it, because this is a correctable problem that is greatly to your child's benefit to fix now, not later. Do not let your pride and your child's pride increase his risk of social and legal repercussions. Your child most likely has a lot of energy and talent than can be used more positively and productively in any number of ways other than bullying! Limit-setting and clear behavior guidelines with parental reinforcement, and more outlets for energy, are effective for many children. Professional help can be of benefit, and newer approaches are emphasizing behavioral therapies over medication even for the few tougher cases of difficult and aggressive children (for example, some kids with Attention Deficit-Hyperactivity Disorder, and Conduct Disorder, Oppositional Defiant Disorder; see resources at the end of this chapter).

If you are a family with a bullied child and you have gone through school channels without relief, you may decide that escaping an abusive and unresponsive school is your healthiest option, and less traumatic than staying to fight. This choice is likely to be confirmed when the new school (which you have investigated and felt welcomed at!) is like going from night to day and an end to the family's nightmare. But at least make it clear to school authorities why you are leaving, and also, strongly consider letters or emails to the school board. Other families will be coming behind you and are counting on you, because nothing will change if you keep it to yourself. Going to the media about what has happened to your family is fraught with dangers of slanted presentation and misquotes, but can be effective especially if you have support of other parents. Someone has to go first in speaking up, and usually others will follow. Sometimes you are just too angry to stay silent, as we were. One Denver family finally got action from the school district by going public when their middle school daughter's sexual harassment—she had been pushed down and groped in a corner of her school—was ignored by officials. She was finally transferred and is much happier in her new school, saying, "It's totally different and friendly. The teachers in the hallways keep things calm and quiet."[30] Until all schools have come up to speed on leadership, culture and anti-bullying programs, transfer will be an unfortunate necessity. Some day, unrepentant bullies will be inconvenienced with schedule and school changes. Small rural towns, however, present a unique challenge as there is no close-by new school and retaliation for school criticism can be crushing. It is a wrenching decision to move for the sake of your child, or to make lifestyle changes in order to homeschool.

It is advisable to get professional help if things are bad enough to consider school transfer or moving. But be wary of glib diagnosis of mental illness in your bullied child, or prescription of medication; get second opinions. Psychotherapy, i.e. intensive counseling, is first line treatment for most children with stress, anxiety and depression.[31] Unfortunately, the school counselor may not be helpful and in fact back up the school, not your child. If finances are an issue, local mental health centers may be able to help, and many therapists have sliding scale fees.

Other families, especially those with teenagers who don't want to leave their friends, or run from bullies, will want to stay and challenge the status quo. You and your child must believe in what you are doing, and not be embarrassed to be identified as a target of bullying, one with less social power in a non-inclusive school culture. Just as those victimized by other types of interpersonal violence such as domestic violence and sexual abuse/assault are beginning to come forward

---

30. "Middle school taunts take frightening turn," Denver Post, January 13, 2005. This girl bravely came forward with her family by name, and also said, "The bullies, they'll do what they want...even when someone saw what was happening, they wouldn't say anything because then they'd come after them."

31. Numerous studies support this well-accepted clinical guideline.

and say, "I did not deserve what happened to me, and I am not a lesser human being because of it," so must the families of bullied children stand up.

Note: This chapter is not meant to be an authoritative, complete guide to bullying, but its purpose is to stimulate new thinking on the issue of bullying, and to encourage families to consult a wide range of newer resources in tackling the problem, and get professional help when needed.

Recommended Resources

1. Stop Bullying Now Website. www.stopbullyingnow@hrsa.gov (start here)
2. Gabarino and deLara, *And Words Can Hurt Forever: How to Protect Adolescents from Bullying, Harassment and Emotional Violence*. Free Press, 2003. (excellent, geared toward high school students, every chapter ends with practical ideas)
3. Coloroso, *The Bully, the Bullied, and the Bystander*. Harper Resource, 2003 (good basic primer, geared toward younger students; lots of self-help information for families; I disagree with some portions which seem to over-analyze children and families.)
4. Resources for parents of difficult children:
    Parent Management Training. www.childconductclinic.yale.edu/
    The Incredible Years Program. www.incredibleyears.com/
    Multisytemic Therapy. www.mstservices.com/
5. The Anti-Defamation League. www.adl.org/education.
6. Educators for Social Responsibility. www.edunational.org (Partners in Learning and Resolving Conflict Creatively Programs)

Other Resources

1. Dulmus and Sowers (Eds.), *Kids and Violence: The Invisible School Experience*. 2005, Haworth Press. School violence is often covert, and adults contribute through silence or support of school culture; discusses interventions.
2. Bluestein, Jane, *Creating Emotionally Safe Schools: A Guide for Educators and Parents*. 2001, Health Communications. Advises teachers and parents on how to transform schools from fear-torn arenas into learning sanctuaries.
3. Hyman and Snook, *Dangerous Schools: What We Can Do About the Physical and Emotional Abuse of Our Children*. 2004, John Wiley and Sons. An expose of institutional abuse of students and how-to guide for parents confronting these issues.
4. Epp and Watkinson (Eds.), *Systemic Violence in Education: Promise Broken*. 1997, State University of New York Press. Examines school practices contributing to racism, harassment and child abuse.

5. Dellasega and Nixon, *Girl Wars: 12 Strategies That Will End Female Bullying.* 2003, Simon and Schuster. Practical and succinct how-to information for parents and girls.

6. Garrett, Ann, *Bullying in American Schools: Causes, Preventions, Interventions.* 2003, McFarland & Co.Publishers. Details negative long term consequences of bullying behavior, discusses myths, and offers solutions.

7. Smith, Rigby and Pepler (Eds.), *Bullying in Schools: How Successful Can Interventions Be?* 2004, Cambridge University Press. Reviews strategies in other nations.

Epilogue

"I didn't speak up.... Then they came for me ..." German Pastor Niemoller, 1945[1]

Growing up white, middle class and Protestant in America was a privileged existence, even though we wore used clothing and drank powdered milk at times in our family of seven. My mother was a Catholic, disowned by her family and excommunicated by her church for marrying outside the faith. She was a Navy WAVE who worked on the Manhattan Project to build the atomic bomb, probably as a secretary; we don't know, it was secret and she has passed away. She married my dad after WWII in a civil ceremony, both in their uniforms. Benson's Landing, Vermont, is where my great-great uncle is buried. On our family's Sunday drives after church, we picked up trash by the roadside for the Keep America Beautiful campaign started by President Johnson's wife, Lady Bird. We got a new car every ten years. In many ways it was a typical childhood of the 1950's and '60's.

I never experienced discrimination as a girl, and benefitted from the feminist revolution. My family was certainly not racist, and no such sentiments ever passed their lips. But I absorbed the culture around me. As a 10 year old in 1960, the civil rights unrest on the television and no doubt what swirled around me in our dusty little New Mexico town prompted a letter to the President. "If they don't like it here, tell them to go back to Africa." In high school, the gym teachers separated out the Hispanic kids, and called them "suntans." The townsfolk and students called them spics and wetbacks (which someday will be the s- and w-words), and the n-word was used as a casual insult, like gay is today. I said nothing, but never used these words and even had the school's only black girl as one of my friends on campus. We did not think of getting closer because it just wasn't done then. Only one teacher objected to these epithets. Somehow, one day, the

---

1.　 "First they came for the Communists, and I didn't speak up because I wasn't a Communist. Then they came for the Jews, and I didn't speak up because I wasn't Jew. Then they came for the Catholics, and I didn't speak up, because I was a Protestant. Then they came for me, and by that time there was no one left to speak up for me."

casual n-word came out of my mouth in front of my friend and this teacher! He let me have it. I lost my friend. I have never told anyone, not even my husband, of these two shameful acts, but now I say it very publicly.

We moved to a Chicago suburb when I was 16, where the Jews were the butt of discrimination, because there were no blacks or Hispanics? My dad worked in a large corporation in the neighboring town of Skokie. I said nothing when it was called Skokikie (the k-word?) because it was home to many Jews. The reader may recall this is the place where the Aryan Nation chose to march a few years ago. Even as some of my friends said nasty things about Jews, I went with others to march against the Vietnam war in Lincoln Park in 1968, to hear railing against the killing of yellow people called gooks (g-word?). I was starting to wake up. This was a normal upbringing in America, infused with racism even if it was of a lighter variety than in other parts of the country and earlier times. Now things are definitely better, but not totally better.

So it shocked me to the core, to realize that my son was being discriminated against by my own co-religionists. I just wasn't accustomed to that subtle knowledge of being an outsider, that is in the back of the minds of minorities, that whispers be careful, this is the world we live in. Was this my own payback, my karma? More likely, fate handed me a job to do, knowing I had the temperament and resources to do it.

Mark's story is that life is not fair, but you must work hard to succeed despite this. Both sets of grandparents escaped pogroms in Eastern Europe and Russia to come to America. One great-grandma is said to have fled on foot to Paris with valuables sewn in her coat and two young children in tow, after shooting the Cossacks invading her house. His dad experienced discrimination about which Mark won't speak, but he became a well-regarded psychiatrist. His aunt was turned down at every medical school because of her sex and older age, until she applied to Howard University, a black medical college. She too, became head of her department. His stepfather was denied membership in the local fire department because he was Jewish, but persevered and became a teacher, and a park ranger in the summers. Mark grew up in New York State in a secular home where there was a Christmas tree in the window, and a Passover seder on the table. When he snuck out of elementary school with the Catholic kids to the church one Wednesday afternoon, after the cookies one girl pointed at him and said "Father, he doesn't belong here." Mark was mortified until the priest said, "All are welcome here." In the high school play, he was given the role of the Jewish merchant in Shakespeare's The Merchant of Venice. So the discrimination in his family had faded over time to next to nothing. He broke off young adult friendships over black slurs. He sat in Zen Buddhist practice in graduate school and still has an affinity for it, but he doesn't openly talk of his atheist beliefs because it is not very accepted in America.

Jeff's uncle once said that it may be beneficial to experience a little discrimination when you're young, so as to know how it feels to be on the receiving end, and have the empathy to intervene if you see it happening to others. I do know that the rising anti-Semitism in Europe chills me more because now I know what it was like to be the outsider. I don't appreciate evangelical Christians using Jews and Israelis as pawns in their sick end-times mythology, salivating about the Rapture every time it looks like Armageddon is about to happen in the Middle East. It's nearly as bad as the 72 virgins. Jeff became completely turned off to my faith by feral children at his old school, still uncorrected by adults, 40 years after my school days! I have never worn religious jewelry to work, but for sure I never will now, because I don't want anyone to think I'm intolerant. My church is very moderate, but I have slipped in my attendance lately, feeling diffusely angry at Christians. The words of forgiveness have been whispered but not felt. I wouldn't doubt that some observers of my crusade think I want my pound of flesh.

Our attorney Howard said the solution to our problem was political, not legal, and now I get it. Although I had significant final success in the school reform fight, it should not have been that hard. At 21, I took on my mom's Democrat affiliation. This faded in middle age, concordant with the dictum of former British Prime Minister Margaret Thatcher, which states: if you're not a liberal when you're young, you have no heart, but if you're not a conservative by 45, you have no brain. Accordingly, I switched parties about 10 years ago, and have voted for George W. Bush twice. The last time we were both wishing Lieberman had somehow gotten the nomination, but knew the country would not yet elect a Jew. It is a bitter pill now to realize that the strong defense stance we approved of came with Bush's Faith-Based Initiatives and the Ashcroft Justice Department that have had direct consequences for us. Our politics have definitely returned leftward as a result of our experience.

Mark lost some faith in the justice system, and found that being called for jury duty elicited more sympathy for defendants, and doubts about police reports and prosecutors' motivations. People reading the paper about juveniles arrested for minor crimes or no crime at all, will never know what a helpless, horrible feeling it is to have your child taken away in handcuffs until it happens to you. If it does happen to you, mortgage the house or sell everything you own to get the best attorney, because the system will not deliver justice on its own. He lost less faith in the school system than I did, and thinks that not all schools are as bad as our former charter school. But he gives this advice to any parent: If your kid is not one of the in-crowd, be careful, and get the hell out if something happens, because the school will not be on your side. My challenge has been to act positively for change, after being burned by the institutions of religion, education and justice that I completely trusted before. But I'm nothing if not persistent, probably to a fault. And while there was success in culture change at the charter school which will hopefully provide an example to other charters, it remains to be seen whether zero tolerance will moderate in our school district. I hope so, and I'm still working on it.

Originally, I thought Jeff, now 16, might want to contribute to this last chapter. But, as mentioned before, he is "so over" his bad experience. This is the best positive way that I could end this book. He is too busy with school (getting A's and B's again and wants to be an attorney), girls, first job, new driver's license and mom's old wagon to think about the past. He builds custom computers for friends and family, still enjoys on-line computer games and has organized and managed player guilds, but has a much wider range of interests now. Our fear that he would develop a bad attitude toward police did not materialize, and he told one friend recently that it was really stupid to call cops pigs, and even initiated a conversation with a policeman in a fast-food place about curfew times and driving rules! He is way ahead of us on the recovery scale. This is as it should be. A child's role is to learn and grow, and an adult's to correct injustice. I am comforted that he has spoken openly of his Russian Jewish heritage to his friends, and has expressed some interest in Buddhism. Both sides of our family are a motley crew of religious cross-fertilization: Jews, Christians of all stripes, and atheists. Jeff is beginning to be able to pitch in on the conversation at big family gatherings, and this is no easy task. He now feels generous enough to be open to activities that benefit others, such as volunteer trail-building at a childhood summer camp. We are bursting with pride. I do believe that the support he was given instead of punishment made all the difference in the world, and that every child who makes a cry for help, or makes harmless, naive mistakes deserves the kind of support he had.

When I read to him out of the paper about kids getting arrested and expelled for saying dumb stuff on Myspace.com, he said once, "I sure learned my lesson, and they will too." I found this comment sad; yes, he has learned that speech can be dangerous for children, and that the hammer comes down very hard. This is how it is now, but I hope for change through this book.